Contemporary Approaches to the Teaching of Physical Education

Neil J. Dougherty
Diane Bonanno
Rutgers College
New Brunswick, New Jersey

Burgess Publishing Company
Minneapolis, Minnesota

Editor: Wayne Schotanus
Production Editor: J.D. Montgomery
Production Manager: Morris Lundin
Art Director: Joan Gordon
Sales/Marketing: Travis Williams
Cover design by Joan Gordon

Printed in the United States of America
Library of Congress Catalog Card Number 78-73039
ISBN 0-8087-0446-X

0 9 8 7 6 5 4

preface

This text is designed for students preparing for a teaching career in the field of physical education. It covers the wide variety of topics necessary for successful teaching and relates them to one another in a succinct and meaningful fashion. The text progresses logically from an understanding of the role of the physical educator through the process of planning, developing, and implementing teaching techniques to the delineation of administrative responsibilities of teachers. Each chapter contains a variety of well-substantiated ideas necessary for teaching success, not only today, but in the foreseeable future as well.

Good teaching requires a great deal more than mere mastery of the subject matter. It is a complex process which demands, among other things, a broad repertoire of alternative teaching techniques, an ability to objectively analyze teacher/student interaction, and effective communication of program goals and accomplishments to the public.

Unlike traditional "methods" texts, this book does not contain a voluminous listing of lesson plans and activities. Rather, we have chosen to provide prospective teachers with a broad range of professional skills which will allow them to develop effective individualized lessons to suit the demands of their particular teaching situations. The skills thus acquired are virtually independent of subject matter and age-group bias and, hence, should benefit the competent teacher in practically any teaching situation.

We feel that the development of such skills and the concomitant absence of dependence upon trite predeveloped materials will prepare the student for a successful career as an independent and resourceful professional.

acknowledgments

To Richard J. Levinson, an excellent attorney and a very good friend, we would like to extend our sincere thanks for his assistance in the writing of chapter 10.

Thanks are also extended to our friend Georgjean Gillis, who always managed to make the time to do the typing we needed, and to our friends Sam Bonanno and Sunny Regalado, who spent countless hours of their free time helping us illustrate this book.

To our students at Rutgers College and the students and faculties of the many elementary and secondary schools throughout Central Jersey who helped develop, test, and redefine many of the ideas represented in this text, we would like to extend our most sincere appreciation.

Finally to our families, whose support and understanding have been such an integral part of this or any other venture we have undertaken, we offer our love, our heartfelt thanks, and the dedication of this book.

Neil J. Dougherty
Diane Bonanno

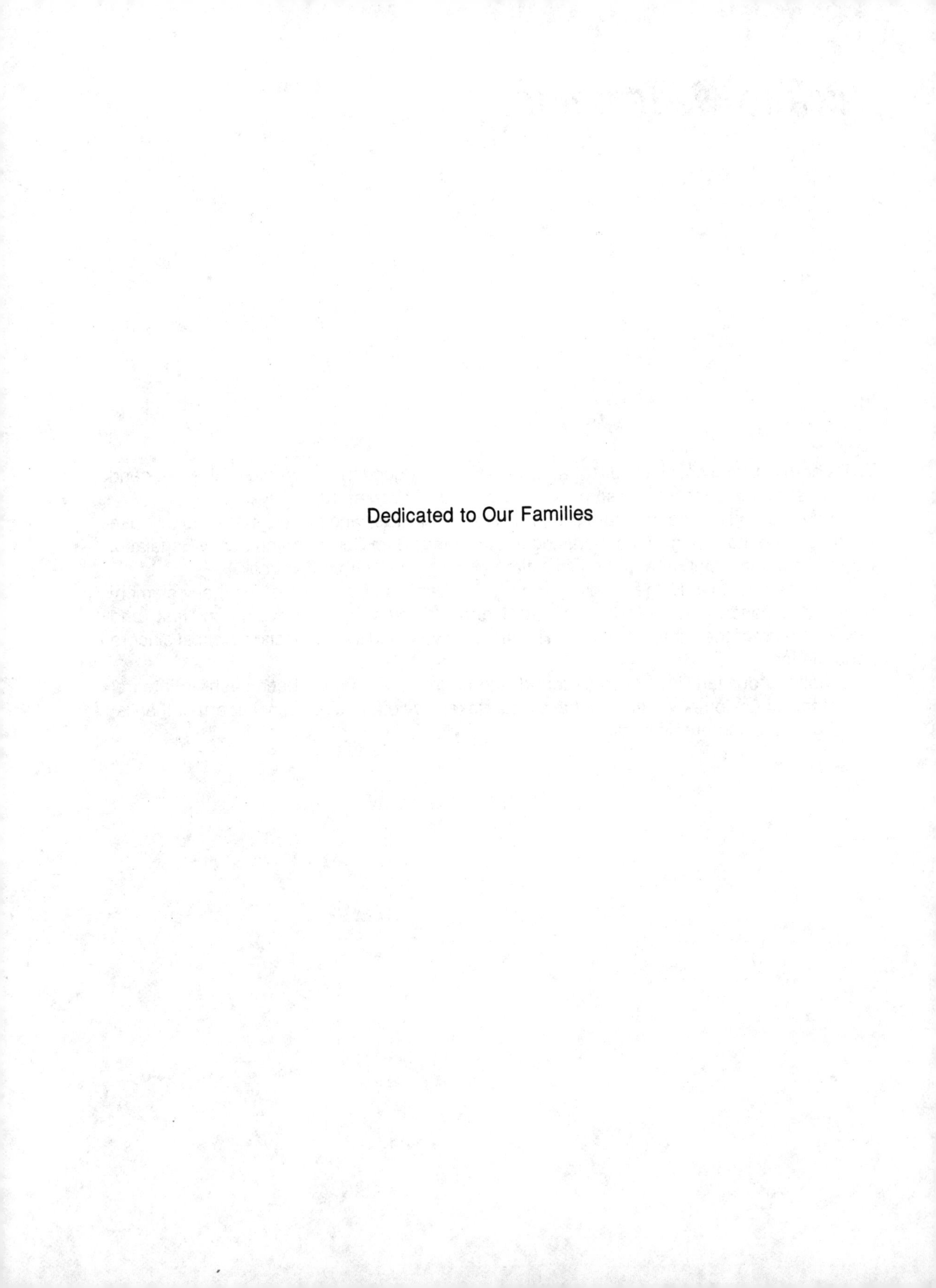

Dedicated to Our Families

contents

chapter one

Perspective: The Future

Educators in the year 2000 will probably classify the physical educator of the seventies and eighties as one of the last vestiges of that creature known as the "jack-of-all-trades," whose sole purpose and function in the school setting was to transmit and improve motor skills. They will probably also view this period of time as having been one of transition and change, when the emphasis in physical education shifted from a "subject-centered" curriculum, where the teacher's main concern was imparting specific sports skills, to a "people-centered" curriculum, where the teacher's main concern focused more on individuals and their ability to achieve maximum potential through movement.

This shift from physical education as a vehicle for skill acquisition to physical education as a tool for self-development is taking place now. Every philosophy, ever tenet, every facet of the physical education program has come under close scrutiny. The net result has been change, incessant demanding change which has left us in a state of flux. Permanence in the field is fast becoming a thing of the past and physical educators are finding that what is considered innovative and positive today will almost assuredly be considered outdated long before its merits are discovered or evaluated tomorrow.

This trend is not merely a reflection of transition; it is the hallmark of the future. Physical education as well as many other professions is experiencing overwhelmingly rapid growth in terms of its field of knowledge. Professionals have had to specialize in order to cope with such accelerating growth, and the profession itself has been splintered into many small fragments in an effort to compartmentalize and channel the research.

If the present trend is predictive of the future, the question confronting every professional is, How should we prepare to meet this seemingly endless wave of uncertainty? Should we specialize and try to keep pace with the research as we are doing now, should we reverse course and try to gain a broad-based understanding of all the specialties, or should we seek other alternatives? The solution to the problem probably lies somewhere between these choices.

Unfortunately, the best solution may be somewhat long in coming, for the educator's response to change has traditionally been exceedingly slow and usually the result of external pressure rather than internal vision. This is largely due to the fact that educators have been trained to perform for the present with little concern for the future. Within the security of the educational institution they are content to believe that the future will come and they will be part of it — so why be concerned? It is exactly this type of listlessness which "has resulted in the static teaching and learning atmospheres that currently threaten the viability of educational institutions."[1] Furthermore, "physical educators cannot tolerate such ennui."[2] They must turn their minds toward the future and *involve themselves in* rather than *react to* our rapidly changing society. They must begin to anticipate possible future changes and thus prepare themselves and their students for what may lie ahead.

> Since a people's shared collective image of the future tends to shape their behavior in the present, inaccurate images about the future — images that are out of phase with the changing reality — can be dangerously misleading. The challenge to us as contemporary men and women is therefore that we restructure our images of the future in light of a rapidly changing world in order that our present behavior can be consistent with the demands of the future.[3]

Unfortunately many physical educators have failed to recognize the importance of this type of preparation. They have blithely ignored the changing world around them and clung blindly to the security of the past until transition has been forced upon them. This conservative, anachronistic attitude has prompted many individuals to express concern with physical education's apparent inability to respond adequately to society's ever-changing needs. If there is to be a change, if physical educators are to respond to and service the needs of their students in the future, regardless of what those needs may be, they must 1) learn to accurately assess individual needs and desires; 2) be creative and help their students to be creative when responding to future needs or demands; 3) learn to project and evaluate future alternatives; and 4) learn to cope with change by being adaptable and flexible. If the professional is able to do this, he or she will be prepared for the transitional phase as well as for whatever might come in the future.

DEVELOPING AN ATTITUDE TOWARD THE FUTURE

Before individuals can envision a possible future, they must believe that forecasting the future is not only possible but necessary and that they have the potential to make forecasts become reality, for "there is a growing realization that man's future may be literally what he chooses to make it, and that the ranges of choice and the degree of conscious control which he may exercise in determining his future are unprecedented."[4] This attitude is important, for if one views a particular future as desirable, one will work toward attaining that future by molding the present into a form which will lead toward projected goals.

The challenge to you as a student is to prepare yourself for your role as educator in the future by learning to view education not in terms of *present* societal goals but in terms of *projected* societal goals. As instructional techniques and educational strategies are assimilated throughout your career, you must evaluate their potential in terms of a long-

1. Celeste Ulrich, "The Future Hour: An Educational View," in *Physical Education: A View Toward the Future,* ed. Raymond Welsh (St. Louis: C. V. Mosby Co., 1977), p. 124.

2. Ibid.

3. Raymond Welsh, "Futuristics: An Emerging Science," in *Physical Education: A View Toward the Future,* ed. Raymond Welsh (St. Louis: C. V. Mosby Co., 1977), p.4.

4. John McHale, "The Sense of the Future," *Quest,* Monograph 21 (January 1974): p. 7.

range rather than an immediate outcome. As one devises courses or selects activities, one must ask what possible consequences one's decisions might have in the future. In short, one's "time-bias," as Alvin Toffler calls it, must shift from the present to the future tense if one is to successfully fulfill the responsibilities of an educator in the future.

A POSSIBLE TOMORROW

As John McHale has suggested, "The future of the future is . . . what we determine it to be, both individually and collectively. It is directly related to how we conceive of its possibilities, potentials, and implications. Our mental blueprints are its basic action programs."[5] Whether such programs are carried out in total or at all will depend, however, on society's priorities.

The important point about future-oriented blueprints is that they not only give credence to educational innovation but actually give rise to it. Many of the educational innovations that are currently in vogue were developed as a result of work which has been done in futures research.

Individualized instruction, humanistic education, movement education, and values clarification are educational strategies that anticipate alternative futures where humankind must, generally speaking, be creative, adaptable, self-actualized and self-motivated in order to be successful.

But what will the future be like? What can we expect in the next twenty or perhaps fifty years? How might people view physical education? What might our programs be like? Where might they take place? What will our responsibilities be? And most importantly, what is the projected relevancy of that which the future physical educator is learning today?

One View of Physical Education

Many futurists, regardless of their perspective or their professional background, agree with Ronald Podeschi when he writes:

> As a society, we shall have ever increasing time and energy to concern ourselves with what Maslow calls the growth or meta needs, not just our basic physical and psychological needs. The enhancement of ourselves as human beings will receive more and more of our attention as our maintenance or survival needs are satisfied easier and earlier. The dimension of physical activity as part of this enhanced human activity will undoubtedly be affected and affect the twenty-first century. If we are to become a society whose needs are being more rapidly rooted in the higher psychological, aesthetic, and spiritual dimensions of life, physical activity can no longer be a separate and sideline activity.[6]

Writing in regard to Abraham Maslow's "third force" psychology and the potential of physical activity based on this philosophical foundation, Podeschi continues to develop his thesis by stating that:

> The child's living body, which is at the center of his life, would be at the center of his education. Emphasis would be on process and movement rather than on static

5. Ibid., p. 8.

6. Ronald Podeschi, "The Farther Reaches of Physical Activity," *Quest*, Monograph 21 (January 1974): p. 13.

content at an unmovable desk. Rather than playing the usual inferior role to the so-called real curriculum, physical-aesthetic activities would lead the way for the child to learn reading, writing, and even arithmetic in a more creative, natural, and integrated way.[7]

If this position gains acceptance in the future, the mind/body distinction which has pervaded Western thought since the sixth century B.C. will be dissolved and the concept, esteemed by the Greeks, of the mind and body as one will be restored. Physical activity will be engaged in for purposes of self-actualization, creativity, and self-trust, and such activity will be viewed as a basic and necessary feature of an individual's education, not as a separate, unrelated experience in and of itself, apart from the mainstream. In the future we may find that George Leonard, author of *The Ultimate Athlete*, is correct when he says that "sports and physical education, reformed and refurbished, may provide us the best possible path to personal enlightenment and social transformation in this age."[8] Furthermore, as Podeschi has suggested, "we may even find that sport may help us dissolve the masculinity/femininity dichotomy and other such dualities which have bound both men and women in a stereotyped role for centuries."[9]

The advent of this revised and enlightened view of physical education may well be accompanied by an enlightened view of education as well. Results from numerous studies have indicated that we are prolonging formal education unnecessarily and that the custodial school as we know it today will vanish. At first glance this would seem to suggest that the role of education in our society will diminish. If children are no longer required to go to school, what will the status of education be?

At present, *schooling* and *education* are in most people's minds synonymous terms, both being defined as that period of time during which a child acquires skills that will be needed in adulthood. According to this definition, education takes place in a formal setting, under the supervision of an authority figure, for a prescribed amount of time. Upon completion of the required number of years, an individual is considered educated and is graduated into the next phase of life.

In the future, education will be defined in completely different terms; it will no longer be thought of as a segment of time in which youth absorbs the practicalities of life. Instead, education will be described as a continuous process that is engaged in throughout life for purposes of rejuvenation, reorientation, self-actualization, and socialization. Classrooms of the future will be filled with adults as well as children. No longer chided to master courses in reading, writing, and arithmetic, people will revisit the school many times throughout their lives, each time striving to achieve a higher level of self-actualization. Education consequently will not be limited by fixed periods of time. Man's imagination and desire will be the only delimiting factors. Rather than be diminished, the role of education in our society will be greatly enhanced in the future.

Education and the Work-Play Ethic

As this more enlightened approach to education is accepted, the work-play ethic will undergo changes as well. Working on the premise that man will no longer have to work to

7. Ibid., p. 14.
8. George Leonard, *The Ultimate Athlete* (New York: Viking Press, Inc., 1974), p. 20.
9. Podeschi, "Farther Reaches," p. 17.

satisfy basic maintenance and survival needs, one can speculate that human energies will be directed toward self-fulfillment and that the aspects of play which are now viewed as unrelated to work will combine with work concepts to form a totally new concept. If this occurs, "the traditions in physical education that relate to a study of the whole person moving and interacting with others throughout life can contribute immensely to such a synthesis."[10]

The New Curriculum

This enlightened view of physical education and the work-play ethic will place new responsibilities upon the profession. Society will expect programs which will enhance an individual's physical and inner awareness. Individuals will expect activities which will help them realize their full potential. In order to fulfill these responsibilities, professionals will have to develop curriculums and methods based not only on their knowledge of man and his ability to achieve but on their knowledge of the inner dimensions of sport as well.

Activities selected on the basis of their ability to heighten the individual's senses or increase his or her self-knowledge will dominate the curriculum. Eastern sport forms, such as aikido, will be introduced because of their emphasis on process rather than product. In aikido, for example, there are no winners or losers and no competition — only cooperation. As such, aikido is like a "lifelong journey with no fixed destination,"[11] a search for harmony with the universe or, in other words, a perfect sport for enhancing one's physical and inner awareness.

While this enhancement is important, it will not be the only objective of the new curriculum. Activities will also be expected to teach concepts which society deems important. Such concepts as community or harmony will be transmitted through sport or dance forms which have been developed explicitly for this purpose. Here, as in aikido, process rather than product will be emphasized. The transmitting of such concepts will be more important than the outcome of the activity.

The new curriculum may also include elements of *softwar* which would allow the individual to give vent to his emotions by allowing him to form his own conflict forms. *Softwar*, as defined by its inventor Stewart Brand, refers to "conflict which is regionalized (to prevent injury to the uninterested), refereed (to permit fairness and certainty of a win-loss outcome), and cushioned (weaponry regulated for maximum contact and minimum permanent disability)."[12] In essence, softwar resembles our present form of athletics; the major difference be ing its lack of time and form restrictions. According to Brand, softwar has no time limits and is not played according to fixed rules of form. The game continues to evolve each time it is played. This in itself makes it much more desirable for the curriculum of the future than the games offered in our present system of athletics.[13]

In contrast to and yet in combination with this psychosocial orientation of physical education, there will probably exist a scientifically based orientation towards detailed analysis of human motion for purposes of perfecting performance in any aspect of human movement, whether it be in sport or some regimen of daily living or working. This type of

10. Ginny L. Studer, "Synthesis and Coalescence," in *Physical Education: A View Toward the Future*, ed. Raymond Welsh (St. Louis: C. V. Mosby Co., 1977), p. 28.

11. Leonard, *Athlete*, p. 53.

12. Andrew Fluegelman, ed., *The New Games Book* (Garden City, NY: Doubleday & Co., Inc., Dolphin Books, 1976), p. 9.

13. Gideon Ariel, "Physical Education: 2001," *Quest*, Monograph 21 (January 1974): p. 51.

analysis will permit the formulation of principles, and guidelines based on such principles will not only help the teacher plan appropriate activities for people of varying ages, conditions, or abilities but will also aid in the development of individually prescribed training programs for achieving optimum efficiency in overall movement.

In the future, computers will be used by physical educators to monitor and continually evaluate the performance of any individual in their charge on the basis of specifically designed criteria. The computer will not only have the capabilities to evaluate performance, it will also have the ability to determine the intensity and duration of the work period as well as the energy expended throughout.[14]

> Children will be classified automatically into activities on which they are more likely to succeed. This will be determined by a program whose models are used to optimize the performance based on factors such as muscular make-up, individual link systems, psychological make-up, individual desire, and geographical location.[15]

Classification by such a system would be purely voluntary and in no way binding. If an individual chose a sport other than the one for which he or she was biomechanically best suited, the computer would also be capable of designing a program which would help maximize the individual's potential in that sport.

Thus the new curriculum will be a conglomeration of activities designed to help humans achieve self-understanding and determine their place in the world. It will serve as a vehicle for transmitting societal values and mores by direct experience and also as the means for achieving a higher degree of self-actualization regardless of an individual's age or inclination. The new curriculum will provide unlimited possiblities for the creative physical educator.

The Future Environment

Activity programs such as those previously described will be conducted in many settings throughout the community. In the public sector, where they will reach the greatest number of individuals, however, these programs will be provided through a modern-day "service center."

If the concept of the custodial school disappears, as was previously speculated, the question remains "What will become of the edifice known as the school?" The answer is simple, it too will disappear. The schoolhouse as we know it, a formalized structure set apart from the community at large, will be reclaimed as public space for use by all the people, not just the young.

It is conceivable that "under the pressure of increased public demand for a variety of social services dispensed from a single place, the schoolhouse may well become the community center and vice versa."[16] Under one roof then, one may find schooling for the young and old, medical and dental services, facilities for leisure, and government-operated services such as the post office and the library. In some cases the center may include such commercial units as pharmacies, bakeries, and even supermarkets, which will make the center somewhat of an old-fashioned marketplace.

14. Ibid., pp. 51-52.

15. Ibid., p. 52.

16. Harold B. Gores, "The Future File: Schoolhouse 2000," *Phi Delta Kappan* 56 (January 1975): p. 310.

It is within this setting then that the physical education program will be conducted in the public sector. This arrangement has many advantages. The housing of multiple services within one complex will permit great savings to be realized in energy and building costs, as well as in operating and maintenance expenses. Because of this, the center will be used to its fullest potential even in a society which is forced to frugally budget both its natural and financial resources.

Because the complex will be an amalgam of distinctly separate units, its layout will be designed to allow for maximum use. Similar services located in clusters will in turn be connected by enclosed walkways allowing access and egress both internally and externally. Within the education-and-leisure cluster, great expanses of open space will dominate the interior, thus permitting flexible scheduling. At a moment's notice walls will be erected, ceilings lowered, and lighting adjusted to create whatever environment is necessary to insure productive learning.

"Many of the larger cavities of space — stadiums, field houses, gymnasiums, and student activity centers — will be great bubbles of space, encapsulated in long-life translucent membranes, and where large spans or great heights are required, they will be air-supported."[17] These areas will be designed to allow programming flexibility as well. Unlike the basketball emporiums of the present, the gymnasium of the future will not be geared toward the comforts of spectators. Floor surfaces will be highly adaptable, thus allowing golf, ice skating, gymnastics, and volleyball to take place simultaneously, each on its own individualized surface. Nylon nets or collapsible walls will serve both as temporary dividers and as activity facilitators. A nylon or canvas net, for example, could serve both as a room divider for partitioning a golf class off from the main gym and as a natural backdrop into which golf balls could be safely driven. A collapsible wall might become the third wall of a racquetball game one period and a wall to rappel in a mountain-climbing class the next period. Located within the confines of the gymnasium will be computer terminals complete with videotape monitoring equipment, programming stations, and immediate feedback units so that students will have the benefits of individually prescribed instruction whenever the teacher feels it is appropriate.

Indeed the outstanding feature of the gymnasium of the future will be its great flexibility, its ability to be all things both swiftly and easily. Unlike the gymnasium of today, which is geared toward the spectator and used primarily as a refuge during the winter or inclement weather, the gymnasium of tomorrow will assume new dimensions, for it will have the ability to accommodate human movement needs in an environment which is flexible and free.

The Physical Educator of the Future

Earlier discussion of education's potential for helping people become self-actualized now prompts us to consider education's responsibility to help people cope with change and learn how to function in the twenty-first century. Where survival once depended upon knowing the ways of the marketplace, survival will soon depend upon the ability to cope with change. Alvin Toffler, author of *Future Shock*, paints a vivid picture of education's role in the future:

> For education the lesson is clear: its prime objective must be to increase the individual's "cope-ability" — the speed and economy with which he can adapt to con-

17. Ibid., p. 311.

> tinued change. And the faster the rate of change, the more attention must be devoted to discerning the pattern of future events.
>
> It is no longer sufficient for Johnny to understand the past. It is not even enough for him to understand the present, for the here and now environment will soon vanish. Johnny must learn to anticipate the directions and rate of change. He must, to put it technically, learn to make repeated, probabilistic, increasingly long-range assumptions about the future. And so must Johnny's teachers.[18]

And so Johnny's teachers, the teachers of the twenty-first century, must learn to anticipate change and make long-range assumptions. They must be informed, future-oriented, and adaptable individuals that are capable of envisioning future alternatives and devising suitable courses of action for themselves and their pupils.

Some believe that the teacher's role in the future will be little different than it is today, and in part they are right. Throughout time, teachers have been expected to understand the individual needs of every student placed in their charge and to account for individual differences in their presentation of material. But, in the future this will become a much more complex task. Teachers, in addition to being students of human identity and group dynamics, will have to be students of movement technology and instructional technology as well, for the "study of nonverbal behavior patterns, the genesis of human movement, the functional aspects of human movement, and theories of human movement will be woven into the existing matrix of sport, dance, techniques gymnastic, and aquatic skills and techniques."[19]

Teachers must be able to integrate, synthesize, and coordinate diverse concepts representing both the psychosocial and bioanalytic dimensions in a way such that the individual needs of their students are best served.

Without a doubt, the demands made on physical educators in the future will far outweigh those made on their contemporary counterparts, for today we will deal with only the physical aspect of the individual, whereas, tomorrow we will be responsible for the whole person.

What Is the Projected Relevancy of What the Future Physical Educator Is Learning?

To answer this question one must consider the students being taught in the schools today and ask what their needs will be tomorrow. Contained in the following list are characteristics of life in the future which most experts agree can be expected and which will most likely have bearing on this question:

1. The normal life span will probably exceed ninety years
2. Vitality will probably be retained throughout one's life
3. Change will escalate at a tremendous rate
4. People's basic needs for comfort will be met
5. Life will not be viewed in time sequences of work versus play but in periods of work, rejuvenation, revitalization, etc.
6. Greater emphasis will be placed on self-actualization
7. The individual will explore several professions or vocations in a lifetime

18. Alvin Toffler, *Future Shock* (New York: Bantam Books, Inc., 1970), p. 403.
19. Ulrich, "Future Hour," p. 128.

In view of the changes forseen, students in the future will need to learn how to: 1) value education as a continuing process; 2) cope with change; 3) respond creatively to problems; 4) be self-directed; and 5) keep in tune with their inner self.

Teachers in turn will need to learn how to provide opportunities for creativity and individual development, and how to provide opportunities for decision making and group dynamics. Most importantly, teachers will need to work closely with individuals in the community and be able to respond to their needs by implementing those methods and activities that will best permit self-actualization to occur. If the present schooling program for physical educators does not meet these needs and fails to develop the abilities which the future demands, if its primary goal is only to train sports buffs and athletes, then its projected relevancy is zero and the program must change.

chapter two
Styles of Teaching

Much of the theorization and research in the field of education has been devoted to the effects of various instructional methods on learning. Most authors in the field have tended to view the teaching process as being polarized into two styles: the formal teacher-centered style and the more informal student-centered style. A few others have attempted to identify a third style, falling somewhere between the two extremes, which combines several components of each. Teachers, too, have traditionally tended to follow one or the other of the major styles of teaching to the exclusion of other alternatives. Muska Mosston, on the other hand, has developed a catalog of seven distinct styles of teaching which covers the entire continuum from teacher-centered to student-centered behavior.[1] This work has had considerable impact upon the teaching profession.

A style of teaching, as defined by Mosston, is basically a set of decisions made in conjunction with the teaching act. The shift from one style to another is facilitated by the transfer of certain of these decisions from the teacher to the student. At the theoretical extremes of the continuum, one finds styles where the decisions are made exclusively by either the teacher or the student. The relative position of any teaching style along this continuum is determined by the number and the type of decisions that the student is allowed to make in the planning, the execution, and the evaluation of the lesson. The shift from any given style to one on a higher level of the continuum is characterized by the transfer of more decision making from the teacher to the student.

CATEGORIES OF DECISION MAKING

Mosston contends that all teaching decisions can be assembled into three categories which must be present whenever the teaching/learning process is in effect. These three categories are the *pre-impact* or planning phase, the *impact* or execution phase, and the *post-impact* or evaluation phase. Table 2.1 illustrates some of the types of decisions which are included in each of the three decision-making categories. These three sets of decisions make up what Mosston calls the anatomy of a teaching style.

1. Muska Mosston, *Teaching Physical Education* (Columbus, OH: Charles E. Merrill Publishing Co., 1966).

Table 2.1. The Anatomy of a Style.

Decision set	Decisions to be made
Pre-Impact (content preparation)	1. whom to teach 2. what to teach 3. where to teach a. starting b. stopping c. duration d. rhythm/pace e. interval f. termination 4. quality 5. quantity 6. communication 7. teaching style 8. anticipated learning style 9. class climate 10. why 11. evaluative procedures and materials 12. others
Impact (content execution performance)	1. implementing and adhering to the set of pre-impact decisions 2. adjustment 3. others
Post-Impact (content evaluation)	1. about feedback; a. reinforcement: (1) immediate (2) delayed b. correction: (1) immediate (2) delayed 2. about interpreting and evaluative data procedures and materials a. instrumentation b. frequency c. norms 3. about the teaching-learning transaction itself 4. others

SOURCE: Muska Mosston, *Teaching: From Command to Discovery* (Belmont, CA: Wadsworth Publishing Co., Inc., 1972). Reprinted with the permission of the publisher.

Any given teaching style can, therefore, be explicitly defined by describing the relative involvement of the teacher and the student in each phase of the decision-making process;

and the act of moving from a particular teaching style to the next one along the continuum calls for an increase in the number and type of decisions made by the student. The following specific teaching styles move progressively from minimal to maximal involvement of the student in the decision-making process.

THE COMMAND STYLE

The essense of the command style of teaching is the complete domination of all phases of decision making by the teacher.[2] The teacher makes all decisions in every phase of the anatomy of the style. The only student decision which is even theoretically possible is whether or not to comply with teacher directives and participate. And, since there is really only one acceptable answer to that question (at least in the eyes of the teacher), one can only conclude that, in the practical sense, the student makes *no* decisions. Probably the best example of pure command behavior is seen in military drill sergeants. They control everything from the choice of activity to the rate of performance to the evaluation of that performance. The individuals in their command are expected to comply with every direction, attend to every explanation, and perform essentially as a single unit, much like a group of robots.

The theoretical support for this type of teaching is found in the stimulus-response learning theory. This theory assumes that stimulus *x* will produce response *y* and that the student, through his or her participation in a planned series of S-R situations, will learn and/or achieve the desired physical skill. It is assumed, consequently, that development and learn ing will, of necessity, accompany planned, directed participation. The role of the teacher, therefore, is to control all variables in the preparation, execution, and evaluation phases. The student's role, on the other hand, is expected to be one of total compliance.

An important element in this schema is the demonstration. If the teacher is going to demand adherence to a restricted set of performance criteria (as, indeed, he or she must in executing the command style), then it is necessary that these criteria be clearly explained and illustrated to the students. The demonstration provides the most common and probably the most efficient means by which the desired criteria can be made clear to the students. It sets a standard to which the students are expected to conform and serves as a valuable adjunct to the verbal presentation of the teacher. Great care must be taken, however, to avoid the pitfalls which can, in some cases, undermine a teacher demonstration. An imprecise or poorly conducted demonstration, for example, can set an unsatisfactory model for student behavior and actually lead to the development of incorrect motor skills. A second pitfall can result from the fine distinction between a demonstration which serves to effectively illustrate a teaching point and one which serves primarily to bolster the teacher's ego. While the former enhances learning, the latter can, and often does, impede it — either by generating a "show-off" image of the teacher or by illustrating a level of performance which is far beyond the reach of the students.

The command style, like any other style of teaching, has both advantages and disadvantages. Done well, the command style (and its classroom corollary, the lecture) is the most efficient of all styles in terms of the amount of information or practice which can be provided

2. Ibid., p. 19

in a given period of time. It provides for a high degree of uniformity in student performance, as each student is required to conform to a teacher-designed pattern. This uniformity in performance also lends an "eyewash" effect to command teaching found in no other style: a large group performing any given activity in unison or an individual accurately performing a skill "by the numbers" looks impressive. While research on the styles of teaching is scant, there is some evidence to show that if one has only a relatively short period of time within which instruction and practice can take place, for example six weeks, command teaching will result in greater fitness and motor-skill development than other styles of teaching.[3] Another advantage of command teaching is that, compared to other styles, it requires a less thorough knowledge of the subject matter in order to succeed. Because the teacher has complete control, he or she can, and in fact must, control the rate of flow of information. There is no give-and-take, and therefore, little likelihood of unpredictable questions and/or responses. The teacher, therefore, can avoid the necessity of either dealing with unpredictable questions or individualizing instructions to suit the needs and ideas of each student. This same situation, however, gives rise to one of the major shortcomings of the style: it is insensitive to individual needs and differences.

Even if a class happens to approximate that elusive Gaussian bell curve, and even if the teacher is capable, whether through skill or guesswork, of approximating the present average of the class in terms of some skill, any program designed for that average still fails to meet the needs of those students on either extreme of the curve, or about 30 percent of the class. An additional shortcoming of the command style is that it hampers the development of creativity and individuality. Students are required to conform to a specified pattern at a predetermined rate. Behaviors which deviate from the prescription are regarded as inappropriate and are either modified or eliminated by the teacher. A further consideration which has some research support is the fact that students taught exclusively through the command style tend to devote less extra classtime to the skills being taught.[4] It would appear, therefore, that the command style fails to provide some factor necessary to the development of self-motivation, which is a major shortcoming if we truly seek to prepare our pupils for the future.

Before leaving the discussion of the command style, one further point deserves mention. Rarely, if ever, does the command style exist in a pure form. It is virtually impossible and certainly impractical for a teacher to attempt to control each and every decision concerning a lesson. If, for instance, the teacher says "Jump up, using the following prescribed form," the student can still select a starting time. If the teacher also prescribes the starting time, the question of how high to jump still has to be resolved, and so on. In the authors' experiences, we have never seen *pure* command teaching in any but the most restricted demonstration circumstances. In the practical situation, the question is more one of how many decisions can be controlled and with what degree of consistency. Consequently, while that extreme on the decision-making continuum where the teacher makes every decision is theoretically possible, it is extremely improbable in the practical sense. Without doubt, however, one can, if one so desires, control a sufficient majority of the teaching decisions to be clearly labeled a command teacher.

3. Neil J. Dougherty, "A Comparison of the Effects of Command, Task, and Individual Styles of Teaching in the Development of Physical Fitness and Motor Skills," Ed.D. diss., Temple University, 1970.

4. Ibid.

THE TASK STYLE

As was previously stated, the pure command teacher is a rare entity. Almost invariably, either by change or by design, teachers will allow their students to make a limited number of decisions during the impact phase of the lesson, and in so doing, they approach the next level of the continuum, which Mosston has labeled the task style.[5] In teaching by task, the teacher must permit students to make certain decisions during the impact or execution phase. For example, a teacher might organize the class and begin a warm-up drill, using traditional command techniques, but then say, "When I say 'begin,' I want each of you to do ten push-ups and then sit upright on your spot when you are finished. Ready ... begin." This assignment, with its implicit permission to set one's own rate of performance, would be a simple task. To carry the example a step further, the teacher might then say: "Based upon your success at that task, I am going to allow you a little more responsibility. On my signal, find a new spot on the floor and do ten sit-ups, ten jumping jacks, and fifteen side-stretches. When finished, just sit in place. Ready .... begin." The students are now free to make geographical decisions, decisions as to the rate of performance, and even, if they so desire, decisions as to the order of performance. The teacher still retains control over the type and quantity of the exercises as well as starting time and gross geographical limitations.

It is particularly important here that the students understand that the teacher is *allowing* them to make a limited number of decisions. While this may seem like a minor point that is probably self-evident to any reasonably alert student, it is not. Consider, for example, a situation where the teacher is conducting what he or she considers to be a command lesson, but, because all execution variables are not being controlled, the students are actually performing at a variety of rates. This is not an example of task teaching, it is simply sloppy command teaching and, moreover, the students know it! The message they get here is not that the teacher is willing to allow them to make a decision, but that the teacher cannot prevent them from making it. This is a subtle but infinitely important distinction which has a tremendous impact on class control and discipline as well as on any further modifications one may attempt to make in the decision-making continuum.

Once the student has been permitted to make decisions regarding such factors as geographical location, rate of performance, and order of execution, another problem arises: there is a functional limit to the memory of the student. Can one, for example, realistically expect an entire class of fifth-graders to remember that the teacher asked them to do ten sit-ups, fifteen jumping jacks, eight push-ups, twenty-five toe-touches, and twelve straddle-hops? Of course not. The solution is simple. Put it in writing. Design a card or paper which gives the exercises or activities and the quantities desired. If the reading level of the students is a problem, simple stick figures help tremendously.

The use of the task sheets provides several advantages:

1. They help the student to remember what to do
2. They provide a record for the teacher and the student of what was accomplished during a given period
3. They provide an immediate visual reference for the teacher when dealing individually with a student. This reference includes the student's name and the skill he or she is working on.

Figure 2.1 is an example of a single sheet that presents the student with several tasks.

5. Mosston, *Physical Education*, p. 31ff.

FIGURE 2.1. Simple Task Sheet.

Name____________________ Date____________________

Check off each skill as you complete it.

1.	Jumping jacks	25	Completed_____
2.	Sit-ups	20	Completed_____
3.	Balance beam — walk entire beam heel-to-toe, arms free		Completed_____
4.	Fingertip push-ups	10	Completed_____
5.	Inverted balance — tripod, 5 seconds		Completed_____
6.	Toe-touches, feet together	10	Completed_____

While this task sheet allows more freedom to the student than the command style, it still allows no choice as to quantity, and, therefore, fails to recognize the wide variety of individual differences likely within any given class. Therefore, the simple task sheet serves as a necessary preparatory step in developing the individual decision-making ability of the student, or it can be an end in itself. A more satisfactory solution, however, and one which is still within the scope of task-style teaching, is to provide a range of tasks as illustrated in Figure 2.2. The students are now free to set their own performance levels in keeping with their individual abilities. The tasks should be designed such that the lowest level is below that of the poorest performer in the class and the highest level is above that of the best performer. The result of such an arrangement is that no one is programmed for failure and everyone has higher goals to seek.

Aside from the obvious need for pre-planning and task-sheet preparation, there are also some very important features of teacher role behavior implicit within the task style. Foremost among these is the responsibility for individualized instruction. The teacher has been released from the role of stimulus-emitter which was imposed by the command style. The students now receive their performance initiation cues from the task sheet. The activity becomes the stimulus. The teacher, therefore, is free to move about the class giving individual attention and guidance where needed. Praise and criticism can now be administered privately along with corrective feedback, personal encouragement, or whatever other teacher/pupil interchange may be appropriate. This does not eliminate the possibility of directing feedback and comments to the class as a whole, but it does, however, open the door to other possibilities which did not exist with the command style. Another important factor is the teacher's ability to adjust to a situation in which thirty pupils may be doing thirty different things simultaneously. One must learn how to spot individual needs and achievements within such a framework. Furthermore, there must be an acceptance of diversity and a dedication to individual accomplishment. If the teacher cannot see his or her students as individuals within a class, no matter how large or small, then the full potential of task-style teaching will never be realized.

While the opportunity to individualize instruction is the primary advantage of task teaching, there are other values which are important and bear mention. Because a variety

FIGURE 2.2. Task Sheet With Ranges.

Name____________________ Date____________________

Instructions: Check each level as you accomplish it. Work for *continual improvement.*

1. Jumping jacks — 2 minutes
   Number completed: 25____ 30____ 35____ 40____ 45____ 50____ over 60____

2. Sit-ups — 2 minutes
   Number completed: 30____ 40____ 50____ 60____ 70____ 80____ 90____ over 100____

3. Balance beam (use spotters)
   (a) walk entire beam, heel-to-toe, arms free____
   (b) walk entire beam, heel-to-toe, arms behind back____
   (c) walk half beam, heel-to-toe, backwards____
   (d) walk entire beam, heel-to-toe, backwards____

4. Fingertip push-ups — maximum without stopping
   5____ 10____ 15____ 20____ 25____ 30____ 35____ over 40____

5. Inverted balance (use spotters)

(a) tripod	5 seconds____	7 seconds____	10 seconds____
(b) tip-up	5 seconds____	7 seconds____	10 seconds____
(c) headstand	5 seconds____	7 seconds____	10 seconds____
(d) handstand	3 seconds____	5 seconds____	7 seconds____
(e) handstand	180-degree turn and stop____	270°____	360°____

6. Straddle toe-touch: Place toes along the edge of one floorboard, feet shoulder-width apart. Score the number of boards you can touch behind toes without bending your knees. 10 repetitions
   1 board____ 2 boards____ 3 boards____ 4 boards____
   feet six inches apart: 1 board____ 2 boards____ 3 boards____ 4 boards____
   feet together: 1 board____ 2 boards____ 3 boards____ 4 boards____
   more than 4 boards____

---

of tasks can be designed for a single class and because it is not necessary to have each pupil perform each task at the same time, or even in the same order, there can be a more efficient use of equipment. Tasks on the balance beam, for instance, can be included with balance tasks on the floor, on practice beams, and even with tasks on other pieces of apparatus. The opportunity for maximal participation within existing equipment limitations is increased greatly. A further advantage of the task style is that it is relatively independent of class size. If well planned, this style works equally well with either large or small groups. A final advantage, but by no means the least important, is the psychological impact of task-style teaching on the student. The successes and failures of each student are no longer known to the entire class. Criticism and praise can now be administered privately, thus removing any stigma from the underachiever as well as reducing the "hero" image of the star athlete. It is easy to imagine the potential benefits this style affords in terms of improved pupil self-image and better teacher/pupil relations.

While the possibilities for task individualization give rise to the major advantages of the task style, they also constitute its greatest shortcoming. Reduced to simplest terms, the problem is that a student can hide! Because of the diversity of activities being conducted at any given time, students can, if they are so inclined, lose themselves in a mass of activity, avoid most personal contacts with the teacher, and perform only as much as may be absolutely necessary to escape detection. After awhile, of course, the attentive teacher will become aware of such a situation and take the steps necessary to correct it. In the meantime, however, the student has lost valuable developmental opportunities. The more experience teachers have with the task style, the easier it is for them to divide their attention among the total group of individuals rather than a selected few and thereby effectively lessen the opportunities for hiding. Furthermore, if the additional decision-making opportunities are presented gradually and with careful planning, the students are far less likely to deviate from the behavior patterns which the instructor has outlined as being acceptable.

THE RECIPROCAL STYLE

Having allowed the student to enter into the decision-making process in the execution phase of the task style, the teacher can now extend this involvement by increasing the number of available decisions. The reciprocal style begins to shift the evaluation variable to the student. Two restrictions are, for the time being, imposed. First the area of evaluation being manipulated with the reciprocal style of teaching is specifically limited to the correction of performance errors. The second restriction involves the decision-making shift itself, for one cannot, at this point, assume that the students are able to evaluate themselves. Instead, the teacher allows them, with careful guidance, to evaluate one another. Therein lies the crux of Mosston's reciprocal style of teaching: one student acts as the performer while another student evaluates his or her performance according to criteria carefully established and outlined by the teacher.[6]

The advantages of this arrangement are obvious. There is a one-to-one student/teacher ratio. Each student has, in effect, his or her own private tutor to provide immediate feedback. The potential for skill improvement through immediate feedback is well documented in the literature and the concept is brought to a practical application for every student with the reciprocal style. There is, additionally, an enhancement of self-image when students can see that they have been of assistance to their peers. One need not know how to execute a given skill in order to tell whether another's performance of that skill meets a certain set of well-defined criteria. It is necessary only for one to understand the criteria and observe the performance to note discrepancies. This technique has succeeded in a wide variety of activities ranging from gymnastics to volleyball and even swimming. It is, in fact, an excellent technique for teaching beginner swimming. One student standing on the pool deck giving feedback on a specific, well-defined set of performance criteria can greatly accelerate the learning of a partner in the pool. Moreover, the evaluator, as he or she constantly reviews the necessary performance criteria, goes through a process of mental practice which provides a much firmer mental picture of the proper technique when the roles are reversed.

The reciprocal style, however, is not without its potential hazards and drawbacks, and these problems are intimately tied to the specific behavioral changes required of the

6. Ibid., p. 71ff.

teacher if the style is to succeed. Most of the hazards center around the role of the student-observer and the importance of such a position in the teaching/learning process. There are, for example, very real dangers to the emotional state of any student who is teamed with a teaching partner who tends to be overly critical. There is a limit to the amount of negative feedback that even the most secure student can withstand. It is, therefore, the responsibility of the teacher to insure that students using the reciprocal style learn to praise as well as to criticize one another. In many instances this is not a simple matter, and the most effective solution lies in a series of preparatory lessons. These lessons concentrate first on praise only and later on a specified number of praises and criticisms until the students become accustomed to presenting a careful, balanced review of a demonstrated skill. The quantity and nature of the feedback given by the teacher is also a major determinant of the corrective techniques which the students are likely to employ.

A second potential drawback to the reciprocal style is the possibility that a teacher-partner may reinforce incorrect performance. This possibility is reduced most effectively by the preparation of exceptionally clear evaluative criteria which are spelled out in detail. In this manner, the teacher-partner has but to compare the established criteria with the performance of his or her classmate. The better the written or pictorial description and accompanying explanation and demonstration, the less the likelihood of observational error.

Another source of potential breakdown is seen in the status of the teacher-partner. The teacher must be careful to reinforce the status of the students and help build their partner's confidence in them. This is done primarily by speaking only to the teaching partner. If the teacher wishes to affect change in a student's performance it must be accomplished through that student's teacher-partner in as subtle a manner as possible. Such questions as "How is your partner doing?" "What areas still need work?" and "How is the position of the feet?" guide the observer toward those areas needing further work. Comments such as, "John is doing very well, you are a fine teacher," or "That's a good point, Mary, that's the way to help her," give an indication of the teaching partner's success and value and can, at the same time, provide praise for the performer. The point is that, in either case, the status of the teaching partner is elevated. Every time the teacher steps in and corrects or "teaches" the performer, the unspoken message is that the teaching partner is doing an unsatisfactory job and the status of the teaching partner is lowered accordingly. After a few such incidents, the performing partner will begin to ignore corrections and comments regardless of their validity. This is a very difficult aspect of the reciprocal style for a teacher to master.

Stepping in to assist in learning difficulties is a very natural reaction for a teacher. The let-me-help-you syndrome becomes almost habitual. In order to succeed with the reciprocal style, a teacher must overcome this instinct and replace it with a subtler means of guidance, i.e., guidance that is channeled through an intermediary. There is only one instance when this concept of intervention through an observer should be violated, and that is in the case of impending physical danger to the performer. The student-observer may not be able to detect physical dangers as quickly as an experienced teacher; and while careful instruction and demonstration will reduce the incidence of dangerous situations, emergencies may, nevertheless, arise. If they do, the teacher should not hesitate to intervene immediately. There is never any excuse for endangering the safety of one's pupils, and an unsafe situation that is quickly and quietly remedied by the teacher is far less destructive to the status of the student-observer than a painful injury to his or her partner.

Figures 2.3 and 2.4 illustrate the types of worksheets used in reciprocal teaching in a variety of subject matter areas.

THE SMALL-GROUP STYLE

The small-group style of teaching is a simple extension of the reciprocal style that utilizes more than two students.[7] The key here is that each member of the group has a functional role to perform in the learning task and, as in reciprocal teaching, the students each take their turn at each task as the lesson progresses. A small-group arrangement in basketball, for example, might have one student as the shooter, another as the observer giving feedback on the quality of the shooting form, and a third student as the rebounder and scorer.

While this style provides the same general advantages and disadvantages as the reciprocal style, it also permits more efficient utilization of equipment. In the preceding example for instance, three students are productively and simultaneously occupied with each basketball. However, more or fewer students can be occupied in any activity depending upon the availability of equipment and the teacher's own ability to modify the subject matter.

FIGURE 2.3. Reciprocal Worksheet — Sidestroke.

Directions: Check ✓ all items that apply to the performance of this skill. Add other noted errors in the spaces provided.

Name ______________________
(of performer)

Name ______________________
(of analyzer)

Illustrations of correct techniques	Analysis of performance

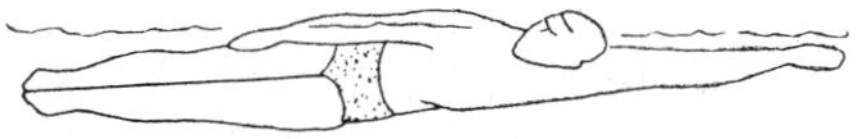

BODY POSITION

___The form *is* acceptable.
___The form is *not* acceptable because:
 ___Arms and legs not fully extended.
 ___Legs not together.
 ___Body not stretched and straight.
 ___Body turned toward stomach-down position
 ___Body turned toward back-down position
 ___Head not turned toward the upper shoulder to facilitate breathing.
 ___(Other)______________________
 ____

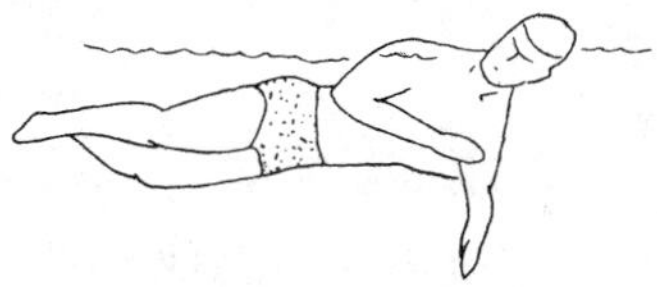

LEGS

___The form *is* acceptable.
___The form is *not* acceptable because:
 ___Legs separated vertically; resulting in a breaststroke kick.

7. Ibid., p. 93ff.

FIGURE 2.3. Reciprocal Worksheet (cont'd).

____Inverted scissors kick used.
____Legs do not bend enough at knees during recovery.
____Knees brought too far in front of stomach during recovery.
____Legs recovered too vigorously.
____Legs not straightened before the squeeze.
____Too little effort during squeeze.
____Ankles not extended to point toes during late part of squeeze.
____Legs pass each other at end of squeeze.
____(Other)________________________

ARMS

____The form *is* acceptable.
____The form is *not* acceptable because:
____Pull of the leading (lower) arm too short.
____Pull of leading arm too deep.
____Leading arm not recovered with finger tips leading.
____Elbow of leading arm not brought to ribs before recovery of that arm.
____Trailing (upper) arm does not pull to thigh.
____(Other)________________________

COORDINATION AND BREATHING

____The form *is* acceptable.
____The form is *not* acceptable because:
____Both arms pull toward feet at same time.
____Leading arm begins pull immediately after recovery.
____Leading arm pulls at same time kick is delivered.
____Kick delivered before leading arm ready to recover.
____Exhalation is at a time other than during leg kick or during glide.
____Inhalation does not follow immediately after exhalation.
____The duration of the glide is too brief.
____(Other)________________________
____

SOURCE: John A. Torney, Jr., and Robert D. Clayton. *Aquatic Instruction Coaching and Management* (Minneapolis: Burgess Publishing, 1970), pp. 86-87.

FIGURE 2.4. Reciprocal Worksheet — Inverted Balance (Headstand).

Name ______________________ Partner's Name ______________________

Activity: Inverted Balance (Headstand) Task Card **#1**

Tasks	Complete	In-complete	Comments and Corrections
Task 1 — Base position Kneel on one knee, place hands on floor, shoulder-width apart. Place your head (at hairline) on mat in front of hands so that head and hands form an equilateral triangle. Things to look for: equilateral triangle, head contacting mat at hairline. 5 times			
Task 2 — Tripod From the base position in Task 1, move your right leg forward onto right arm just above the elbow. Then move left leg onto left upper arm. Hold position for ten seconds. Things to look for: knees firmly resting on arms, solid base of support, both feet off floor. 5 times			
Task 3 — Headstand Shifting weight slightly forward, slowly straighten and raise both legs. Point toes and extend body as high as possible. Hold position for ten seconds. Things to look for: toes pointed, body steady, back straight. 5 times			

THE INDIVIDUAL-PROGRAM STYLE

The aim of the individual-program style of teaching is to extend the opportunity for self-motivated learning and decision making over a more prolonged period of time than was the case with any of the preceding styles.[8] This is accomplished primarily through a further

8. Ibid., p. 97ff.

shifting of the decisions in the area of evaluation, so that in the individual-program style, the student is given the opportunity for self-assessment.

While the individual program can take a variety of forms ranging from quantitative evaluation to programmed instruction and qualitative evaluation, certain identifiable characteristics remain constant:

1. Each separate individual program focuses on a single unit of subject matter.
2. Individual programs require a gradual freeing of the student from the traditional teacher stimuli. The aim is to develop greater independence over a longer period of time.
3. The individual program should serve both as a means of assessing present performance levels and encouraging self-improvement.
4. The teacher, who is now freed from the role of group leader and motivator can concentrate on individual guidance and consultation during the class period.

Of the several possible forms which the individual program can take, the most elementary would call for a simple quantitative self-evaluation. For example:

Attempt each task each day and circle your score:

Task	*Level 1*	*Level 2*	*Level 3*
pushups	5,6,7,8 9,10	11,12,13, 14,15	2 sets 10, 2 sets 15 3 sets 15, 3 sets 20
headstand	3 seconds	5 seconds	15 seconds
volleyball service to a designated target (20 serves)	1-7 on target	8-14 on target	15-20 on target

---

One can see that each of the tasks, when combined with others in the same subject matter area, could constitute the basis for several practice sessions, and it is to this end that they should be designed.

Having learned to evaluate themselves quantitatively, students are then ready for the more difficult task of qualitative self-assessment. A general format for a qualitative individual program might be as follows:

Perform each of the following tasks four times each, circle the level of performance, and complete the evaluative comments to the right of each:

Task	*Fair / Good / Excellent*	*Errors*
Break down into its component parts. Explain clearly and in great detail.	Include a clear description of the specific criteria making up each category.	Allow space for students to list the specific criteria they failed to attain.

It is absolutely essential that the qualitative individual program be very carefully planned and well written. Without a crystal-clear delineation of the factors involved in the performance, students cannot hope to accurately assess themselves. Since many students will, in all probability, lack an accurate sense of kinesthesis, it would help if they were provided specific visual and/or tactile clues. For example, instead of merely directing the student to "keep the legs together throughout the forward roll," one might instead say, "Place a single piece of paper between the knees and complete the roll without dropping it." Or, in the case of the set shot, rather than merely saying, "Follow through," one might say, "After release, the index finger of the shooting hand is pointing at a spot just above the rim of the basket." Obviously, the more thought and imagination one is able to bring to bear on the various evaluative criteria, the more valuable they are likely to be to the student.

The third major form of the individual program is programmed instruction. In designing a programmed lesson, one must first decide upon the final target or goal. Once this decision is made, the goal must be analyzed and broken down into its component parts. Having decided upon the component parts, one must then organize them into a sequence of tasks (ones that most students will be successful at) which, upon completion, will lead the students to the accomplishment of the final goal. Examples of qualitative and quantitative individual programs and programmed lessons are shown in Figures 2.5, 2.6, and 2.7.

FIGURE 2.5. Individual Program (Quantitative).

Name______________________________ Team______________________________

Do each of the items listed below as soon as you enter class on the next four dates. Record the date of each trial, circle the number of completions, and hand in to the instructor after the final session.

Item One — Overhand Serve: Serve the volleyball into the opposite court fifteen times. Record the number of legal serves.

Item Two — Forearm Pass: Pass the volleyball to the wall above the color change repeatedly for 30 seconds. Execute at least two trials. Record the number of legal passes that hit above or on the color line in the most successful trial.

Item Three — Overhand Pass: Execute a 30-second trial with a volleyball (VB), a soccer ball (SB), and a basketball (BB). In each trial, attempt to pass the ball repeatedly against the wall above the color line. Record the number of *legal* overhand passes that go over or hit the line.

Date________________________

	Level 1	*Level 2*	*Level 3*
Item One	1 2 3 4 5	6 7 8 9 10	11 12 13 14 15
Item Two	0-10____	11-20____	21-45____
Item Three (VB)	0-10____	11-20____	21-45____
Item Three (SB)	0-10____	11-20____	21-45____
Item Three (BB)	0-10____	11-20____	21-45____

FIGURE 2.6. Individual Program (Qualitative).

Name_______________________

Be sure you can do (a) before (b), (b) before (c), and (c) before (d).

1. Compact forward roll
   a. From a squat with hands on mat outside knees; push off toes, tuck head, do forward roll; end up sitting holding knees (maintain compact position).
   b. From standing; squat and repeat step 1a.
   c. From standing; squat and do step 1a but get enough momentum to end up standing.
   d. Form check: repeat step 1c with slip of paper between knees (see if you can end up without losing paper).
2. Compact backward roll
   a. From squat; roll backward, immediately placing hands on mat (or fists if easier) along side of ears — do not do the roll yet.
   b. From squat; repeat step 1a but go through roll, pushing off with the hands to return to squat.
   c. From standing; squat and do backward roll; return to standing.
   d. Form check: use paper between knees and do backward roll.

FIGURE 2.7. Programmed Instruction: Volleyball — Forearm Pass.

Section A

1A____ Bounce ball to self, bend low, bump it up at least 10 feet and catch it without moving more than one step. Repeat 5 times. Record the number of successes.

2A____ Stand 5 feet from the wall. Bounce the ball, bump-pass to the wall above the 10-foot line, touch the floor with both hands and catch the ball before it bounces. Repeat ten times. Record the number of successes. If the number is 8 or greater, proceed to 3A, if less than 8, try 2B.

2B____ Stand 5 feet from the wall. Bounce the ball, bump-pass to the wall above the 10-foot line, clap and catch the ball before it bounces. Repeat 5 times. Record number of successes. Proceed to 3A.

FIGURE 2.7. Programmed Instruction: Volleyball (cont'd).

3A____Stand 5 feet from the wall. Bounce the ball, bump-pass to the wall above 10-foot line. Take two slides to left, touch the floor and slide back. Catch the ball before it bounces. Repeat 5 times to the left and 5 times to the right. Record your score. If the number is 6 or greater, proceed to 4A; if it is less than 6, try 3B.	3B____Stand 5 feet from the wall. Bump-pass the ball over the 10-foot line, execute a full turn and catch the ball before it bounces. Repeat 3 times turning to the right and 3 times to the left. Record your score.
4A____Toss the ball to self. Bounce-pass the ball repeatedly to the wall. Do not allow it to bounce in between passes or to strike the wall below the line. Make 3 separate attempts. If you accomplish 10 passes in succession, record and proceed to 5A. If the number of successive passes is less than 10, try 4B.	4B____Toss the ball to self. Bounce-pass to the wall above the 10-foot line, allow it to bounce on the floor and bounce-pass again. Continue until a miss occurs. Repeat twice. Record greatest number of successive passes. Proceed directly to 5B.
5A____Toss the ball to self. Bounce-pass the ball upward at least 10 feet, execute a half-turn while keeping foot stationary and bounce-pass again, catch the ball. Repeat 10 times.	5B____Toss the ball to self and attempt to bump-pass the ball upward over your head. Repeat 5 times without missing. Make 3 separate attempts.

The individual-program style of teaching offers the possibility for increased individual freedom and develops students who can function as self-motivated, self-assessing learners. It is not, however, a style that can be implemented without a great deal of preparation and planning. First, the students must be led to the point where they can cope satisfactorily with the extended period of independent decision making called for in the style. It is highly improbable that a class taught primarily with the command style could shift abruptly to the individual-program style of teaching. The decision-making ability of the students must be carefully developed over time. Second, because the students will need specific cues by which to evaluate themselves, and because each task must be broken down in such detail, it is essential that the teacher have excellent command of the subject matter and plan each task in minute detail. Finally, if the programs are to realize their fullest potential, the teacher must review them after each class session to determine whether any portions of the program need further explanation and which students will need additional individual attention during the next class session.

THE GUIDED-DISCOVERY STYLE

Thus far the styles have gradually increased the independence and decision-making ability of the student. They have increased the potential for individualized practice and physical development, and they have offered increased opportunity for social interaction with other members of the class. They have not, however, developed one very important aspect of the total student, the intellectual capacity. Up to this point the student has merely been required to follow a set of guidelines, to select within a framework, or to evaluate according to a rigidly defined set of criteria. While these things may require a certain degree of attention and concentration, they do not make use of those higher-level thought processes usually associated with the development of the intellect. Such processes as synthesis, inquiry, comparison, invention, and discovery have been conspicuously absent in the framework up to this point.

The guided-discovery style, however, offers a solution to this dilemma in that it uses the process of inquiry to lead the students to the discovery of the desired end product.[9] That end product can be as specific as a performance technique or a fact, or it can be as general as the relationship between several different skills or the concepts underlying their development. The real key is the inquiry process through which the students are led to the desired end.

The teacher must first set the scene. Through a process of questioning, all students must be brought to the point where a common background or a common starting point can be assumed. Having established this background and made whatever preliminary statements may be necessary, the teacher then leads the students through a series of carefully designed questions to the discovery. The questions must be designed so that question 2 is based on the answer to question 1, question 3 is based on the information gleaned from the solution to question 2, and so on. Each succeeding question should narrow in on the target until the solution to the final question results in the desired discovery. The following diagram illustrates the funnel effect of the questioning process.[10]

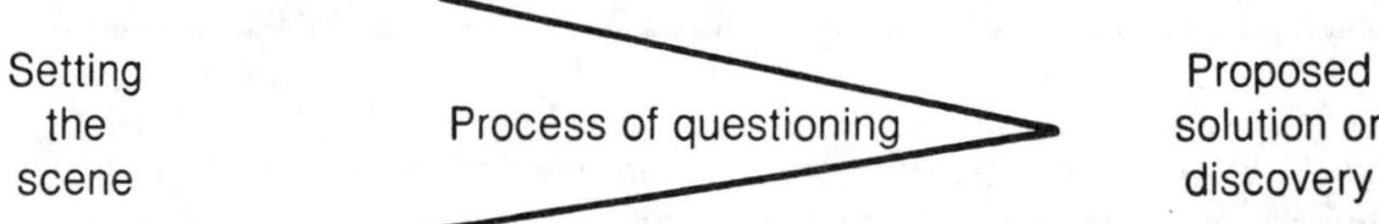

Teaching by guided discovery is an interesting but, at times, difficult process for the teacher. During the preparatory phase, the teacher must decide on the target to be sought. Having decided on the target, the teacher must next determine the tentative sequence of steps or questions which will lead students to that target.

Although these steps must be planned, it should be understood that since each question is to be predicated upon the previous answer, it is quite likely that the sequence will be changed during the execution phase due to the diversity of possible student responses and the teacher's inability to accurately predict all of them. In this regard, the student is in a very real sense beginning to exert an influence over the pre-class or planning phase of the lesson.

9. Ibid., p. 143ff.

10. Adapted from Muska Mosston, *Teaching: From Command to Discovery* (Belmont, CA: Wadsworth Publishing Co., Inc., 1972), p. 131.

During the execution phase of the lesson, the teacher must follow the question-and-answer format through to the planned conclusion. This calls for in-depth knowledge of the subject being taught and a great deal of confidence in one's own ability to manipulate the subject matter. There are, in addition, several ground rules which will facilitate smooth development of the guided-discovery process:

1. *After asking a question, always wait for a student response.* Do not be afraid of a few seconds of silence, it takes time for students to *think.*
2. *Reword the question if you must, but never give the answer.* If after a reasonable wait, no answers are forthcoming, you may have taken too big a step. Ask a simpler question based on the previous response.
3. *Always reinforce student responses.* The whole idea of the guided-discovery style is active involvement of the students. Teacher responses such as "That's wrong," "No," or "Of course not," tend to inhibit further student response. Responses such as "Go on," "That's a possibility," or "That's one alternative, are there any others?" tend to maximize further student involvement.
4. *Accept off-target responses and then lead the group back onto the track with additional questions.* This is best illustrated by the following diagram:

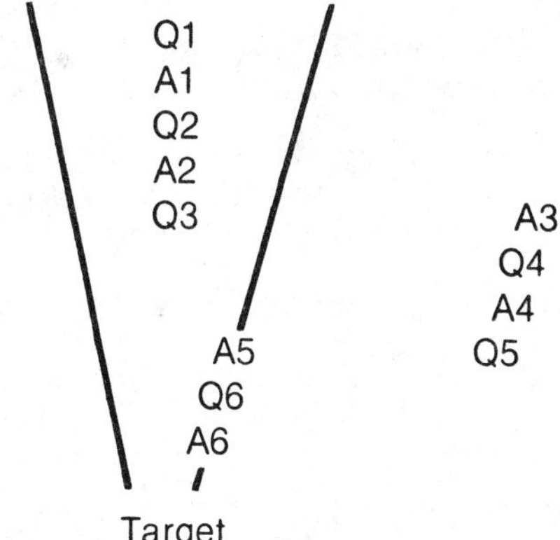

While the planned sequence may have called for five questions and five answers, answer 3 was well off the planned track. It then becomes necessary to structure several questions to bring the class back into the planned pattern. Since such situations cannot be pre-planned, they obviously require a thorough knowledge of the subject matter.

The primary advantage of the guided-discovery style is the intellectual involvement which it affords students. Students are led to think about the subject matter of the lesson. Progressive development of the subject matter with the question-and-answer technique helps develop their understanding not only of the final solution, but of the process through which it evolved as well. This is a two-fold benefit, since not only is the subject matter retained longer, but the deductive process, which is itself learned, can be applied by the student in other situations. Finally, the constant reinforcement and encouragement of student response helps to develop a positive self-image in the students and generate greater interest in and involvement with the subject matter.

The primary disadvantage of the guided-discovery style of teaching is that it is extremely time consuming. It takes a considerably longer period of time to lead the students to a solution with the question-and-answer process then to merely tell them the facts. The style also works better with small groups or when it is used in written form with each student working at his or her own rate. The larger the group, the more difficult it is to keep all students involved and abreast of the development of the question-and-answer process. Individual worksheets allow students to respond to the question sequence at their own rate and also permit the teacher to give individual assistance to those who need it. At the conclusion of the lesson, the teacher can lead a brief summary discussion, using the question-and-answer technique to draw together the major points developed in the worksheets. In this manner, the complete involvement of the total class can be maintained. Figure 2.8 illustrates a worksheet designed to teach the concept of place-hitting.

FIGURE 2.8. Learning to Place-hit — Guided-Discovery Approach for 6th, 7th, 8th Grades.

Statement: Place-hitting is an extremely important offensive tactic in baseball and softball. Being able to place the ball in a specified area in a tight ball game will make you a valuable player on any team.

If you can bat you can learn to place-hit. It's really simple if you understand the principle that governs the skill.

Hypothesis: Pretend you are at bat. See yourself swinging and making contact with the ball so that it flies to whatever field you'd like it to. Try to decide why it happens. Write your idea below.

I think the ball flies to the field I want it to because:

____

____

Let's see if your idea is correct.

Procedure:

Step. 1. Get into groups of four. Move to any station. Check to be sure you have 10 balls, 1 bat, 1 batting tee and 2 gloves.

Step 2. Appoint the following jobs to the people in your group:
One batter who will bat 10 balls in each position.
Two fielders to shag the batted balls.
One recorder who records the direction each ball flies.

Step 3. Have the batter hit 10 consecutive balls off the batting tee using each of the foot patterns seen below. Record the flight of each ball on the appropriate diagram. Before you begin, try to predict, using your idea, where the balls will go for each foot pattern.

Fig. 1 Fig. 2 Fig. 3

FIGURE 2.8 (cont'd).

I predict the balls will go: Fig. 1 ______________

Fig. 2 ______________

Fig. 3 ______________

Were your predictions right? ____________

Step 4. Have everyone change jobs. Be sure you get a different job each time.

Step 5. Repeat step 3 but use the foot patterns shown below.

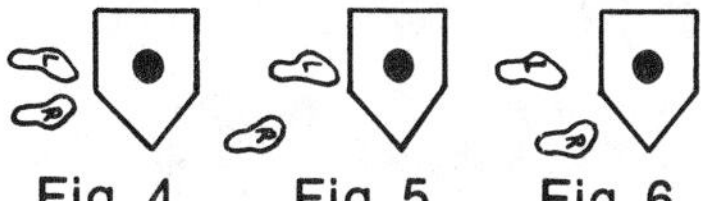

Fig. 4 Fig. 5 Fig. 6

I predict the balls will go: Fig. 4 ______________

Fig. 5 ______________

Fig. 6 ______________

Were your predictions right?

Step 6. Switch jobs again. Do step 7 twice so that everyone gets a chance to bat.

Step 7. Repeat step 3 but use the foot patterns shown below.

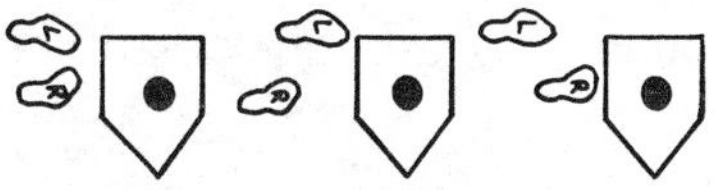

Fig. 7 Fig. 8 Fig. 9

I predict the balls will go: Fig. 7 ______________

Fig. 8 ______________

Fig. 9 ______________

Were your predictions right? ____________

Conclusion:

1. Identify the number(s) of the foot pattern(s) where the ball usually went to the right.

   Do any of these foot patterns have something in common?

   What did you notice about the angle of the ball?

2. Identify the number(s) of the foot pattern(s) where the ball usually went to the left.

   Do any of these foot patterns have something in common?

   What did you notice about the angle of the ball?

FIGURE 2.8 (cont'd).

3. Identify the number(s) of the foot pattern(s) where the ball usually went straight.

   Do any of these foot patterns have something in common?

   What did you notice about the angle of the ball?

Can you identify principle no. 1 in regard to the relationship of your body to the ball as you hit it? Write your statement below.

Can you identify principle no. 2 in regard to the sharpness of the angle of the ball when it flies? Write your statement below.

How did your first idea and your final conclusion compare?

THE PROBLEM-SOLVING STYLE

The problem-solving style of teaching is designed to bring the student closer to the highest level of the decision-making continuum.[11] By employing this style, the teacher encourages students to use their creative and organizational talents to the fullest. The concept can be most simply described as a reversal of the funnel effect that was developed by the guided-discovery style. With guided discovery, the student was led, by a series of questions, from a general concept to a specific goal or target, as illustrated by the following diagram:

With the problem-solving style, on the other hand, the student is given a specific question or task, and is directed to seek out a variety of alternative solutions. The process goes from the specific to the general, as is illustrated by this diagram:

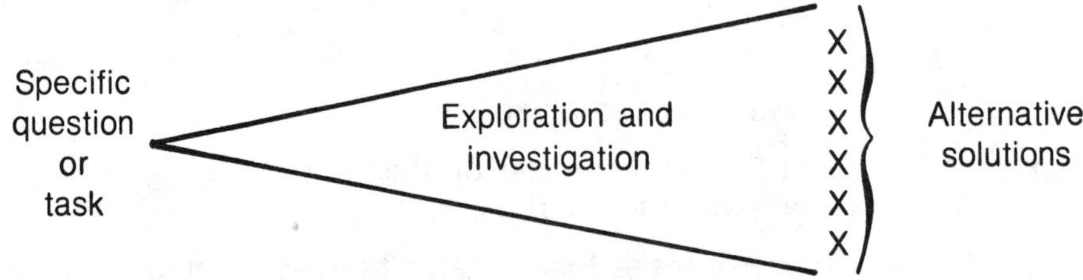

With the problem-solving style of teaching, each new and different problem should lead students to a variety of solutions which, while challenging, are within the limits of their ability. Any solution developed by a student which meets the criteria set up by the teacher must be considered correct and, therefore, praiseworthy. For example, if the teacher asked, "How many ways can you get over this horse by touching it with only your hands?" any

11. Mosston, *Physical Education*, p. 183ff.

recognized gymnastic vault would be an acceptable solution to the problem, but so would any vault which involved placement of only the hands on the horse, regardless of the form or configuration. It would be inappropriate, therefore, under these circumstances, to criticize a student for unpointed toes or an asymmetrical body position. As long as both hands were on the horse as the body went over, the vault met the criteria and was, therefore, worthy of praise. It should be mentioned here, for those of you who may have already concluded that the secret to success lies in structuring the criteria in such a way that only a very limited

FIGURE 2.9. Problem-Solving Exercises.

Student directions:

1. Read the following statements
2. Proceed on your own to find solutions to these problems
3. When *you* think you have found a solution, try it a few times. Then write it down and check with your teacher
4. Don't hesitate to try "crazy" ideas — they are welcomed

Balance Beam

1. *Mounts*
   Can you find two ways to get on the beam while you are facing it?
   a. ______________________
   b. ______________________
2. *Positions*
   Design two positions on the beam that are other than vertical.
   a. ______________________
   b. ______________________

Mats

Problem: Design and list five ways of traveling from one end of the mat to the other.
a. ______________________
b. ______________________
c. ______________________
d. ______________________
e. ______________________

Movement Exploration

1. Can you jump up and make your body into a different shape in the air?
   Can you now do four more different shapes?
2. Can you do two different shapes in one jump?
3. Can you take the same movement in the same path at a different level? Say lower or higher?

---

number of predictable solutions are acceptable, that such is very definitely *not* the case. The problem-solving style is designed to *develop* diversity and individuality of thought and performance, not *limit* them. If you, as a teacher, are aiming for a single correct response, either lead the students to it or tell them, but do not expect the entire class to select it as the only solution to the problem-solving situation. Examples of viable problems in a variety of subject-matter areas are presented in Figure 2.9.

Although problem-solving style teaching is not designed to develop specific skills, it is an excellent vehicle for conceptualization and acclimatization. It will not be the most efficient means of teaching a straddle mount or an arabesque on the beam, for example, but it will be an excellent tool for introducing the beam, helping students become familiar with it, and giving them the opportunity to develop some confidence in their ability to successfully remain on it. Once such a groundwork has been established, specific skills and techniques are much more easily developed.

If the teacher is able to design problems which are relevant and motivating to the students, there will be a tremendous increase over previous styles in the amount of cognitive involvement and the degree of individualization and, one would hope, an effect on decision making later in life. A student is presented with a situation and required to develop a solution according to the presented criteria and his or her own particular capabilities and interests. This is, in a very real sense, the same kind of decision making that adults are required to perform every day. It does not, therefore, seem unreasonable that students should be provided an opportunity to develop similar problem-solving skills in our classes. If one accepts this, however, one must, at the same time, accept the fact that a wide diversity of acceptable responses will occur simultaneously in each class and that uniformity of performance will not only be impossible to achieve, but deliberately discouraged.

IMPLEMENTATION AND APPLICATION OF THE SPECTRUM OF STYLES

The preceding section presented the seven primary styles of teaching, as developed by Muska Mosston, in terms of their characteristics, special teaching considerations, advantages and disadvantages. The summary chart shown in Table 2.2 provides a capsular view of this information for the purposes of reference and review. Before leaving this topic, it would be well to discuss a few ground rules which should be considered in regard to the total spectrum of teaching styles.

1. *No style is "best" all the time.* Each style has advantages and disadvantages which are peculiar to that style alone. These factors must be weighed in relation to the particular objectives for the lesson, the students' readiness for decision making, available equipment, the suitability of the subject matter, and any number of other factors. There is, in addition, a considerable body of research which would suggest that the most effective teachers are those who vary their teaching behavior from class to class and even within classes.
2. *There is a weaning period which must be observed if one is to successfully move toward the student-centered end of the continuum.* People who have never had the opportunity to make decisions in the classroom cannot, for both intellectual and emotional reasons, be expected to make a great number of decisions without a gradual period of development and practice. Conversely, teachers who have been accustomed to making all the decisions must learn to curb this behavior and allow more freedom to the students if

TABLE 2.2. Summary Sheet for Styles of Teaching.

Style	Teacher Decisions	Student Decisions	Distinguishing Characteristics	Advantages	Disadvantages
Command	All	None	S-R learning Teacher dominated	Uniformity Efficiency	Not sensitive to individual needs and differences
Task	All Pre-Impact Some Impact All Post-Impact	Some Impact decisions, e.g., rate, geography, start and stop times	Initial decisions for student in Impact phase	Individualization of instruction Private feedback Better equipment utilization	Student can avoid teacher contact Need for more Pre-Impact planning and preparation
Reciprocal	All Pre-Impact Some Impact Some Post-Impact	Some in Impact Some Post-Impact, i.e., evaluate another student	Evaluation is carried on by another student Speak only to the teaching partner	One-to-one teacher/student ratio Immediate feedback Mental practice	Student interaction gives rise to potential physical, intellectual and emotional dangers
Small Group	Same as Reciprocal	Same as Reciprocal	Same as Reciprocal Three or more people each with a functional group role	Same as above More efficient use of equipment Planned use of spotter reduces physical hazards	Same as Reciprocal
Individual Program	Same as Reciprocal	Some in Impact Some Post-Impact self-evaluation	Student self-evaluation Longer period of independence Single SM objective	Increase ability for self-motivation and self-assessment	Must be planned in minute detail Qualitative evaluation requires specific cues Teacher/student readiness
Guided Discovery	Same as Task but many decisions must be modified as a result of student responses	Post-Impact decisions become interwoven with Impact and teacher now provides reinforcement for all responses	Q and A process to a single goal Funnel effect	Intellectual involvement Understand process by which SM was developed Self-concept	Extremely time consuming More difficult with very large or very heterogeneous groups
Problem Solving	Reduced decision-making in all three phases	Some involvement in all three phases	Multiple responses elicited for each problem posed Reverse funnel effect	Develops conceptualization and acclimatization Great cognitive involvement Learn problem-solving technique Creativity and individuality are developed	Does not teach specific skills No uniformity of performance

they wish to move from command teaching. This transition is most effective when undertaken slowly and deliberately. It is far better to increase decision making by one or two small decisions at a time than to go too far, too fast and suffer almost certain failure.

3. *When a lesson proves unsuccessful, carefully evaluate all the variables in the teaching situation before condemning the style itself.* As in any other teaching, there is a

multitude of possible pitfalls for each of the various styles. Some of them are specific to the styles, others are not. If a lesson fails, consider all variables before blaming the failure on the style itself. Ask such questions as:

a. Were the students prepared to make the kinds of decisions I expected them to make?
b. Did I provide them with sufficient preparatory information?
c. Did I execute the style correctly?
d. Did I provide them with feedback regarding not only physical performance, but adaptation to the style?
e. Did the style suit the subject matter?

4. *Do not be afraid to mix and combine styles.* There is nothing so sacred about any particular style of teaching that it cannot be combined and modified to suit individual needs and desires. Once the teacher and the students are comfortable with the entire range of behaviors, there is nothing wrong with combining elements to form new teaching styles. The important factor here is that the new styles must be consciously manipulated and developed based upon considered judgment. There is no value in putting a label on a mistake merely because it is easier than correcting it. Learn the styles well *first*, then feel free to modify them to suit your individual needs and desires.
5. *Do not become locked into a steady diet of any single teaching style.* Nothing is as monotonous as complete predictability. The constant repetition of any teaching style, regardless of subject-matter changes, is stifling to students and teacher alike. While a certain amount of security and repetition is necessary, particularly with younger children, too much of anything is not good. The best teachers are inevitably those who have a wide repertoire of teaching behaviors and who vary their behaviors according to the particular situation. This is, in fact, the primary value of the spectrum of styles. It provides a clearly codified means of selecting and developing alternative teaching behaviors. The more alternatives a teacher has at his or her disposal, the better able the teacher is to suit teaching behavior to student needs and lesson content, and, therefore, the greater the likelihood of success.
6. *Remember that the method is only as good as its practitioner.* No style can succeed without thoughtful preparation and careful attention to detail. No style can compensate for a lack of expertise in the subject matter being taught or for a lack of sincere concern for one's students. Teachers who are not willing to work hard or who do not really care about their students would be well advised to pursue a different profession rather than alternative teaching styles. For those of us who regard the student as the most valuable link in the teaching/learning process, however, the spectrum of styles offers a variety of interesting and productive teaching strategies which can be adapted and modified to suit the needs of each new teaching situation.

REFERENCES

Hyman, Ronald T., *Ways of Teaching* (New York: J. B. Lippincott Co., 1974).

Mosston, Muska, *Teaching: From Command to Discovery* (Belmont, CA: Wadsworth Publishing Co., Inc., 1972).

Mosston, Muska, *Teaching Physical Education* (Columbus, OH: Charles E. Merrill Books, Inc., 1966).

chapter three

Creativity in Education

In the minds of many, creativity is a quality associated solely with the realm of artists, poets, and others who pursue the arts. As such, creativity training is considered important in those areas of the curriculum known as the humanities but quite irrelevant, if not frivolous, in those areas most closely aligned with mathematics and the sciences.

In physical education, creativity training is a main ingredient in dance education but is often unheard of in sports training. Why is this? Consider for a moment the performance of a skilled guard in basketball as he or she weaves in and out in a constant, persistent drive toward the basket. At the last moment, inches from the goal, two defenders block the way. Undaunted, the guard jumps to shoot but instead passes the ball in a deft but unorthodox manner to a teammate, who then scores the goal easily. In the stands cheers go up not so much for the goal as for the pass — the unorthodox, creative pass.

Coaches attribute unorthodox play to "good ball sense," but what is good ball sense? It is a creative act that imaginatively utilizes the skills associated with a particular sport. If good ball sense is creative and highly valued, then should not creativity training be highly valued in sports training?

The answer to this question lies with the individual teacher and coach; but the decision should not be based solely on what can happen in a game or the type of player that can be developed. The answer should be based on the needs of the student not only in the present but in the future. Lack of attention to the creative development of the child can be a costly oversight, one which society may soon regret.

Today, vast segments of our population have been relegated to gathering data, memorizing facts, and solving problems in the most logical manner. Instead, they should be learning to expand their curiosity and explore the world around them; for in the future, society will need creative minds to solve the world's problems, not minds that have been trained to absorb facts like a sponge.

If students are to be prepared to cope with the problems of the future, our attitude toward creativity must change. Educators must come to recognize the importance of creative thinking for all people and learn to incorporate creativity training into their teaching. For physical education the matter is a simple one. The opportunities that present themselves are numerous. The purpose of this chapter is to acquaint the physical educator with the creative process and to help define the teacher's role in regard to both teaching creativity and teaching creatively.

UNDERSTANDING CREATIVITY

Research has demonstrated that creativity is not a quality inherent only in artistic individuals. Creativity is a quality that each person is born with and has the potential to develop. It has been proven that once this potential is developed, the ability is transferable, i.e., creative children can become creative scientists as well as creative artists, depending upon their individual talents.[1] The creative qualities for each are the same. This being the case, educators have the responsibility of developing creative as well as critical minds. Each should receive at least equal attention in the school.

If the challenge of developing flexible and imaginative minds is to be met, teachers must 1) have a working definition of creativity, 2) be able to recognize and encourage creative ability, and 3) be able to create an atmosphere that fosters creativity. Most importantly, however, teachers must develop their own creative potentials. In addition, the following assumptions must be accepted:[2]

1. That every child possesses the ability to be creative
2. That these abilities can be enhanced through instruction
3. That it is the duty of the schools to provide such instruction
4. That the ability to be creative is most evident in early life and that care must be taken to encourage not inhibit its growth

CREATIVITY DEFINED

In order to discuss creativity, we must understand the concept and set limits on its meaning. The poet John Ciardi has defined creativity as "the imaginatively gifted recombination of known elements into something new."[3] It has been further defined as "the process of forming ideas or hypotheses, testing hypotheses, and communicating the results."[4] Inherent in both of these definitions are the following conditions: 1) that the creative act result in a product or idea that is unique and is considered worthwhile by the creator or the community, and 2) that the act be a result of imaginative thinking to the extent that previously held ideas must be modified or discarded.

Please note that neither the definition nor its qualifiers mention the "doer." The "doer" could be a four-year-old child who has recycled a cardboard box into an obstacle course, a scientist who has discovered a replacement for petroleum, or a young teacher who has designed a game to suit the needs and abilities of a particular class. The doer *does not* have to be a grand master like daVinci to be considered creative. This idea must be fully accepted from the start, or teachers will impose upon themselves and the classes they teach a bias that will be more inhibiting than not teaching creativity at all.

1. Viktor Lowenfield, "Creativity: Education's Stepchild," in *A Source Book for Creative Thinking*, ed. Sidney J. Parnes and Harold F. Harding (New York: Charles Scribner's Sons, 1962), p. 8.

2. E. Paul Torrence, "Creative Thinking through School Experiences," in *A Source Book for Creative Thinking*, ed. Sidney J. Parnes and Harold F. Harding (New York: Charles Scribner's Sons, 1962), p. 33.

3. John Ciardi, "What Every Writer Must Learn," *Saturday Review*, 15 December 1956, p. 7.

4. Torrence, "Creative Thinking," p. 32.

THE CREATIVE PROCESS

Having defined creativity and two of its conditions, the next logical step is to explore the creative process. Understanding the creative process will help the teacher identify creative behavior and those situations which encourage and develop it.

Graham Wallas defined the creative process in terms of four stages: preparation, incubation, illumination and verification.[5] During *preparation* the individual defines the problem, gathers facts, and in general learns as much about the problem as possible. In the case of a child, the period of preparation would include all of the child's previous experiences in regard to a particular object or situation. This previous experience may be extensive if the problem is defined in terms of an everyday object or situation, or it may be minimal if defined in terms of a situation that has only been experienced once or twice.

The teacher is an extremely important influence during this phase. Acting as a vital resource, the teacher can help the child define the problem, gather the necessary data, and, most importantly, encourage the child to take the risk of searching for the answer. The teacher must be careful, however, not to prejudice the data or push the creative process in a direction of his or her own choosing.

Incubation is that period of time in which the individual actively seeks an answer to the problem. The time lapse is not important. It may take a few seconds, a few days, or a few months. Although the individual may not be consciously aware of the search, researchers have observed that he or she seems preoccupied with trying to discover an answer. At this point, the person often appears to be restless or unsettled. The teacher should be cautious during this stage for the individual often experiences feelings of inferiority and will probably need reassurance.

Incubation ends when a good idea appears. Having completed the incubation phase, the individual enters the *illumination* phase. This phase is characterized by a sense of achievement. The individual is satisfied with the idea and feels it must be shared with others.

The act of sharing, evaluating, and refining the ideas or illumination is called *verification*. This is the final phase of the creative process and it must occur or there is no creation. Teachers must be supportive during this period. They must encourage the students to believe in their idea — believe in it to a point where they will risk peer disapproval. The teacher must also focus attention on the other students as well. They must be taught to keep an open mind and learn the art of constructive criticism rather than destructive opinion. If this atmosphere is not established, there will be very little verification and, therefore, very little creation.

The creative process has been described in terms of other phases as well. These descriptions are based on the orientation of the researchers. The teacher should not conclude that there is only one method of arriving at an answer to a problem. If this is done, teachers may find themselves imposing a rigid set of guidelines on the learners, thereby depriving them of their freedom to create. A teacher's guidance should always be kept to a minimum, and the information received from researchers should provide greater awareness of the creative process and not help to smother it.

5. Richard P. Youtz, "Psychological Foundations: Applied Imagination," in *A Source Book for Creative Thinking*, ed. Sidney J. Parnes and Harold F. Harding (New York: Charles Scribner's Sons, 1962), p. 194.

THE ROLE OF THE PHYSICAL EDUCATOR

If asked to define their role in the school, most physical educators would probably respond by saying that they prepare students for leisure-time pursuits or that they help youth gain that elusive condition known as physical fitness. There are probably many more stock-in-trade answers that can be provided, but the question is, will they be assessed worthy goals by the community or, more importantly, by the students?

Creating any environment where students can learn to move efficiently and effectively in prescribed activities is certainly an important function of physical education but only in regard to the schooling or training of the individual. If teachers are to stimulate creative development, they must restructure their own value systems as well. There is a vast difference between training the individual to perform and educating him or her to think creatively in terms of physical activity. There is also a vast difference between training students to react to certain stimuli and sensitizing them to the details of a problem and encouraging them to work out imaginative responses. In the school setting then, teachers must search for an equitable balance between the two.

The styles of teaching have been discussed earlier in this text. It becomes immediately evident that if one is to instruct for creativity as well as skill acquisition, one must lean toward guided discovery and problem solving. Although it has been pointed out that problem solving does not result in the acquisition of a skill as quickly as, say, the command style, the teacher must keep in mind that in this case, physical activity is not an end unto itself but rather the medium for teaching creativity as well.

Elementary school physical educators seem to find many more ways of incorporating the concept of teaching for creativity than secondary school physical educators. A common example of the application of creative development techniques in the elementary schools is movement education. Movement education seeks to free children to work at their own ability levels while it poses thought-provoking problems which encourage creative responses. It is extremely effective in achieving the balance previously mentioned because it results in not only a good movement vocabulary, which can be used in any activity, but because it also enhances a child's self-concept and provides a training ground for creative thinking. (See chapter 4 for a discussion of movement education.)

E. Paul Torrence, a noted leader in studies concerning the identification and development of creative thinking among children, offers the following practical suggestions to teachers who are concerned with developing creativity:[6]

1. Value creative thinking.
2. Make children more sensitive to environmental stimuli.
3. Encourage manipulation of objects and ideas.
4. Teach how to test systematically each idea.
5. Develop tolerance of new ideas.
6. Beware of forcing a set pattern.
7. Develop a creative classroom atmosphere.
8. Teach the child to value his or her creative thinking.
9. Teach skills for avoiding peer sanctions.
10. Give information about the creative process.
11. Dispel the sense of awe of masterpieces.

6. Torrence, "Creative Thinking," p. 46.

12. Encourage and evaluate self-initiated learning.
13. Create "thorns in the flesh." ("Thorns in the flesh" refers to controversial issues or even seemingly unanswerable questions which can stimulate creative thinking.)
14. Create necessities for creative thinking.
15. Provide for active and quiet periods.
16. Make available resources for working out ideas.
17. Encourage the habit of working out the full implication of ideas.
18. Develop constructive criticism — not just criticism.
19. Encourage acquisition of knowledge in a variety of fields.
20. Develop adventurous, spirited leaders.

Suggestions are only as good as their practical application. Scanning these suggestions, one can probably think of numerous ways of implementing them in the gymnasium or on the playground, but each of these implementations must be accompanied by an attitude, an attitude implied in Mr. Torrence's first suggestion: a teacher must truly value creative thinking. Children are no different than adults, they become proficient in that which the community values. Holding a certain quality in high regard, however, is not enough. This attitude must be communicated to the students. It must, therefore, become evident in teacher behavior as well. Take, for instance, the following example. Ms. Wilson asked her class to create a movement sequence in gymnastics using the following criteria.

Each sequence must include:

1. Three rolling movements
2. Three locomotor skills
3. Two transitional moves
4. Four balanced positions
5. One inverted position
6. One wheeling movement

The assignment gave the students direction but also provided enough latitude so that each of them could create a routine according to their own ability and imagination. Each student knew exactly what was expected of them and they were given ample time to accomplish the task. As Ms. Wilson moved among the students her comments sounded like this:

> Jane, as you describe that movement it sounds like one I'm familiar with that's been tried before and doesn't seem to work. Why don't you try something else?
>
> Tom, that sequence looks awkward, why don't you replace it with a more standard sequence. Perhaps incorporating a roundoff would be the best possible solution.
>
> Sherry, that position on the floor is really unique, but I doubt if you'll be able to get out of it in a graceful manner.

Ms. Wilson had devised a situation in which her students could create their own responses but instead of encouraging their creativeness, she criticized it in a manner which was destructive rather than constructive.

The problem was compounded by her final evaluation of the project. Seventy-five percent of the grade was based on execution rather than composition. This communicated to her students that she was much more concerned about bent knees and unpointed toes than she was about original moves or imaginative sequences. Throughout the performance, she would yell, "Point those toes," "Reach for that cartwheel," or "Smile." In essence, what she had done was defeat her original purpose by communicating her displeasure with every movement that had the slightest flaw. Her students quickly responded by attempting to give the teacher what she wanted — perfect execution of standard movement patterns.

If creativity had been really valued by the instructor her comments should have sounded more like this:

> Jane, that movement sounds fine. Something similar has been tried and part of the difficulty in execution was related to balance. You might keep that in mind as you experiment with your new movement.
>
> Tom, that sequence is really imaginative. Can you find a way to make it more aesthetically pleasing without losing its originality?
>
> Sherry, you've discovered a really unique balance. How many ways can you find to move from that level to another level?

By addressing her students in this manner, Ms. Wilson can give them the benefit of her professional opinion at the same time she is able to indicate to them her high regard for their efforts.

Ms. Wilson could have also based seventy-five percent of her grade on composition rather than execution. She could have made notes about each student's performance and shared them with the student at a more appropriate time — when performance was the main purpose of the lesson. By acting in this manner, Ms. Wilson's behavior would have reflected her stated value, not implied an opposite one.

Values are not only reflected by behavior, they are reflected by the implementation of an idea as well. Free play can be a perfect activity for promoting creativity or just an exercise in reinforcing set patterns and ideas. The difference occurs when the teacher establishes the rules and sets out the equipment. Use Figure 3.1 to compare Mr. Grant's idea of a free-play period for his second-grade class with Mr. Howard's.

When Mr. Grant's class arrived at the play area, they were quickly organized into two lines and taken on a tour. As Mr. Grant introduced them to each activity, he gave them the rules and stressed the safety aspects needed. There was a basket-shooting contest the children could enter, a rope-skipping contest (the winner would be the child that skipped the greatest number of times without missing), a chart that showed suggested activities on the scooters, a field set up for a mini-kickball game, a pile of hoops where they could play a target game, and ten pictures which Mr. Grant had taped to the mats that illustrated the stunts that could be performed.

Mr. Grant knew exactly what he wanted the children to do and so did they. He kept the decision making to a minimum, maintained a relative uniformity of performance, and kept the lesson from looking disorganized.

Claudia, who was a creative child but somewhat of a loner, was quickly reprimanded when she took a rope from the prescribed area and began playing a game of her own inven-

FIGURE 3.1.

MR. GRANT	MR. HOWARD
Rules: 1. Everyone must engage in an activity. 2. Once an activity is chosen you must remain at that area until the whistle blows. 3. When the whistle blows, you must choose another activity. 4. The equipment can only be used for the activity indicated 5. All safety rules must be followed.	*Rules:* 1. Everyone must engage in an activity. 2. All safety rules must be followed. 3. You cannot leave the general area.
Equipment: 6 jump ropes 1 basketball 6 scooters 6 hula-hoops 2 playground balls 3 mats 1 set of bases	*Equipment:* 2 large refrigerator boxes 6 tires 2 twenty-foot ropes 12 balloons 3 playground balls 6 traffic cones 1 box of chalk 1 set of stilts 12 weighted milk cartons 2 mats
Responsibilities: 1. Be sure students are engaged in an activity. 2. Be sure children use the equipment properly. 3. Referee games when necessary. 4. Help students improve skills.	*Responsibilities:* 1. Encourage students to see relationships between the different pieces of equipment. 2. Encourage the students to use the equipment in an original way. 3. Create quiet as well as active areas for play.

tion off in an isolated area. Mr. Grant reminded her that the ropes were only to be used for the rope-jumping contest and other jumping games.

When six boys excitedly pulled Mr. Grant aside to show him a game they had devised during their recess periods, Mr. Grant listened and responded with "That's fine, fellas, but what are you supposed to be doing now?"

What Mr. Grant had done was package a lesson for activity. He presented it to his students and expected them to conform regardless of their individual differences or ideas. By the time he had conducted a free-play period for the fourth time, Mr. Grant managed to gain compliance with all of the rules from all of his students.

Mr. Grant's principal was very pleased with the activity he observed on the playground. Little did he realize that Mr. Grant was teaching the children that conformity was best, and the sad thing is that Mr. Grant didn't realize it either.

Mr. Grant's lesson may have been organizationally sound and well implemented in regard to basketball shooting, kickball, and the like, but was it well suited for a second-grade class? Remember that the ability to be creative is most evident in early life and that care must be taken to encourage creative growth not inhibit it.[7] Children will decide soon enough that a basketball is for basket shooting, why not give them an opportunity to experiment with its other uses and qualities? If someone were to ask Mr. Grant whether he wanted his students to grow up to be unique individuals, he would probably answer yes. He, like so many others, is concerned with developing individuality but, because of his teaching techniques, is ineffectual when dealing with children and their creativity.

Using the same activity as Mr. Grant, Mr. Howard approached the lesson in the following way. He started by making a list of the action words that first came to mind when he thought of his second-grade class. The list included such words as jumping, running, fleeing, dodging, weaving, and touching. He then carefully picked out equipment that had the potential to stimulate the imagination and enhance the action words. He was careful not to pick equipment that immediately suggested an organized activity, such as football or baseball.

When he was satisfied with his selection, he placed the equipment strategically around the area so that there were quiet areas as well as active areas, large open areas as well as small cozy ones. He then waited for his class.

When his class arrived, he made sure that his presence was not felt. He wanted to give the children ample time to get acquainted with all the equipment and get their imaginations working. Mr. Howard's students did just that. They moved about the equipment touching, looking, and rearranging.

When Mr. Howard decided that their imagination had been sufficiently aroused, he called the class over and explained the rules. He reminded the children that they were to engage in an activity throughout the period and that they were to remain in the general area prescribed by a set of yellow cones. He also reviewed the safety rules that applied to this particular situation, being sure to explain why such rules were necessary. Then, just as he was about to let them begin, he said, "Oh yes, I'll be teaching the kindergarten children tomorrow, so if any of you discover a new game today, let me know about it at the end of the period." With this one comment, Mr. Howard invited them to give order to the equipment they saw scattered in front of them. He challenged them to make something from nothing and, before he got the words out of his mouth, they were off and trying. Mr. Howard ap-

7. Ibid., p. 33.

proached his students that day the same way he did every day — with an openness and an eagerness that were infectious. His classroom atmosphere was free of the tension that invades so many classrooms. His students felt secure. They knew that their ideas would be accepted and that they were truly free to experiment within accepted guidelines. Mr. Howard had succeeded in setting conditions for creativity by implementing his lesson in a way that helped avoid set patterns and ideas. He taught his students that equipment was meant to be manipulated and that the only number of limitations to its uses were the limitations imposed by the inventor's mind. During this lesson, for instance, Mr. Howard's class used a twenty-foot rope to:

1. crawl under
2. swing back and forth on
3. jump over
4. swing around
5. twirl
6. make letters and numbers
7. serve as a boundary
8. climb up
9. make geometric figures
10. make an obstacle course
11. balance on
12. tie two or more objects together
13. hang on to
14. pull an object with

There are many more uses. The point is that, like Mr. Howard's students, individuals must be flexible in order to begin seeing them.

Mr. Howard's lesson ended that day with twelve suggestions for games, three obstacle courses, and twenty-two requests to repeat the lesson the next time. Mr. Howard was beginning to succeed. His students were beginning to refine their techniques in divergent thinking and they were enjoying it.

Flexibility Is a Must

There seems to be something sanctimonious about the height of a balance beam or the configuration of the even parallel bars. Why can't a balance beam look like this:

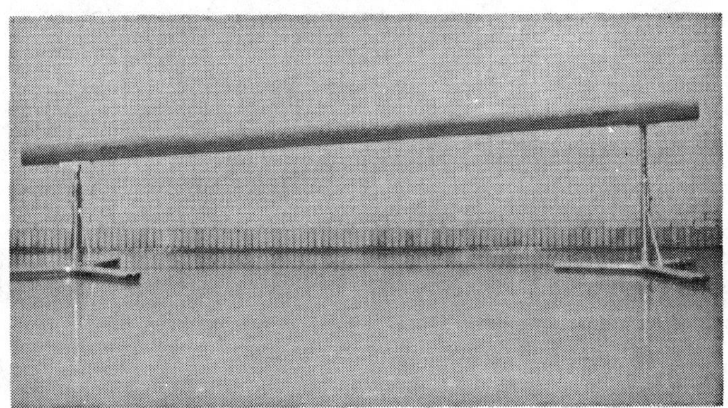

Or why couldn't the parallel bars look like this:

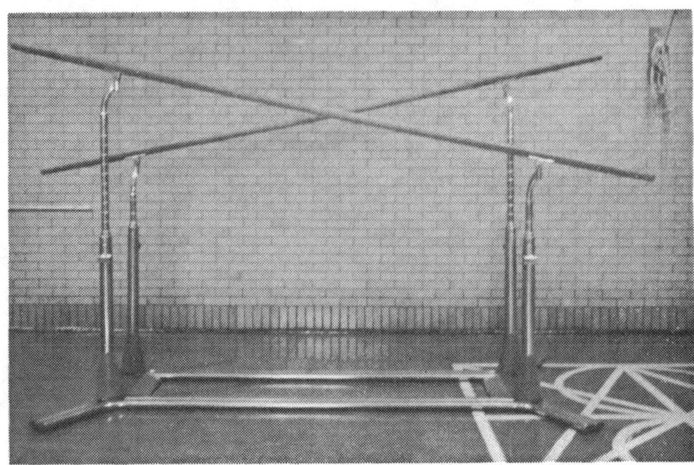

If the teacher demonstrates this flexibility, the students will soon learn to do the same. Here are a few examples of the kinds of problems which are applicable to any grade level and which encourage the manipulation of an object so that it is seen in a different light.

Task 1: Can you design an obstacle course that requires the use of strength, using only the uneven parallel bars and the loose hand apparatus found in the middle of the floor?

Task 2: Using two cardboard boxes, a ten-foot pole, and a fifteen-foot length of rope, can you get your entire team from one side of the imaginary ravine to the other and have all of your equipment on the same side as well?

Task 3: Using everyday articles, such as a plastic container, a rolled up sock, paper plates, and a stick, can you design a game that would teach a sports skill or a concept in math?

Task 4: Can your group design a pyramid any place in the gym other than on the floor or on the mats?

Ms. B. once assigned Task 4 to a class of college sophomores — build a pyramid any place in the gym other than on the floor or the mats (mats were used for safety purposes). She had imagined a few solutions in her mind, but was anxious to see what her students would create.

During the course of the period, one group sat in the corner of the gym excitedly discussing their ideas. Finally, the spokesman asked her to lower the ropes. Her initial reaction was "What in the world could . . .?" but that's as far as she got. She kept her reservations to herself, immediately lowered the ropes, and waited for the results.

The results came the next day. The group came dressed in costume and asked that their demonstration be accompanied by background music. She quickly complied with this request, then sat back and watched. Using the horse below and the ropes as their base of support, the group began to perform what they called a rope ballet. They moved smoothly from one pyramid to another, using the ropes not only to support those at the top of the pyramid, but also to enhance the lines of the pyramid.

The response to this exhibition was overwhelming. The class applauded enthusiastically and quickly got in line to try their luck. The most gratifying part of the exhibition was the fact that the students had seen the ropes as something other than an apparatus for climbing and that they had devised a way to share it with their classmates that was unique as well. Flexibility of this sort cannot help but carry over into a person's everyday life.

In summary, a teacher teaches creativity by creating opportunities and conditions that set off the creative process. He or she must design lessons that will provoke a new discovery or a new idea through divergent thinking. Teachers must be sure that their tasks and their comments are open-ended or they will stifle the creative act. They must be careful not to impose set patterns or preconceived ideas on the students. They must withdraw from the creative process during the first phase and let the students arrive at their own answers. They must value creative thinking and communicate this to their students with praise for creative ideas and self-initiated learning. They must permit their students to manipulate equipment and ideas, and help to develop flexible and open minds by setting an example and constantly providing students with tasks of this nature.

Teaching Creatively

"When an individual is trying to do something creative as a teacher, what is the product? It is clear what the product is not. It is not people, for teachers do not mold people as if they were clay. The 'product' of the teacher's creativity is *opportunities* for individuals and groups to experience and learn."[8] Providing students with the opportunities for creativity requires a creative approach. A teacher cannot simply use any style of teaching to derive the desired results unless the problem is approached in a unique manner.

The problem itself becomes the starting point. One must learn to ask the right questions in order to define the problem and begin gathering data. Just as the journalist asks the what, when, where, why, and how of things, so must the teacher. There is one important addition, however, and that is asking about the "what if" of things. This last question helps keep the fantasy alive.[9]

Learning to ask the right question is extremely important. Asking a question in a way that it has never been asked before could tap a resource deep in one's experience that may eventually lead to a discovery.

When the right question has been formulated, the search begins for the answer. There are many techniques that have been developed by researchers since the early 1950s. Two will be described so that readers can become acquainted with them and perhaps start experimenting on their own to find the most effective method for themselves.

Alex Osborn designed a checklist to help people expand their abilities to conceive creative ideas. For a physical educator, this technique can be invaluable when he or she is trying to design a new piece of equipment or modify an old one. Osborn suggests that the individual ask the following questions:[10]

1. *New Use* — What new use can I find for this object in its original state? What new use can I find for this object or idea if I modify this thing?

8. Alice Miel, ed., *Creativity in Teaching* (Belmont, CA: Wadsworth Publishing Co., Inc., 1962), p. 8.

9. John E. Arnold, "Education for Innovation," in *A Source Book for Creative Thinking*, ed. Sidney J. Parnes and Harold F. Harding (New York: Charles Scribner's Sons, 1962), p. 131.

10. Adapted from John E. Arnold, "Useful Creative Techniques," in *A Source Book for Creative Thinking*, ed. Sidney J. Parnes and Harold F. Harding (New York: Charles Scribner's Sons, 1962), p. 254.

Table 3.1. Modified Attributes of Volleyball.

MODIFICATION	REASON
1. Make the court circular or triangular. If triangular, the diagram would look like this: 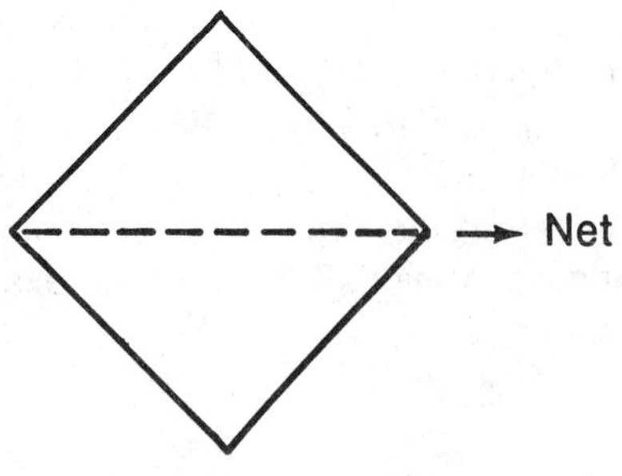	1. To help develop depth perception.
2. Divide the court unevenly.	2. So that one side must move rapidly to cover all areas while the other side has coverage and more time to develop plays.
3. a. Lower the net to six feet. b. Raise the net to nine feet. c. Set the net at angle from six feet to eight feet.	3. a. So that everyone can spike. b. So that no one can spike. c. So that everyone has an opportunity to spike somewhere at the net.
4. Played by two teams of two.	4. So that there is much more vigorous play.
5. a. Play with a light-weight vinyl ball. b. Play with a medicine ball. Catching it rather than volleying it.	5. a. So that every student has an increased opportunity to play the ball successfully. b. So that arm strength can be developed during play.
6. a. Give points whenever a specific play is made. b. Give points every time the ball is touched legally.	6. a. To encourage the use of plays. b. To eliminate competition between two teams, to encourage legal hits.
7. Eliminate points	7. To eliminate the pressure of competition.
8. Ball put in play by the referee tossing it to the center back, who must impart immediate impetus to the ball.	8. To eliminate the advantage of the powerful serve, to give the referee more control of the game.

2. *Adaptability* — What other idea or object does this remind me of? What other ideas does this suggest?
3. *Modify* — Can I change the meaning, color, sound, odor, taste, shape, purpose . . .?
4. *Magnify* — What can I add? Can I make it higher, stronger, longer, thicker . . .?
5. *Minify* — What can I subtract? Can I make it lower, smaller, thinner, lighter . . .?
6. *Substitute* — What can I substitute? What about another ingredient, material, power, place, process . . .?
7. *Rearrange* — Can I rearrange the pattern, the sequence, the layout, the schedule, the pace?
8. *Reverse* — Could I reverse roles, turn it upside down, turn it inside out, turn it backward?

There are many types of checklists that can be used to increase one's productivity. Probably the best one a teacher could use would be one of his or her own design, one which could be easily remembered and which would be practical in his or her field.

A technique known as attribute listing, which can be quite useful in modifying an existing idea or game, was developed by Robert Crawford.[11] Using this technique, one lists all the attributes of an object or idea in descriptive phrases and then proceeds to modify one or more of the attributes so that it better fits one's needs. Below is a simple attribute listing for volleyball:

1. Played on a rectangular court
2. Rectangular court divided in half
3. Net suspended across width of court at least seven feet, four inches high
4. Played by two teams of six
5. Played with a light leather ball
6. Points received only while serving
7. A game is fifteen points
8. The object of the game is to make the ball drop on the opponent's side
9. Ball is put into play by a serve

There are many other attributes which can be listed for volleyball. These have been chosen because they best describe the basics of the game. Table 3.1 lists the modifications made and the reasons why they were made. Please note that by the time the ninth change is made, although it still resembles volleyball, the modified game if allowed to evolve could become an entirely new game.

Whatever technique is used, the teacher must remember to keep an open mind and defer judgment on any idea until the incubation phase. The greater the quantity of ideas, the greater the likelihood of finding a quality idea. Creativity relies on inquisitive, imaginative thought. If teachers wish to develop this trait in their students, they must exhibit it themselves.

11. Ibid., p. 255.

chapter four

Movement Education

Physical education in elementary schools is in a state of transition today. The old approach to teaching young children, which has relied heavily upon command-style teaching and a games-oriented curriculum, is slowly giving way to a newer approach, one more closely aligned with contemporary educational thought.

For the first time, physical educators are beginning to understand that the education young children receive will not only have an effect upon what they are able to learn in the future but, whether they will want to learn and, just as importantly, whether as adults they will be inclined to use what they learned as children.

Based on this understanding, the sports-oriented curriculum, which was designed to produce a select group of Olympic athletes, is slowly shifting to a task- and challenge-oriented curriculum that is designed to produce a generation of informed and confident movers, children who are adaptable, creative, and independent.

Relay races and fixed formations, which are alien to the typical play behavior of children, are being replaced with games and other activities which are more in keeping with child development. Games such as "Duck, Duck, Goose" or "The Beater Goes 'Round," which require that the majority of those participating sit and watch while only a few perform, are being discarded and games that require maximum participation from all participants are being introduced.

Even traditional running and fleeing games are acquiring a new orientation. Where once they were used to simply develop agility, fitness, and competitive spirit, they are now being used to explore spatial relationships among objects and other individuals.

The one-on-one competition and the humiliation of defeat and elimination from the game are also being minimized. In their place, competitive spirit of a new form is emerging, one which is inner directed and self-paced. This type of competition is intended to help the child gain self-confidence so that he or she is better prepared to meet the challenges and frustrations of individual or team competition.

All of these changes and others, which are so characteristic of the "new look" in physical education, are most often referred to as the movement education approach. This approach, while still controversial, has had an impact on contemporary physical education that is impossible to deny.

THE MOVEMENT CONTROVERSY

The movement education concept has no less than three different interpretations, all of which exist side by side. The first interpretation and probably the most extreme is that:

> Movement education is a lifelong process of change. This process of motor development and learning has its beginning in the womb and proceeds through a never-ending series of changes until death. Some of this movement education is the responsibility of an inschool program of instruction called physical education.[1]

At the opposite end of the spectrum and in stark contrast to this global view are those definitions which limit the range and significance of movement education to a method or a unit of study in the overall curriculum.

Somewhere in between these two extremes lies a concept of movement education which is moderate in nature. Proponents of this concept define movement education as the:

> foundational structure and process portion of physical education which is characterized by the experiential study of 1) time, space, force, and flow as elements of movement; 2) the physical laws of motion and the principles of human movement which govern the human body's movement; and 3) the vast variety of creative and efficient movements which the human body is capable of producing through manipulation of movement variables.[2]

Movement education in this case is synonymous with physical education. According to Tillotson and staff, movement education is the:

> action oriented, child-centered Physical Education of today based on the following concepts:
> a. All children move in their own unique fashion yet are encouraged, through problem-solving situations, to develop efficient and expressive ways of moving, to understand how the body moves, where it moves in space, and what its capabilities are.
> b. Movement experiences help children express themselves, and that, in turn, helps us understand them.
> c. Children learn to move for many purposes, gaining success, satisfaction, and positive attitudes toward activity.[3]

Also consistent with this concept of movement is the idea of the movement vocabulary which is common to and therefore serves as a foundation for all physical activity.

> Movement education purports that fundamental skills are not the basis for the physical education program. Rather, the movement elements of time, space, and force underlie the skills. These elements are inherent in every action we perform,

1. Bette Logsdon, et al., *Physical Education for Children* (Philadelphia: Lea & Febiger, 1977), p. 12.

2. Bonnie Cherp Gilliom, *Basic Movement Education for Children: Rationale and Teaching Units* (Reading, MA: Addison-Wesley Publishing Co., Inc., 1970), p. 6.

3. Joan Tillotson and Staff, "Questions and Answers about Movement Education," in *Selected Readings in Movement Education*, ed. Robert T. Sweeney (Reading, MA: Addison-Wesley Publishing Co., Inc., 1970), p. 166.

FIGURE 4.1.

> whether we are children on a playground or adults in a work or play situation. A thorough understanding and practice of the common elements of movement are the real basis for successfully developing fundamental skills and refined movement patterns.[4]

In this interpretation of movement education, the teacher is expected to provide experiences throughout the curriculum which will accomplish the following goals.

1. Enhance the physical development of each child
2. Allow each child to progress at his or her own pace
3. Ensure success and develop confidence
4. Provide multiple challenges simultaneously
5. Allow each child ample time to practice
6. Provide time for individual help
7. Enhance and stimulate creativity
8. Provide opportunities for independent thinking
9. Develop adaptability and flexibility
10. Allow each child to discover his or her own movement potential
11. Help each child understand and interpret movement principles

Throughout this chapter we shall subscribe to an interpretation of movement education which attempts to accomplish these goals. This form should be synonymous with physical education during those stages of life in which efficient movement patterns are being developed.

THE CONTENT AREAS OF MOVEMENT EDUCATION

There are primarily three distinct content areas in movement education: educational dance, educational gymnastics, and educational games. Although all three areas are basically con-

4. Ibid., p. 167.

cerned with interpreting body awareness, spatial awareness, qualities of movement, and relationships to objects and other bodies, each of them has a unique thrust or emphasis which is worth discussing.

Educational dance is the expressive mode of movement. It is viewed as a means of developing self-expression and communicative patterns. Highly stylistic forms of dance, such as jazz or ballet, are excluded from this form of expression.

Educational gymnastics is one of the functional modes of movement and is primarily concerned with body management. This type of gymnastics does not stress the acquisition of predetermined movement patterns or stunts, rather it invites and stimulates the learners to discover their full movement potential on their own.

Educational games is the other functional mode of movement, and it is primarily concerned with developing adaptability and resourcefulness in terms of changing environments and game situations. Games which involve the teaching of specific sports skills are not included in the games content areas.

THE STRUCTURAL FRAMEWORK OF MOVEMENT

The content areas of movement education (i.e., educational dance, gymnastics, and games) are used to help the child discover:

1. *What they can move* — in terms of the body parts they can move and the constant relationship of all body parts.
2. *Where they can move* — in terms of moving in self-space and general space, along different pathways, at different levels, through different ranges, in different shapes and directions, and in relation to objects and other bodies.
3. *How they can move* — in terms of weight, space, flow, and time.
4. *What types of relationships are occurring when they move* — in terms of body parts, objects, other bodies, and the adapting the body must do to be compatible.

These large focus areas are considered the structural framework of movement. It is around this framework that movement education themes are developed in detail.

THE THEME IN MOVEMENT EDUCATION

The movement theme acts as the topic, the objective, and the direction of the movement lesson. It represents the overall problem to be solved by the student.

When selecting themes, one must be careful not to select a theme which encompasses too much territory, for the student will be rushed through a portion of the structural framework so rapidly that it is doubtful whether he or she will receive the full benefit of the experience. Try to be selective when formulating a theme and learn to recognize a theme that can be fully developed in the time you have alotted. The following examples are themes that were developed to teach body awareness:

1. Body parts can travel through different ranges of motion
2. Some body parts can take weight and move weight better than other body parts.
3. Body parts can absorb force and hold balanced positions

Each of these themes is a workable unit of body awareness, but each must be developed further in order to present the material in a fashion that is appropriate for movement education.

THE LANGUAGE OF MOVEMENT EDUCATION

Movement education is conducted primarily in the guided-discovery and problem-solving styles of teaching, hence much of the direction supplied by the teacher is given in the form of a question. In order to reduce a potentially threatening situation, the questions are couched in a "can you" or "how many ways can you" format. Notice the development from the command statement, which is used in the traditional approach, to the "can you" style in the movement approach. "On my signal everyone should try a headstand" is changed to "Can you do a headstand?" and finally to "Can you find five different ways to do a three-point balance?"

There are a number of obvious advantages to this format. The first concerns the matter of safety. If every child must do a headstand, as is implied in the first statement, there is an increased chance of accidents because every child may not be ready to execute a headstand. The second advantage concerns the matter of discipline. With the command statement the students are given no choice. Whether they can do the headstand or not is immaterial, everyone must try. This can often create a situation where the efficient mover is bored by the simple task. To relieve boredom, he or she will invent other avenues for release which often results in a discipline problem. Basically faced with the opposite situation, the inefficient mover may be tremendously afraid to attempt the requested task. In order to save face, he or she will create a diversion which immediately becomes the source of a new discipline problem. The third advantage of the "can you" format involves class morale and cooperation. All things being equal, if children are successful they will experience an increased sense of morale, and if morale is high it is most likely that they will be extremely cooperative. Looking back at the examples, it becomes evident that success is less likely to result from a command statement, because of the restricted demands made on the students, and is more likely to occur with an open-ended question where students are free to move at their own pace.

There are many other advantages to the "can you" format, but as with anything else, a steady diet of "can you?" and "how many ways can you?" will become boring and tiresome, so try to vary this approach with a more direct one.

THE TEACHING METHOD

Bilbrough and Jones have identified three basic methods of presentation which are based on the amount of choice students are given.[5] They include:

1. *The direct method* — where the teacher makes all of the decisions pertaining to the activity that will be performed and the apparatus that will be used.
2. *The indirect method* — where the students are given their free choice of activities, but where the teacher has control of the situation by limiting the choice of apparatus.
3. *The limitation method* — where the students are limited in their choice by some factor other than apparatus.

In essence the direct method and the task style described in chapter 2 (Styles of Teaching) are basically the same, and while these methods would seem completely alien to

5. A. Bilbrough and P. Jones, *Physical Education in the Primary School* (London: University of London Press, Ltd., 1968), pp. 28-38.

a movement education lesson, they have some advantages when working with younger students, students who are unaccustomed to a more liberal approach, or those students who exhibit very little self-control. The direct method would include statements such as "Practice forward rolling on your mat," and "Find a vacant spot on the wall and practice bouncing the ball against the wall."

The indirect method is a valuable means of giving the students an opportunity to practice movements unencumbered, at their own pace, and in a manner that is gratifying to them. The major drawback to this method is that it becomes difficult to communicate with all the learners because they are usually engaged in so many activities. The indirect method would feature statements such as "Get a short jump rope and practice any movement you'd like to do that won't hurt someone else," and "Get a ball and practice freely."

The limitation method is actually a combination of the direct and indirect methods. "While opportunities for a choice of activity are presented, the choice is limited by particular factors, the children being free to practice within the limitations set. The teacher's usual difficulty is to decide what limitations should be set."[6]

THE LESSON PLAN FORMAT

The lesson plan is a necessary part of all teaching, regardless of the method or approach being used. The lesson plan insures that 1) a logical progression has been established in the lesson; 2) all the important aspects of the lesson have been developed fully; and 3) adequate preparation has been made. In other words, it is the teacher's blueprint to the lesson. In order to be effective, the lesson plan format should reflect the spirit of the approach being used, and the following plan does just that. The following are the five basic units that constitute a movement education plan:

1. *The statement of the theme* — All lesson plans need some type of direction. Trying to plan a lesson without first deciding upon a viable theme will only lead to a haphazard collection of activities. Themes should be based on one of the broad structural questions and follow in a logical order so that the student can receive an in-depth experience in one area.
2. *Free play or free practice* — The movement education lesson characteristically begins with free play or free practice. This is a period of time during which the students are allowed to practice:
   a. Activities which were learned previously, so that they become a permanent part of the students' repertoire.
   b. Activities which will be developed in the day's lesson to create continuity and a sense of anticipation.
   c. Activities which will be developed in future lessons, so that the students become acquainted with specific equipment or concepts before they are needed.

   One of the greatest advantages of the free-play segment is the fact that it begins as soon as the students enter the gymnasium. Instructions are given prior to the class's official entrance, perhaps in the classroom. This phase only lasts a short time, usually no more than five or six minutes.

6. Ibid., p. 35.

3. *The running/jumping phase* — This phase should be included in every movement lesson, regardless of the theme that is being developed. The most important reason for this is that running and jumping are fundamentals to all movement activities, gymnastics, sports, and dance alike. For this reason, a great deal of time should be spent perfecting form and gaining confidence. Questions such as "When you come to someone while running at a medium pace, can you change directions quickly without bumping into anyone else?" or "Can you gradually speed up and slow down as you run?" will help the students to practice running while also giving them a basic understanding of what is important during running.
4. *Development of the theme through mini-themes* — Simply stated, the main theme must be strategically scrutinized and broken down into its essential components if it is to be developed satisfactorily. Once this is done, the teacher must create questions and activities which will logically enhance the student's understanding of the entire experience.
5. *Culminating activity or movement sequences* — Each movement lesson should culminate in an activity or movement sequence that utilizes and enhances the theme as it was logically developed in the preceding phase. In this way, the teacher brings the lesson to a close by utilizing the salient points of the day's work and giving the students an opportunity to use what has been learned in a changing environment.

SUMMARY

In summary, movement education seems to be a method which is well suited to nurturing and cultivating those qualities which educators feel will be important to the student in adulthood.

The philosophy of movement education stresses:

1. *Maximum participation* — Movement educators are acutely aware of time, for they know that the time allotted for physical education must be used to its fullest if their students are to explore and discover all the facets of human movement. Relay races and fixed formations are alien to a movement class because they are considered counterproductive. Those activities which allow each child to work simultaneously are preferred, all others are considered undesirable.
2. *Success for every child* — The problem-solving approach is used almost exclusively in a movement class because it enhances maximum participation, allows students a great deal of latitude, and increases the likelihood of success. A task which requires one precise answer is avoided because it has a tendency to evoke both boredom in those it failed to challenge and failure in those challenged beyond their means. The problem-solving approach helps to build self-confidence and thereby seems to increase the child's achievement level.
3. *An understanding of human movement* — Each lesson is based on themes which are intended to increase the student's movement vocabulary. The movement vocabulary is a set of concepts that represent the basic principles common to all movement. It is hoped that students will arrive at a total understanding of each concept through a thorough exploration of the topic.

4. *An understanding of one's own potential* — Many times a student is given a false or overly exaggerated view of themselves in terms of their movement potential. The movement education class is designed to help students understand the scope of their movement potential and to function successfully within that scope. Developing this understanding and helping the individual develop a healthy attitude are extremely important, since future safety and lifetime participation depend upon it.
5. *Creativity* — Creativity is of vital importance to both the individual and society. Throughout the movement education lesson, the student is being challenged to explore the many facets of a problem and to arrive at multiple solutions, each of which is uniquely different from the others. Students are also encouraged to devise new permutations and combinations of known factors such as speed, level, and rhythm. The teacher must be aware of the great difficulty this causes some individuals and be able to guide them through such difficulty with questions, not flat answers. Creativity in movement is transferable. If an individual can solve movement problems creatively, he or she will more than likely be able to solve all other problems in which they are somewhat knowledgeable creatively.
6. *Independent growth* — It is hoped that by helping the individual develop a positive self-concept, a true concept of his or her own movement potential, an understanding of movement principles, and an ability to be creative, the teacher will have provided tools which the student will need in order to develop his or her own understanding of the total realm of movement. And in addition, it is to be hoped that the student will be able to independently transfer this knowledge to new areas of interest. For example, if the student understands the concept of space and how to move efficiently in space, he or she should be able to comprehend and later execute to the best of their ability the dodge-and-weave in basketball.

chapter five
Ideas for Maximum Participation

One universally accepted aim of physical education is that of maximizing student participation. Too often, teachers fall far short of this goal because they are purists and very orthodox in their thinking. Their imaginations are often restricted by a constant desire to teach with official equipment, abundant space, precise and accurate boundaries, and official rules. Granted, it would be ideal if such conditions existed, and one should never stop striving to obtain them, but a crusade for the perfect environment should never overshadow the primary goal, which is maximum participation for everyone.

When asked about the desirability of maximizing student participation, most teachers agree that it is not only desirable but that it is necessary if teachers are to provide the best possible learning environment for their students. Many quickly add, however, that maximum participation in their particular case is relatively impossible due to overcrowding, equipment shortages, poorly designed facilities and/or the wide range of ability levels found in most coed classes. Unfortunately, the real problem for many of these individuals is that they simply cannot cope with such conditions because they are bound by the constraints of their own purism.

In some instances, overcrowding and the like may be valid deterrents which inhibit maximum participation, but in most instances they are merely convenient excuses for justifying long lines of students waiting to use a piece of equipment or practice a skill. In many cases, the real culprit is not the lack of equipment, adequate space, heterogeneous grouping, or proper class size, but rather the teacher's failure to conscientiously organize or rigorously innovate programs specifically designed for maximizing student participation.

This failure to provide maximum student participation is due in part to the teacher's superficial understanding of what maximum participation is. Once the specifics of the condition are understood, the teacher usually discovers many factors in the learning environment which can be controlled or manipulated to maximize individual student participation.

UNDERSTANDING MAXIMUM PARTICIPATION

Maximum participation refers to that state or condition of participation whereby the *greatest possible number* of students is *totally* involved for the *greatest length* of available instructional *time* in *quality activities* or *learning experiences* planned and presented by the instructor. While it might seem obvious that the three aspects of number, time, and quality must be operating simultaneously and continuously in a specified instructional segment in order to guarantee maximum participation, an inordinate number of teachers plan only for the quantitative aspect (i.e., the greatest number) and assume that once this is achieved, the qualitative and temporal aspects will also be achieved. However, this is not so.

Consider, for example, a typical basketball lesson designed to teach dribbling. In the case following, the teacher's main intent is to 1) impart the rudiments of dribbling, 2) have every child attempt to master the skill, and 3) provide an atmosphere that is exciting.

The teacher greets the students and organizes them into squads, making sure that there are no more than seven in each squad in order to decrease the waiting time. There are forty-two students present, hence six squads are formed. The teacher assembles the squads in neat, straight rows at one end of the gymnasium and then takes a place at the head of the rows so as to be seen and heard by everyone. A lecture-demonstration of the dribble in basketball then commences and the teacher tries to illustrate each important point, leaving ample time at the end for questions.

At the conclusion of the lecture-demonstration the teacher describes the first relay, has one squad demonstrate the action, and organizes the start of the race by distributing the basketballs and directing everyone to the proper starting position. After asking if there are any further questions, the teacher gives the command, "On your mark, get set, go!"

The race begins with the teacher standing on the sidelines watching the action intently to be sure that all of the rules are adhered to faithfully and that everyone finishes the race. After everyone is seated, which signifies that they have performed, the teacher announces the first three places and quickly proceeds to describe the next relay. And so the class continues, running relay races for dribbling with the right hand, the left hand, the right hand with a whirl, and so on, until the warning bell rings, whereupon the balls are collected and the class dismissed.

In the plan book, the teacher writes down the eight activities which were covered and notes disappointedly that there wasn't enough time to cover the last four. The teacher also notes that certain objectives were fulfilled; very little time was wasted during the class and every student was totally involved and seemed enthusiastic throughout the lesson.

The question is, was the teacher right, was each student totally involved and, more importantly, did the teacher help the students master the skill as stated in the objectives?

In the lesson previously described, the teacher did manage to involve all of the students in every one of the activities conducted. This being the case, the teacher did achieve maximum participation quantitatively, or, in terms of the total number able to participate, 100 percent was achieved. Qualitatively and temporally, however, the lesson was quite inadequate.

If we were to measure the managerial, the instructional, and the activity phases of the lesson, the results would look like the watch dials shown in Figure 5.1, which represent approximations derived from timing classes where relay races comprised the total lesson.

From the watch on the left, we can tell that the managerial phase, the time used to take attendance, distribute equipment, and so forth, accounted for five minutes or 12.5 percent of the lesson time. The instructional phase, which is represented by the middle watch, accounted for ten minutes or 25 percent of the lesson time, and the activity phase, when students were moving in activity, accounted for the final twenty-five minutes or only 62.5 percent of the time allotted for the lesson.

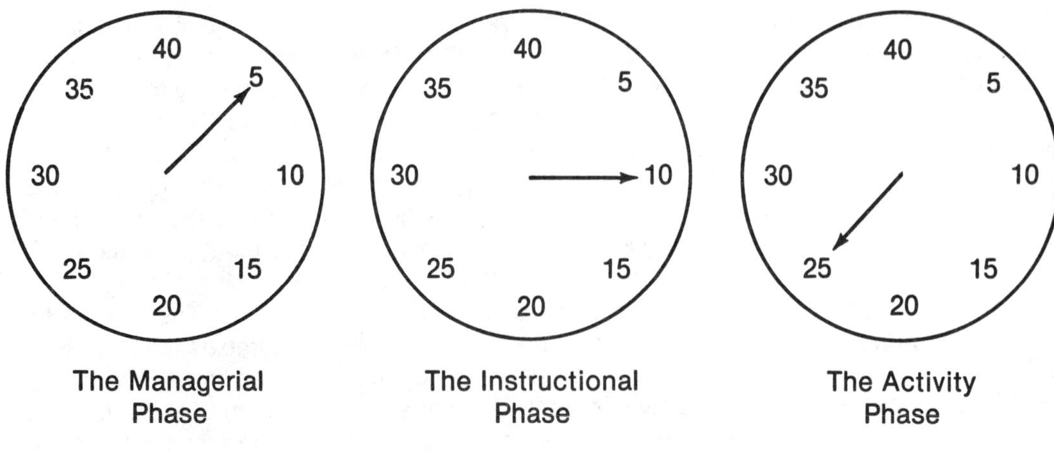

The Managerial Phase

The Instructional Phase

The Activity Phase

FIGURE 5.1.

Comparing the time allotments for this lesson, we find a ratio of one minute of management per two minutes of instruction per five minutes of activity. Even by liberal standards, this lesson was drastically inadequate in terms of activity and instruction. The gravity of the situation does not become apparent, however, until a comparison is done between 1) the total activity time per individual and the total class period, and 2) the total instructional time per individual and the total class period.

Figure 5.2 represents these two comparisons. Note that the total activity time per individual is four minutes or exactly 10 percent of the total class period. Instructional time, in terms of the amount of time the teacher offered criticism or praise to any one individual, is almost nonexistent; remember, the teacher stood on the sidelines, watching intently to be sure that the students adhered faithfully to all the rules of the race and that everyone finished the race. It is quite obvious that the children would receive far greater benefit in terms of moving if they were engaged in a recess period than in the class previously described.

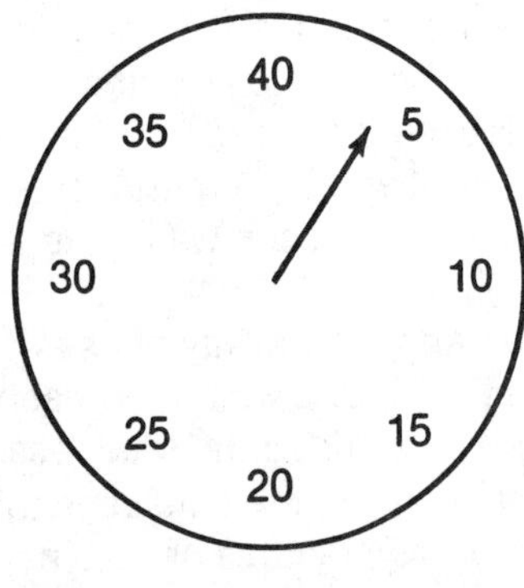

Total Activity Time per Individual

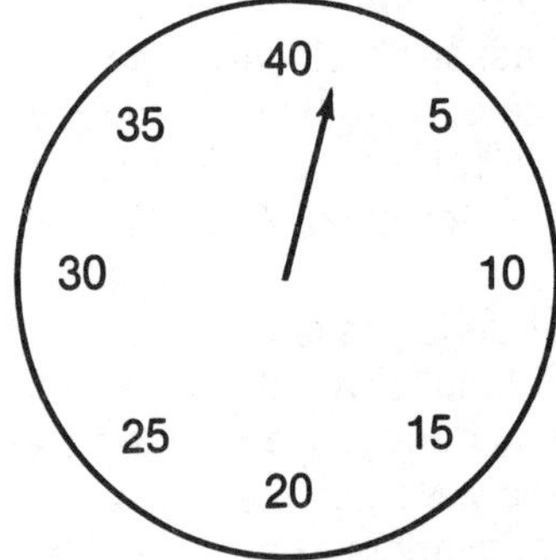

Total Instructional Time per Individual

FIGURE 5.2.

A quantitative measurement of the numbers involved in a specific activity may be an excellent way of justifying financial support for a particular activity, but it is a terribly inadequate way of ascertaining whether maximum participation is being achieved. As a matter of fact, it lulls most teachers into a false sense of accomplishment. When asked about the participation level of the class, the teacher previously described stated emphatically that the students were "enthusiastic and hardworking, and never participated less than 100 percent." When confronted with the facts, this teacher was amazed. Given the myriad movements in a physical education class, it is easy for one to be misled when playing the numbers game.

Becoming concerned about the total time spent by each individual in activity will help the teacher pinpoint the potential roadblocks for maximizing student participation, but it will not guarantee maximum participation even if it is accomplished. The following lesson prepared by Mr. Jones is a perfect example.

When planning his lessons for the week, Mr. Jones decided that he would like to spend an entire class period on ball handling in an effort to improve the throwing and catching ability of his class. After some thought he decided that the game "Keep Away" would be the best activity for his expressed purpose. To be sure that total individual involvement would be increased, Mr. Jones decided to use one ball per three students.

On the day of the actual lesson, Mr. Jones gave a brief lecture-demonstration which highlighted the major components of catching and throwing. He then explained the game, divided the children into teams, and distributed the equipment.

The children played the game, without interruption, until the end of the period, while Mr. Jones walked around the gymnasium the entire time registering students for an intramural track-and-field meet that was scheduled for the end of the week.

Mr. Jones, without a doubt, achieved 100 percent participation in terms of the total number of students he involved in his lesson. He even managed, as can be seen in Figure 5.3, to create a situation in which everyone was involved in some type of activity for approximately 90 percent of the allotted time.

But, did Mr. Jones achieve maximum participation? Did he involve the *greatest number* of students for the *greatest amount of available time* in a *quality* learning experience? The answer to this question obviously can no longer be calculated in terms of numbers, nor can it be measured on a 0-to-100 scale, for the question now focuses upon the key phrase

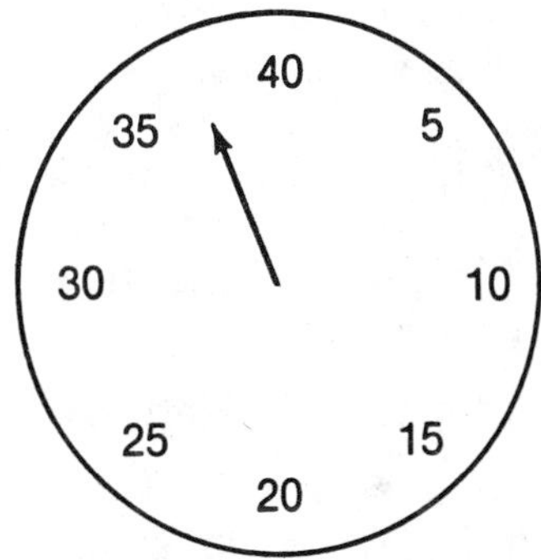

FIGURE 5.3. Total Activity Time per Individual.

"quality learning experience." Did Mr. Jones provide a quality learning experience? Did he choose the most appropriate activity for his students' age and ability level? Did the activity provide for individual differences? Did it allow each child to achieve a measure of success? Did the activity he chose reflect an understanding of children, their developmental stages of learning, and their needs at this specific level? In short, did Mr. Jones avail his students of his expertise in the planning as well as the operational phase of the lesson?

If the answer to these and other questions which seek to determine quality is no, Mr. Jones has fallen short of maximizing participation, regardless of the number of students he involved or the extent of their involvement. Quality is the important qualifying factor in any situation where maximum participation is the objective.

PROVIDING FOR MAXIMUM PARTICIPATION

In order to achieve maximum participation in a specific lesson, a teacher must create an environment in which the student is involved in a gainful experience for the greatest amount of time available, regardless of the number of students assigned to the class, the type of facility provided, or the amount of equipment available. This can be accomplished quite easily if the teacher understands and is willing to employ several options that are readily available.

The first of these options, and the one most often employed to achieve maximum participation, is activity modification. A teacher can easily modify an activity to accommodate any situation by simply manipulating the type of equipment used or the rules that apply. Activity modification requires only an understanding of the situation at hand, the objectives to be achieved, and the ability to analyze the structural components of the activity in question.

The second option involves the manipulation of traditional organizational structures. This option, which is highly effective where overcrowding or equipment shortages are a problem, replaces the traditional structure of one activity per class with a multi-activity design that permits greater diversification of equipment and more efficient use of available facilities. This option requires the ability to choose compatible activities and employ teaching styles that allow the student to be almost totally responsible for the decisions made in the learning environment. It also requires the ability to be highly organized in a complex situation.

The third and last option involves the use of homogeneous and heterogeneous groupings for purposes of individualizing instruction, enhancing self-concepts, increasing social awareness, and promoting cooperation among classmates and teammates. This option requires an understanding of group dynamics and the ability to restructure the emphasis or outcome of an activity to achieve these purposes.

Each of the three options provides the teacher with a means of achieving maximum participation without increased revenue or additional teacher support. Each does, however, require a substantial investment in terms of time and energy and a dedication on the part of the teacher to achieve maximum participation, for partial or ineffectual planning will most assuredly result in inadequate student involvement.

Ideas for Maximum Participation Through Activity Modification

Activity modification is a simple, direct method for increasing the participation potential of a given situation through the use of rule adaptions and/or equipment substitutions. As was mentioned previously, activity modification is the most frequently used and probably the most widely accepted means of maximizing participation. It is even used by children to create game situations that are compatible with their ever-changing needs and desires.

Activity modification can be used to provide an environment in which the beginner can function successfully with a limited amount of skill. It can also be used to create a situation in which a specific aspect of a sport is isolated so that it can be practiced repeatedly. This form of activity modification, which is known as the leadup game, is a widely used method of preparing youngsters for actual game play.

Although the leadup game is an extremely important form of activity modification, it is not the most popular nor the most useful. Because of the recent emphasis on coed participation and activity for the aged and other special populations, the modified game form is becoming increasingly more important in contemporary physical education.

It is being used today to minimize the effects which a wide range of abilities, such as that which exists in most coed classes today, can have on class play and enjoyment. Modified game forms reduce and de-emphasize the advantage of certain attributes such as muscular strength and speed. They are also being used to redesign the rule structure or environment so that the more highly skilled performer will face a greater challenge than an opponent who may be of lesser skill. In order to accommodate the needs of special populations, such as the aged or the handicapped, games are being modified to de-emphasize those aspects of the original game which restricted or excluded these individuals. Full-court basketball, for example, is too strenuous a game for most individuals over 35 years old because of the constant demands made by the fast break. Eliminating the fast break and requiring that the offensive team hold the ball until the defensive team is ready keeps the game within range of the physical capabilities of these individuals.

Modified games are commonly used to resolve unfavorable situations as well. The effects of overcrowding, equipment shortages, and inadequate or inappropriate space can be minimized or eliminated through the imaginative use of modified games. Examples of these and other modified games are given in the section entitled "Games Illustrating Rule Adaption." (See pp. 68-71)

Activity modification is accomplished through equipment substitution and rule adaption. In reading the explanations and examples that follow, it should be remembered that while equipment substitution and rule adaption are discussed separately in theory, there is a definite and essential interrelationship between the two in actual practice.

Equipment Substitution

There are many individual circumstances which may dictate the search for an equipment substitute. Most of these circumstances involve having to:

1. Purchase large quantities of equipment on a limited budget
2. Modify the activity so that it is suitable for the space available
3. Modify the activity so that it is easier and/or safer for the beginner to play
4. Modify the activity to diminish the difference in strength, body awareness, and/or ball sense.

Before searching for the adequate substitute, the teacher must clearly define the problems that an equipment substitution would rectify. Consider, for example, the teacher who is forced by inclement weather to teach a golf lesson inside. At first glance, it becomes evident that the teacher needs a ball which allows restricted flight only. This need immediately suggests a plastic practice ball. Upon closer examination, however, the plastic ball must be ruled out because it bounces too much and may cause a safety hazard indoors. This being the case, the problem must now be redefined; the ball that is needed must be one that has restricted flight and does not bounce or roll excessively. One solution to this problem would be a commercially manufactured yarn ball. This would solve the problem immediately except for the cost factor; each of these little balls costs approximately eighty-five cents. Even if only one ball was purchased for each student in an average class of 35, the price would be $29.75. A somewhat expensive item for a rainy-day class, considering the fact that each student would be provided only one ball with which to practice golf. The teacher could consider making yarn balls, but the number of hours necessary to complete such a task would immediately rule out that idea as well.

Restating the problem as it now stands, the teacher needs a large quantity of practice balls (say, six per student) which have restricted flight, do not roll or bounce excessively, and which can be obtained inexpensively and without a great expenditure of man-hours.

One common item which satisfies all of these conditions is an egg-carton cup. It is sturdy, has restricted flight, does not roll or bounce excessively, and can be procured easily, inexpensively, and in great quantities. Furthermore, an egg-carton cup, even when used as a projectile, will not hurt an individual who has been inadvertently struck by it.

The egg-carton cup would seem to be one of the perfect solutions to this problem; that is unless the teacher cannot accept it as a solution because it is not a bona fide ball. Defining the problem explicitly was the first step to finding a possible solution, but being able to accept the answer is the second step. If the teacher is only concerned with students striking some object with a club so that they can practice their swing, any solution is feasible and acceptable. On the other hand, if the equipment substitute must also look like the original, the teacher has greatly limited the number of possible solutions and perhaps even arbitrarily ruled out the best ones.

In order to effectively use equipment substitution to achieve maximum participation, teachers must not only clearly define the problems, they must also learn to set reasonable and unbiased standards for judging the validity or acceptability of the solutions. Arranged by sport in Table 5.1 are some examples of original equipment items, their substitutes, and the reasons for their selection.

Table 5.1. Equipment Substitution Chart.

SPORT	ORIGINAL ITEM	SUBSTITUTE	REASON
1. Badminton	Birdie	Yarn ball	Easier to use
		Large sponge ball	Easier for beginners to use
		Plastic practice golf ball	Speeds up the game
		Weighted egg-carton cup	Slower flight and readily available
		Small taped sponge cube	Slower flight. Allows game play in restricted space

Table 5.1 (cont'd).

SPORT	ORIGINAL ITEM	SUBSTITUTE	REASON
	Racquet	Racquetball racquet	Easier for beginners to use (shorter implement)
		Pantyhose racquet	Inexpensive and readily available
2. Golf	Ball	Plastic ball	Allows game play in restricted outdoor space
		Yarn ball	For use indoors
		Egg-carton cup	For restricted use indoors, readily available
		Small sponge cube	For restricted use indoors, readily available
		Wadded paper ball	For restricted use indoors, readily available
		Floor-hockey disc	For putting indoors with beginners
		Wooden disc Metal jar lid	For putting indoors with beginners
	Club	Floor-hockey stick	Readily available
		Field-hockey stick	Readily available
		Knotted towel	Used to practice swing
		Flat plastic bat	Readily available
	Tee	Egg-carton cups	Safe and inexpensive for indoor use
		Styrofoam cubes	Safe and inexpensive for indoor use
		Sponge cubes	Safe and inexpensive for indoor use

Table 5.1 (cont'd).

SPORT	ORIGINAL ITEM	SUBSTITUTE	REASON
3. Volleyball	Ball	Dense foam ball	Minimizes range of skill ability. Allows beginners to work on skill without the fear of bent or jammed fingers
		Light-weight vinyl ball	
		Thick-walled punching ball	
		Large material ball	
		Beach ball	
4. Racquetball or Paddleball	Racquet or Paddle	The hand	Easier for beginners
		Round wooden discs attached to hand	Easier for beginners
		Ping-pong paddle	Readily available
	Ball	Thick-walled practice handball	Not as lively. Easier for beginners to work on skill. Makes maximum use of space
		Dense foam ball	
		Sponge ball	Not as lively. Easier for beginners to work on skill
		Tennis ball	

An Example of Activity Modification by Equipment Substitution

Golf can be played on an indoor course quite effectively if precautions are taken for safety and if the equipment substitutions made allow the individual to practice the skill without having to make modifications in style or technique. The following example illustrates how equipment substitution for the game of golf can be used to provide a learning experience indoors.

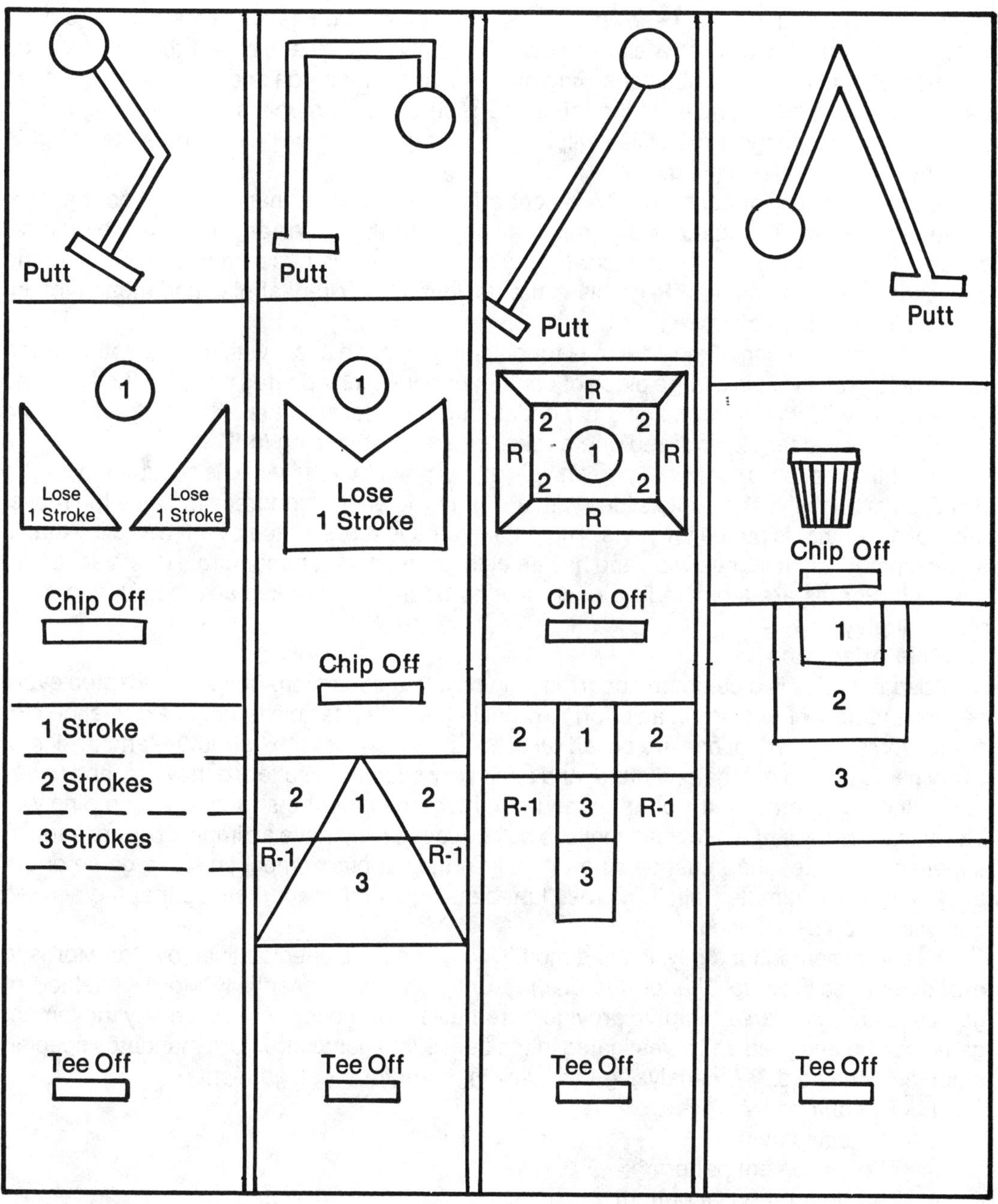

FIGURE 5.4. Floor Plan for Four Practice Holes of Golf.

The diagram in Figure 5.4 shows four practice holes which have been set out in a gymnasium with safety walks between each hole. The only original equipment that will be used are the clubs. One set of clubs consisting of a five iron, a nine iron and a putter are given to each foursome. Each number of the foursome receives a yarn ball, a weighted egg-carton cup, or a taped sponge cube which will be used for driving or chipping, and a metal jar lid which will be used for putting.

The first section of each hole is designed for driving. Tape marks placed on the floor serve as a target. The number of strokes awarded to the golfer depends on the point at which the ball comes to rest on the target. (Only one drive is necessary, except when the ball lands in an area marked R-1. This is the designation for repeat play and means the individual is penalized a stroke.)

The second section of the course is for chipping. In each case, with the exception of the fourth hole, the target is a large piece of contact paper which adheres nicely to the floor and comes up easily without damaging a wooden surface. Hazards are also made of contact paper and the golfer is penalized one stroke for any shot landing in them.

The third section is the putting green. It is at this point that the jar lid is substituted for the ball used previously. The jar lid slides with a slight drag and, therefore, simulates the movement of a ball that is putted on grass. The putting area is represented by a taped alley that is approximately eight inches wide and has an eight-inch contact-paper circle (the hole) at the very end. Scores are tabulated for each hole by adding the strokes awarded during each phase of play.

Rule Adaptions

Adapting rules is a common occurrence in physical education. Rules are adapted every day for a variety of reasons in an effort to provide the best possible learning experiences for the students. Rule adaptions are based on the assumption that the "structure and design of every game played mandate, dictate, and elicit very specific resultant behaviors, and if certain outcomes are desired from a game then the game must be structured accordingly."[1] This being the case, if a rule adaption is to be successful and have an impact on the learning experience, the teacher must be able to analyze the various components of a game or activity which will ultimately elicit the resultant behaviors and adapt them so that the desired objectives can be attained.

A simple method for analyzing and modifying games has been outlined by Don Morris in a book entitled *How to Change the Games Children Play*. Essentially Morris' method of games analysis is "an attempt to provide a framework or model from which any movement game can be analyzed and investigated in the sense that game structure mandates specific outcome behaviors."[2] By analyzing the following structural categories:

1. The number of players
2. The equipment
3. The movement pattern
4. The organizational pattern
5. The special limitations that are imposed
6. The ultimate purpose of the game

1. Gordon S. Morris, *How to Change the Games Children Play* (Minneapolis: Burgess Publishing Co., 1976), p. 2.
2. Ibid., p. 11.

Morris feels that

> by categorizing the many components that make up a game, one is able to provide a model from which teachers and students are able to design, change, adapt and make decisions about the entire structure of any game previously played or any game needed to be played to enhance specific motoric, social, and emotional outcomes.[3]

Once the components of a game have been identified, it is possible to adapt or modify any or all of them so that the actual outcomes of the game are more closely aligned with the intended ones. An illustration of this technique is given for the game of volleyball in Figure 5.5. Note that the salient points of the game appear at a glance, that a structural image of volleyball can be developed, and that changes can easily be made to adapt the game to a specific situation. The usefulness of the game grid is illustrated by the following example.

FIGURE 5.5. Sample Game Grid for Standard Volleyball Game.

Game	Players	Equipment	Movement Pattern	Organizational Pattern	Limitations	Purpose
Volley-ball	Team of six	One leather volleyball One net	Passing, blocking spiking, and serving	W formation with clock-wise rotation	USVBA rules	To win

Mr. Dougherty decided to develop a volleyball unit for his fifth-grade class. After analyzing the basic fundamentals of the game, he decided that he would teach only basic footwork and the overhand pass on the first day. Once this decision was made, he consulted the game grid to see what kind of changes might be necessary if his students were to be successful. After much thought, he decided that his students' best interests would be served if he developed a game based entirely on the forehand pass. To do this, he changed the weight of the ball and the height of the net so that his students would be more successful in their attempts to pass. He also increased the number of players to eight per team so that each student would be responsible for a smaller area. His game grid then looked like this:

FIGURE 5.6. Sample Game Grid for Simply Adapted Volleyball Game.

Game	Players	Equipment	Movement Pattern	Organizational Pattern	Limitations	Purpose
Volley-ball	Team of eight	Vinyl ball Low net	Forehand pass and other striking motions	Scattered formation	USVBA rules	To win

3. Ibid., p. 2.

Because it was the first day of the unit, Mr. Dougherty decided to eliminate the competitive aspect of the game. In order to do this, he removed the USVBA rules and changed the stated purpose. He decided that neither team should win or lose by capitalizing on the others' mistakes but that both teams should cooperate in trying to accumulate the greatest number of points possible in a specified time period by counting the number of times the ball was successfully sent back and forth across the net. In so doing, he placed the emphasis on the overhand pass and footwork, which were his stated objectives for the first lesson. His final game grid looked like this:

FIGURE 5.7. Sample Game Grid for More Complexly Adapted Game of Volleyball.

Game	Players	Equipment	Movement Pattern	Organizational Pattern	Limitations	Purpose
Volleyball	Team of eight	Vinyl ball Low net	Forehand pass and other striking motions	Scattered formation	Only overhand pass scores points	To send the ball across the net as many times as possible in a specified period of time

Another technique that is slightly more elaborate but basically the same as Morris' games-analysis model is attribute listing, which is explained in greater detail in chapter 3 (Creativity in Education).

Regardless of the techniques employed, teachers will find that by being able to analyze and systematically change, eliminate, or expand any aspect of an activity they will exercise greater control over the learning environment and that ultimately games and other movement activities can be used to enhance or achieve the objectives of a lesson rather than be employed to simply culminate a lesson on an enthusiastic note.

GAMES ILLUSTRATING RULE ADAPTION

Following are several games that have been adapted to:

1. Accommodate a wide range of skill abilities simultaneously
2. Offer varying challenges within the same game structure
3. Provide for individual physical differences
4. Achieve a positive learning environment despite unfavorable conditions

Volleyball

A. Name: Insanity
Parent Game: Volleyball
Objective: To accommodate wide range of skill ability by offering two different degrees of the same challenge offered both sides.
Number of Players: Two on one side of the court, four to six on the opposite side.
Court Dimensions:

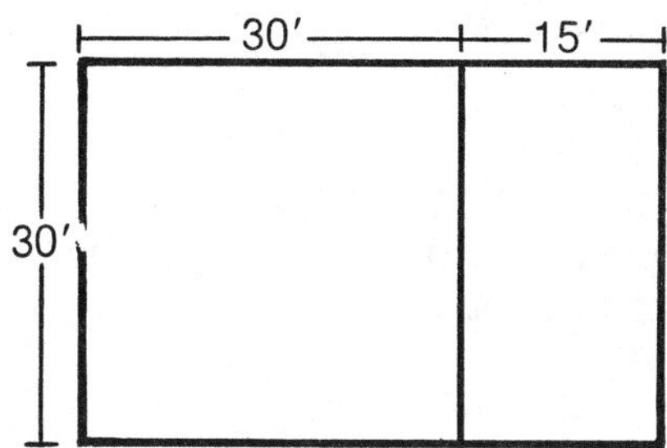

Rules: The same as official volleyball.
Additional Modification: Can be played with a light-weight ball or a dense foam ball.

B. Name: Doubles Volleyball (Triples, Quadruples)
Parent Game: Volleyball
Objective: Allows for much more action in a game. Accounts for the range of skill ability within a class.
Number of Players: Two, three, or four.
Court Dimensions: Court size is reduced. Area measures 30′ x 20′ (see diagram). Court could also measure 15′ x 15′, so that four small courts would fit on an official volleyball court if the net ran in the other direction.

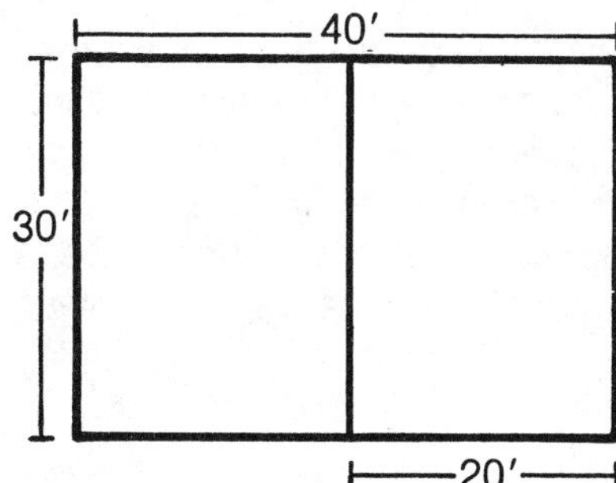

Rules: Same as official volleyball.
Additional Modification: Played with a light-weight vinyl ball or large, dense sponge ball, such as an "all-ball," to reduce the range of skill ability.

C. Name: Lightball
Parent Game: Volleyball
Objective: Slower game. Helps the unskilled player to adapt while learning. Allows full range of play without worry of injury.
Number of Players: Six

Court Dimensions: Official court or half-size court.

Rules and Scoring: Same as volleyball except that one of the following balls is used in lieu of a volleyball: a beach ball, large light-weight vinyl ball, medium-size light-weight vinyl ball, material ball, dense foam ball, thick-walled punching balloon.

D. Name: Wallball

Parent Game: Volleyball

Objective: To make best use of available space. Has the potential to accommodate a large number of individuals.

Number of Players: Two or more.

Court Dimensions: This game is played against the wall. There are two sets of boundaries drawn; one on the wall and one on the floor.

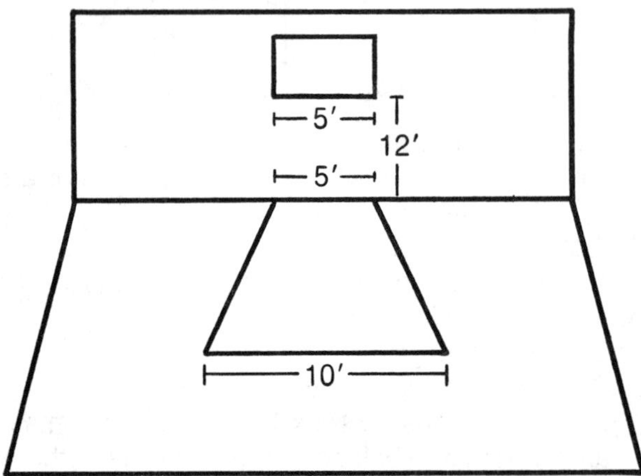

Tape a 5′ square on the wall 12′ from the floor line. Tape a wedge on the floor 5′ wide at its narrowest point, 10′ wide at its widest point. Start the wedge directly at the wall/floor line.

Rules and Scoring: *For two-player game*, points are only awarded when serving. Ball is served from outside wedge into 5′ square. Volley follows. Only one hit is allowed per person. Ball must be volleyed to wall square and must stay within boundaries of the wedge. Game is 15 points.

Badminton

A. Name: Wiffle-Minton

Parent Game: Badminton

Objective: Makes maximum use of space for advanced players. Accelerates game.

Number of Players: Three or four per side.

Court Dimensions: Official badminton size.

Rules and Scoring: Played with a wiffle golf ball and shortened racquet. Rotation same as volleyball rotation. Points awarded only when serving. Game is 15 points.

B. Name: Mini-Minton

Parent Game: Badminton

Objective: Makes maximum use of space. Game slowed down, adjusted to space. Requires increased wrist snap.
Number of Players: One per side.
Court Dimensions: One fourth the size of an official court
Rules and Scoring: Played with a 2″ taped sponge cube. All rules of badminton apply.

C. Name: Ping-Minton
Parent Game: Badminton
Objective: Accommodates wide range of ability. Makes maximum use of wall space.
Number of Players: One per side.
Rules and Scoring: Played with a ping-pong ball against wall. Two-foot line drawn across court 2′ high. All balls must strike wall above line. Racquetball rules apply.

D. Name: Wall Smash
Parent Game: Badminton
Objective: Makes maximum use of wall space.
Number of Players: Two, four, or more.
Court Dimensions: The court should be 7′ wide and extend 10′ back from the wall. The wall should have a similar 7′-by-10′ box marked off 5′ above the floor line.
Rules and Scoring: Birdie is played against wall alternately by opponents. Service alternates every five serves, as in table tennis. Scoring is the same as table tennis. Game is 21 points.

E. Name: Evil-Minton
Parent Game: Badminton
Objective: To offer varying degrees of challenge in the same game by varying the playing conditions.
Number of Players: Three players total.
Court Dimensions: Same as official game of badminton.
Rules: Same as badminton except that players number off 1,2,3. Player 1 occupies one half the court and players 2 and 3 occupy the other half simultaneously. Player 1 serves against players 2 and 3 and is capable of scoring points until he loses the service. Player 2 then exchanges courts with player 1 and serves to player 1 and player 3. When player 2 loses the serve, player 3 moves to serve and so on, until one player scores a total of 15 points. The server in this game is always faced by two opponents. Points are only scored on the serve.

Staging Modified Activities Simultaneously

If forty students were assigned to a tennis class on only four courts, it would be an understatement to say conditions would be overcrowded, and to think that this doesn't often happen in many districts is a total misconception. The question is, "What do you do with forty students on four tennis courts?" The answer to the question relies on a further question: "How often do they have to play the actual game during the course?"

If the answer to the second question is "It doesn't matter," then there are many things that can be done to insure maximum participation; on the other hand, if the answer is "At least once a day," then there will probably be a great deal of waiting against the fence and very little moving.

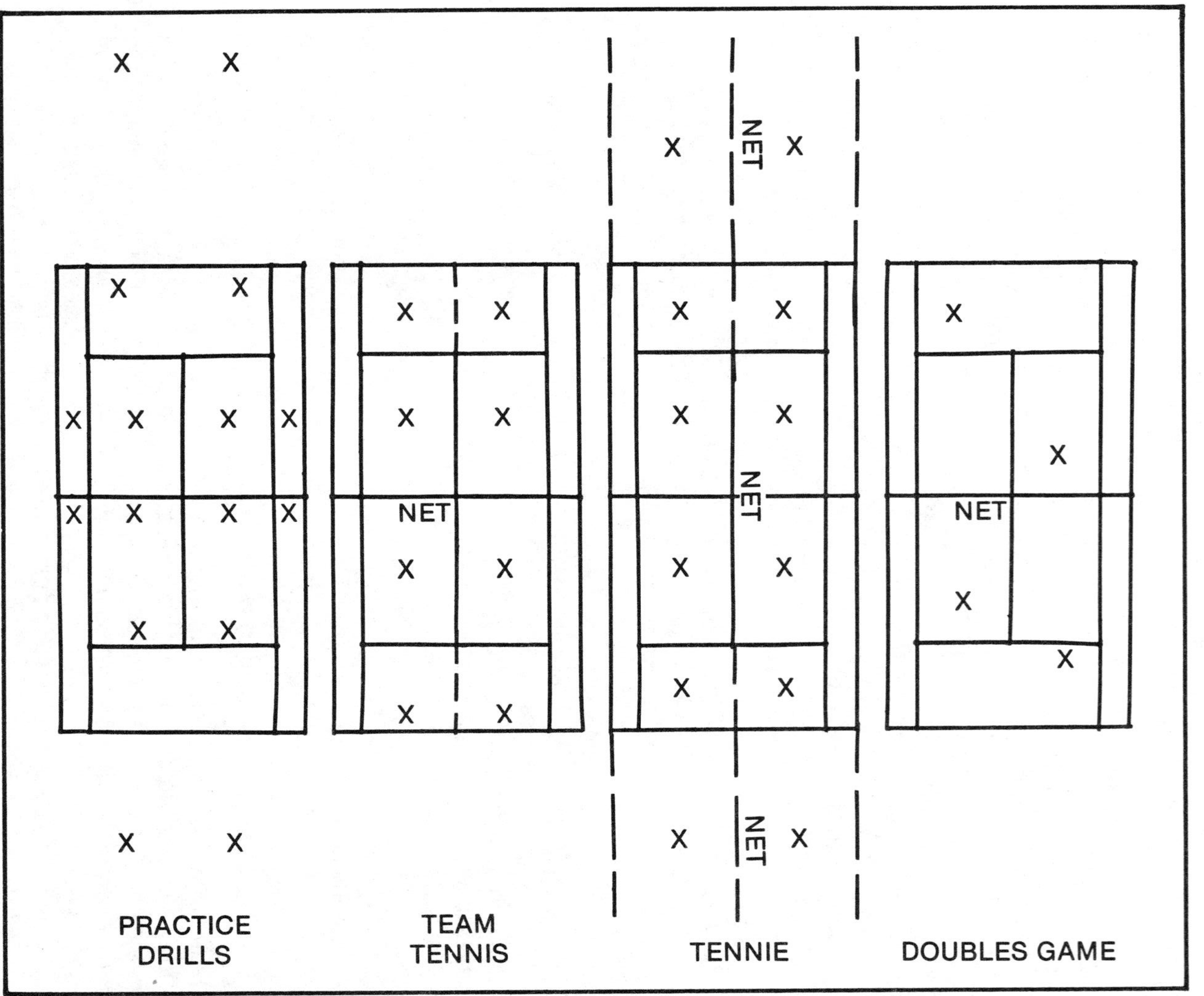

FIGURE 5.8. Sample Diagram of Simultaneous Activity Staging.

Figure 5.8 shows one solution that is possible if a modified, dense sponge ball is used, if boundaries are realigned, and if a variety of activities is staged simultaneously. On the far right-hand court, four students can play a game of doubles. The rules can be altered so that both players on the serving side alternate the serve during a game, thereby giving both of them an opportunity to serve. After two games, a new group is rotated onto the court to play doubles.

Moving to the left, the court labeled tennie can accommodate eight students playing the court widthwise. A rope with ribbons or streamers attached is strung from one fence to the other at the same height as the net. This rope serves as the net on these mini-courts. The ball substitute used here (a dense foam ball) allows students to take a full stroke in a restricted area.

The next court to the left, labeled team tennis, can also accommodate eight students but the court division is different. The court dimensions allow a very narrow court which, in essence, forces the student to make lob shots, smashes, and down-the-line shots.

The court furthest to the left can accommodate any number of students. In the diagram, net drills are marked by *X*'s in the middle of the court, while stroking drills or serving drills are similarly marked on the periphery.

Staging all of these modified activities simultaneously insures maximum participation in a situation that under other circumstances would be considered overcrowded.

Modifying activities by rules adaption or equipment substitution alone is often not sufficient for solving many of the staging problems that have resulted from popularization of individual sports and coed participation. The teacher must learn to stage several activities simultaneously, as illustrated in the previous example, and to help the students accept these modified activities as bona fide experiences for the actual game. If teachers fail to implement this type of staging, it is unlikely that they will be able to achieve maximum participation in its truest and most valuable sense.

Maximum Participation Through Multi-Activity Programming

Activity modification may be the simplest and most popular means of achieving maximum participation, but it is not always the most effective or adequate method of resolving an unfavorable condition in the learning environment. This is particularly evident in cases of overcrowding due to inadequate space or insufficient instructional time. In such situations, the activity modifier can only superficially alter the prohibitive condition in a manner which eventually becomes totally unsatisfactory. The following situation is a typical example of a case in which activity modification fails to achieve maximum participation in terms of a quality experience.

Thirty-two students were assigned to Ms. Regg's paddleball class in the gym annex. While this was not an unusually large class in terms of the student/teacher ratio, Ms. Regg felt it was extremely large in terms of the space provided in the annex, where only four courts could be laid out safely.

Rather than assign eight students to a court where they would only be able to play for half of the period, Ms. Regg decided to make use of an equipment substitute which restricted the flight of the ball and thereby allowed her to double both the number of available courts and the amount of time her students could play. (See Figures 5.10, 5.11.)

This appeared to be a viable solution for increasing the participation level of each student until Ms. Regg realized that she had not really resolved the problems imposed by the

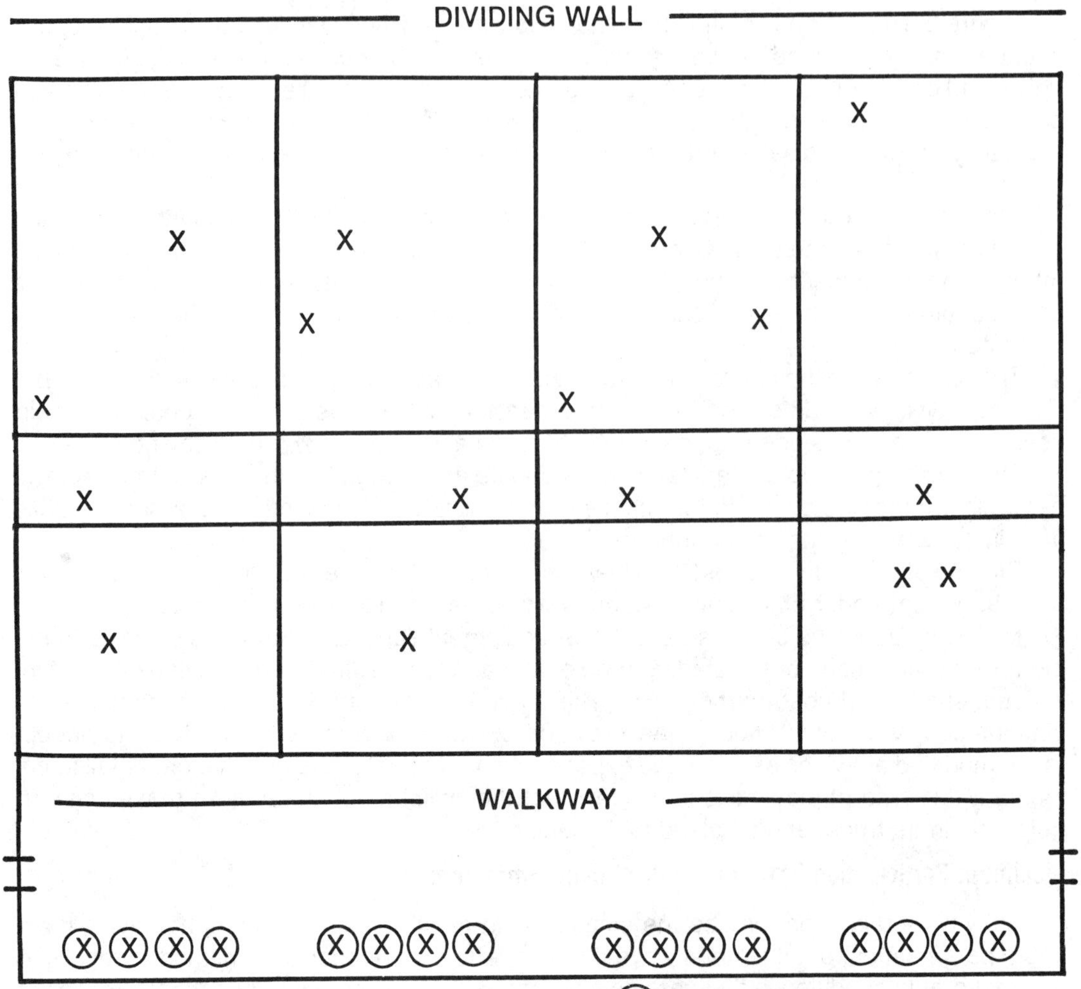

X = Participants   (X) = Spectators

FIGURE 5.9. Conventional Activity Breakdown.

original overcrowded condition, which reoccurred when her class tried to play the actual game of paddleball with a livelier ball. The only satisfactory solution for this type of overcrowding would have been one which increased the amount of playing time per student when the class was playing the actual game of paddleball.

The simple equipment substitution of Ms. Regg's was obviously an inadequate means of achieving maximum participation. What she needed was an entirely different form of programming. If she had broken from tradition and discarded the pattern of one activity per class and substituted a multi-activity design, she would have been able to achieve maximum participation easily.

In a multi-activity design, the teacher selects several compatible or complementary activities and conducts them simultaneously such that maximum use can be made of space,

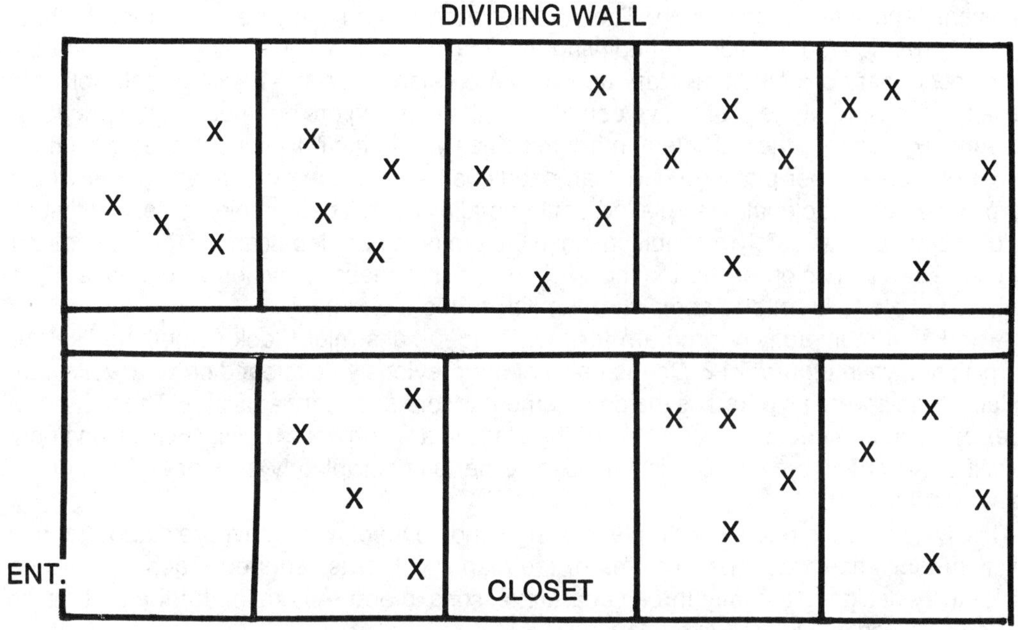

DIVIDING WALL
ENT.
CLOSET

FIGURE 5.10. Modified Activity Breakdown.

DIVIDING WALL
ENT.
(X) = Students playing cutthroat

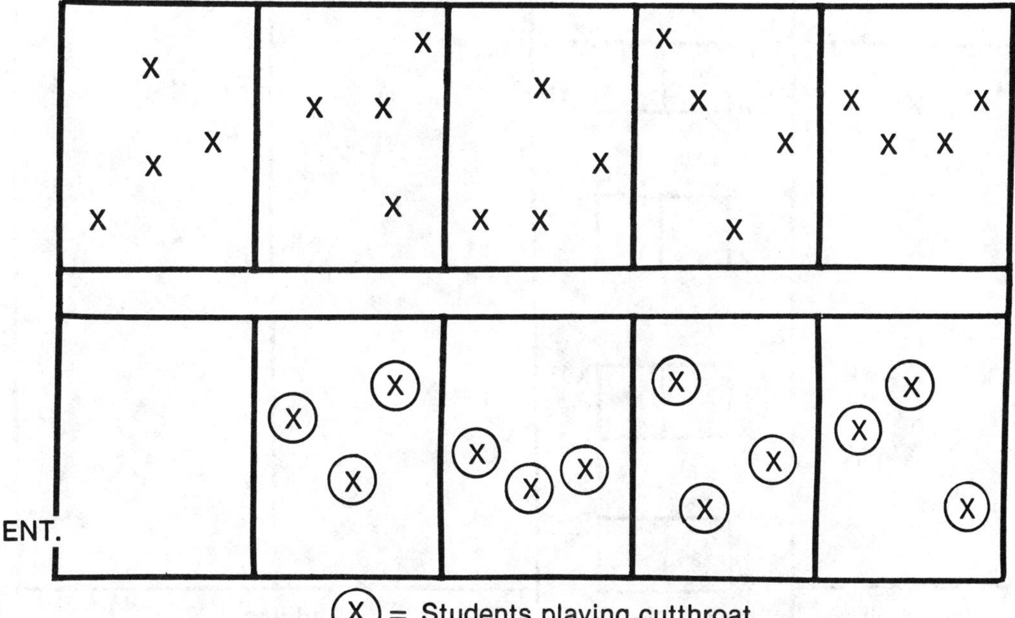

FIGURE 5.11. Modified Activity Breakdown.

equipment, and instructional time. The primary activity can then be conducted without employing restrictive methods or modifying the activity needlessly.

The secondary or complementary activities are selected on the basis of their ability to relieve the pressure of the prohibitive condition in the learning environment. In the previously described situation, the complementary activities would have to accommodate a larger number of students per playing court than paddleball so that the overcrowding that would take place when paddleball was played could be alleviated. The complementary activities would also have to be safely playable in close proximity to paddleball and without the direct and constant supervision of the teacher. In other words these activities would have to be relatively simple to learn and somewhat familiar to the students.

A workable multi-activity program for Ms. Regg's class might look something like the floor plan shown in Figure 5.12. On the basis of the previously developed criteria, volleyball and table tennis were selected as the complementary or secondary activities. These two activities can accommodate three-fourths of the class in a worthwhile activity while using only one-half of the space provided. This leaves the other half completely free for eight students to play paddleball.

This system, while relatively simple in design and concept, is much more elaborate than activity modification would be in terms of the planning that is required. Each lesson in a multi-activity design is actually three separate lessons in one. An outline for the first day in Ms. Regg's class would look like this:

I. Objectives
   A. To develop the forehand and backhand strokes in paddleball

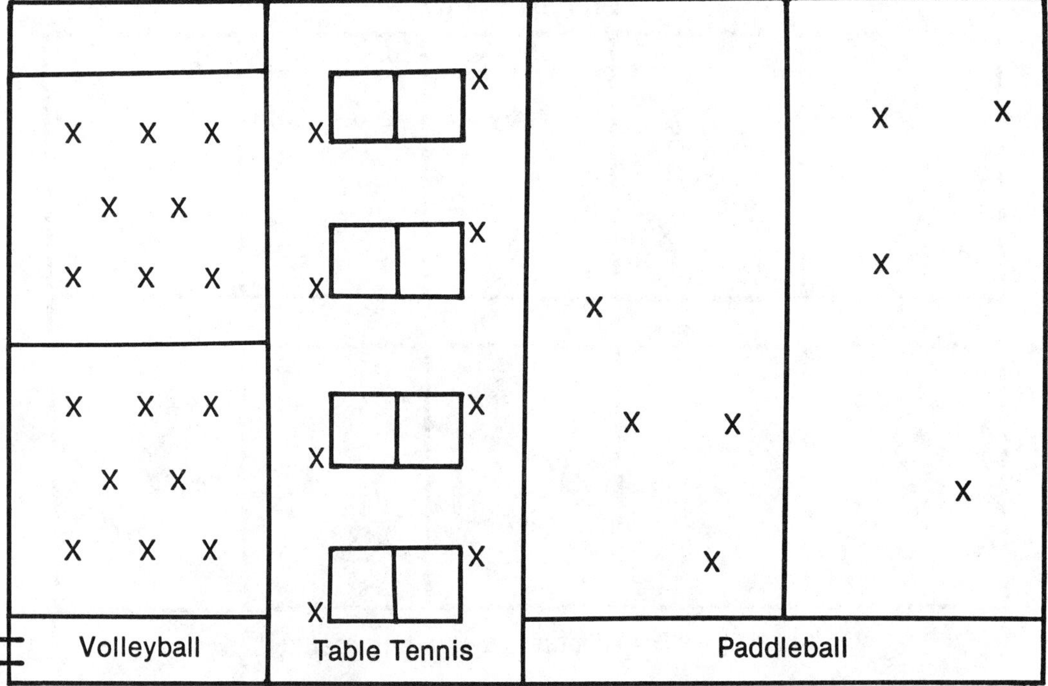

FIGURE 5.12. Workable Multi-Activity Program.

B. To develop the roundhouse serve in volleyball
C. To develop the backhand half-volley in table tennis

II. Procedure

A. Segment A (first 15 minutes)
1. Volleyball — Distribute task sheets to warmup using the overhead pass and the forearm pass.
2. Paddleball — Explain and demonstrate forehand and backhand strokes. Assign drills.
3. Table Tennis — Provide abbreviated set of rules. Assign individual program on the grip and the backhand half-volley.

B. Segment B (second 15 minutes)
1. Volleyball — Explain and demonstrate roundhouse serve. Assign drill.
2. Paddleball — Provide abbreviated set of rules. Play mini-games.
3. Table Tennis — Play game using primarily the backhand for half of each volley.

C. Segment C (third 15 minutes)
1. Volleyball — Play game (use only roundhouse serve).
2. Paddleball — Play an official doubles game.
3. Table Tennis — Play official game. Teacher coaches strokes and makes suggestions.

Notice that this lesson is divided into three segments. This allows the teacher to think in terms of spending a direct segment of time with each group of students giving individual instruction. This type of planning is necessary throughout the unit if the teacher wishes to provide a quality learning experience.

In order to facilitate this design, the class should be divided into four units and assigned to each activity accordingly. Unit 1, for instance, would join Unit 2 for volleyball and then be assigned to paddleball, while Unit 2 had table tennis and vice versa. The same would apply to Units 3 and 4. This arrangement, over a six-week period, would provide each student with seven and one-half lessons in paddleball, seven and one-half lessons in table tennis, and fifteen lessons in volleyball.

Obviously, a multi-activity design can only be implemented successfully by a teacher who is highly organized and adept at using the various styles of teaching to obtain desired results and whose students are self-motivated and responsible. If either of these aspects is missing, the multi-activity design will be doomed before it begins.

Ideas for Maximum Participation Through the Use of Personalized Learning Strategies

Maximum participation can be effectively achieved in the gymnasium if the teacher is sensitive to and can accommodate the individual needs and interests of each student, and it is further enhanced if the teacher can personalize the learning environment. According to Locke and Lambdin, personalized instruction refers to:

> Any version of Individualized Instruction in which there is use of, or emphasis upon, the learner's involvement with others in the learning environment. This either may involve the learner in a tutor/student relationship with the teacher, or may involve the learner in transactions with peers.[4]

4. Lawrence F. Locke and Dolly Lambdin, "Teacher Behavior," in *Personalized Learning and Physical Education*, ed. Don Hellison (Washington, D.C.: AAHPER Publications, 1976), p. 14.

It is the interaction between student and student and between student and teacher that characterizes personalized instruction and makes it an effective tool in maximizing student participation. In this light, the concept encourages teachers to mediate the environment, to make use of child-centered teaching styles such as task and problem solving, to devise contractual agreements between themselves and their students, and, in short, to employ or develop strategies which involve the learner in his or her own learning and focus the teacher's attention on each individual personality.

Creating a Mediated Environment

Today, more than ever before, the physical educator is expected to be an authority on all activities. The list of courses offered in the selective physical education program grows each year but often without regard for the instructor's expertise. This factor, plus the ever widening body of knowledge in physical education, has made it impossible for the instructor to assume the role of the lone authority on any given subject. This phenomenon is not occurring in physical education exclusively, it is happening in other disciplines as well.

Most educators have learned to deal with the situation by recognizing that the teacher does not have to be the all-knowing authority in the classroom. There are others who can and should be brought into the classroom to help present the subject matter. In these instances the primary responsibilities of the instructor should be to:

1. Determine the skill to be mastered
2. Ascertain the performance level of the students in regard to that skill
3. Help students understand the skill that is to be mastered
4. Develop varied alternatives for disseminating information
5. Present the alternatives, using the most appropriate teaching style
6. Evaluate the accuracy of the learning
7. Redesign the methods for imparting the information based on the evaluation

A common method that allows the teacher to fulfill these responsibilities is the use of certain media. Films and books can be used to present the desired subject matter, and this essentially frees the teacher to plan for individual instruction.

Using the Student-Centered Styles of Teaching

After reading the discussion on various teaching styles in chapter 2, it should be obvious that a quantitative form of maximum participation, where the greatest number of people is involved, can be achieved via any teaching style. However, a qualitative form of maximum participation can best be achieved through the use of those styles on the continuum which allow students greater control over their own learning. These include the task, reciprocal, guided-discovery, and problem-solving styles. Examples of these styles can be reviewed in chapter 2.

Using the Contractual Agreement

The contractual agreement is a pact made between the student and the teacher regarding what the student must do to earn a certain grade. Using this method of teaching, the teacher must distinguish the quality and quantity of work which distinguishes a certain grade level long before any student embarks on a series of designated tasks.

Gotts has identified three distinct types of contractual agreements. They include the fixed or required contract, the student-choice contract, and the open-ended contract.

Fixed or Required Contract. This contract insures that each student will cover all the essential material in a unit of work. The distinguishing factor is that students can progress at their own rate and in the order or manner they desire. Here is an example of a fixed basketball contract:[5]

Basketball Contract #1

Performer ___________ worked on these activities in the open gym ___________

1. Free throws. I practiced shooting _____ series of _____ free throws each.
2. Lay-ups. I practiced shooting _____ shots driving from the right side and _____ shots driving from the left side.
3. Jump shot. I practiced my jump shot from _____ different floor locations, shooting _____ shots at each spot. Diagram the locations.
4. Tip-ins. I bounced the ball off the backboard and tried to put the rebound in the basket _____ times.

Student-Choice Contract. This gives the student a greater responsibility in deciding what should be learned. The teacher provides the student with several different options and the choice of grades and concomitant work is up to the student. The following is an example of this type of contract:

Student-Choice Contract for Term Paper

For a grade of "C":

1. Investigate and write a brief critique of two analytical tools. Include: summary, application, advantages, and shortcomings.
2. Select an aspect of the teaching/learning process that interests *you* and justify its importance through a survey of literature.
3. Design a *unique* analytical tool to observe and analyze your selected aspect of teaching.
4. Test the tool on an actual teaching situation: use tapes if at all possible or practical — make appointment to present results orally and in writing to Mr. Dougherty.
5. Make suggestions for modification of tool based upon your experience in its use.

For a grade of "B":

1. Same as for "C" only review *three* tools.
2. Same as for "C".
3. Same as for "C".
4. Same as for "C". Written presentation may be informal.
5. Discuss modification of your system with me in our conference.
6. Implement your modification into your system and retest in actual teaching as in 4.
7. Present final program, with any further ideas for modification or development, in written form.

---

5. Sheryl Leneke Gotts, "Student-Teacher Contracts," in *Personalized Learning and Physical Education*, ed. Don Hellison (Washington, D.C.: AAHPER Publications, 1976), p. 90.

Student-Choice Contract (cont'd)

For a grade of "A":

1. Same as "C" only review *four* tools.
2-7. Same as "B", except all written work to this point may be informal.
8. Clear steps 1-7 with me.
9. Use your system on at least five different teachers, either on tape or in person. Present your analysis of each lesson and draw whatever conclusions or generalizations you feel are appropriate to that aspect of teaching with which you are concerned, i.e., What exists most commonly? What are the options? How can your system help?

Notes:

1. Several examples of descriptive analytical tools are available in my office.
2. You may use any real-life teaching situation for your final analysis, including elementary and/or secondary classes.

Open-Ended Contract. Of the three types of contracts this one gives students the most responsibility. Here the student and teacher come to an agreement regarding the types and numbers of experiences the student should engage in to fulfill the requirements of a specified unit of work. A form of the open-ended contract is presented below.

Contractual Agreement

THIS AGREEMENT, Made on ______________________________, 19_____,
BETWEEN______________________________________as SUPERVISOR
and____as INTERN:
The supervisor agrees to oversee the internship of the above named student from
____________________, 19_____ to ____________________, 19_____.
This internship is granted upon the express condition that if the intern or the supervising agency does not fulfill all conditions of the agreement stated below then a conference will be called between the supervisor, the intern, and the faculty representative with the option to nullify the contract.
THIS AGREEMENT IS MADE UPON THE FOLLOWING CONDITIONS:

1. The intern agrees to prepare at least four news releases and submit them to the appropriate media sources.
2. The intern agrees to prepare a report on the resources which are available from Middlesex County for recreation programming.
3. The intern agrees to prepare a report on the state and federal funds which are available for recreation programming and park development.
4. The intern agrees to spend at least three hours per week working in the recreation office and at least six hours per week working in the field.
5. The intern agrees to plan, implement, supervise, and evaluate one short-term program.

(Contractual Agreement (cont'd)

6. The intern agrees to plan, implement, supervise, and evaluate one long-term program.
7. The supervisor agrees to provide the student with a wide variety of experiences in terms of programming, financing, planning, etc.
8. The supervisor agrees to provide guidance on items 1 through 6.
9. The supervisor agrees to submit to the college a final evaluation of the student's performance for the semester.
10. The intern agrees to submit to the college a copy of all materials submitted to the North Brunswick Recreation Department, a copy of the report on budgeting submitted to the Organization and Administration class, and an evaluation of the total experience.
11. The supervisor agrees to contact the faculty representative immediately upon discovery of a breach of contract by the intern.

THESE CONDITIONS ARE AGREED TO BY: SUPERVISOR:______________________

INTERN: ______________________ FACULTY REP. ______________________

If maximum participation is to be achieved, the teacher must be able to define the specific obstacles to maximum participation and then eliminate them through the creative use of the existing facilities, improvised equipment, and available teaching strategies.

chapter six

Objectively Describing and Analyzing Teaching

Teachers can, as a general rule, easily describe the kind of impact they hope their behavior will have upon their students. They can, and generally do, plan their lessons to include a large number of the particular behaviors which they consider to be most effective in the development of the learning process. Can they, however, say with objective certainty that their actual teaching behavior clearly reflects their pre-class philosophy and planning? In most cases, the answer to this question is clearly and unequivocally no. This ability to clearly understand and describe one's own teaching is critical to the successful planning and implementation of a lesson. It is this clear sense of the manner in which one is perceived by the students and the ability to manipulate it that marks a truly excellent teacher. Therefore, the ability to objectively describe and analyze one's own teaching is critical to teaching excellence.

The type of interaction that occurs in any given classroom is, in most cases, quite different from that which the teacher believes to have occurred. Teachers, like all people, tend to view situations in which they are personally involved in a highly subjective manner. That is, they view situations in the context of their intent and their feelings. There is nothing wrong with subjective analysis, as long as one recognizes the limitations involved and doesn't place too much importance on the conclusions thus derived. In most cases, the teacher sees a class as having occurred one way, each student sees it differently, and each observer sees it in still a different light. The objective truth of the situation probably lies somewhere in the midst of all the subjective opinions.

One means of avoiding the ambiguity inherent in the subjective approach is descriptive analysis. This is an attempt to objectively record and analyze the actual behaviors which occur during the teaching/learning process. Descriptive analytical tools are designed to minimize the possibility of observer bias and to permit a systematic recording of selected teacher and/or pupil behaviors in a manner which facilitates later analysis and study. The knowledge thus derived enables the teacher to take the steps needed to bring actual and desired behaviors into closer alignment. The feedback provided by a descriptive analytical procedure enables the teacher to see where actual behaviors did or did not meet expectations, and once knowing this, the teacher is free to accept or modify the situation accordingly.

The primary concern of virtually all descriptive analytical tools is to collect objective records which accurately describe teaching events, and to organize these records in such a way that they can be analyzed and more readily understood. While a wide variety of recording instruments have been developed within recent years, they all share some common features:

1. All systems avoid qualitative or evaluative judgments. The intent is to present an accurate representation of actual occurrences without bias.
2. Most systems view only a limited portion of the teaching/learning process. The totality of the teacher/pupil interactive process is simply too complex to be efficiently contained within a single recording instrument.
3. Most systems classify behavior into categories. This provides a clear, systematized manner of viewing selected behaviors. It also allows for the development of mutually exclusive, clearly defined areas of interest which tend to increase objectivity.
4. Most systems concentrate on verbal behavior only. Verbal behavior is most easily observed and less easily misinterpreted than nonverbal behavior, and most researchers have assumed that verbal behavior provides an accurate representation of a teacher's total behavior pattern.

A problem which has traditionally been associated with any comparison of teaching methodologies is the lack of distinction among the tested methods. This lack of distinction leads to two problems. First, if the experimenter concludes that differences among the tested methods are significant, he or she is unable to determine whether the differences are due to the style or some other unknown factor. Secondly, an absence of significant experimental findings may have been caused by a high degree of overlap among the methods employed. Descriptive analytical tools help prevent both of these problems by allowing the experimenter to identify, describe, and hold constant experimental teaching procedures in a manner not possible with traditional pre- and post-test type studies.

Tools which provide for the objective description of teaching behavior also greatly facilitate an understanding of the current "state of the art" in teaching. They provide a common language through which actual teaching episodes can be described. These descriptions can be compared with one another to determine similarities, differences, and, if a sufficiently large number of classes are observed, the existence of trends. Further, if one has decided, by whatever means, that certain teachers are better or worse than average, one can now describe their behavior in such a manner that the elusive quality determining their success, or the lack of it, may be defined.

The greatest single value of objective analysis, however, is the impact which it has on teachers and education students. If one is at all concerned with self-improvement, it is virtually impossible to view an objective picture of oneself without also seeking change. Not only can the act of self-analysis lead to change, but training in descriptive analysis tends to make one more aware of teaching behavior as it occurs and thereby better able to teach according to plan and to facilitate change when desired.

THE FLANDERS SYSTEM OF INTERACTION ANALYSIS

Probably the most widely used of the various techniques for analyzing teacher/pupil interaction is the Flanders System of Interaction Analysis. The Flanders system differs from other descriptive analytical tools primarily because it allows one to record not only those verbal events which occur in the class, but also the sequence of their occurrence. This is possible because of the dual interpretation applied to the data recorded by the Flanders system. On the one hand, the actual frequency of each category can be tabulated, thus providing a statistical interpretation of the data observed. Another method of analyzing the data involves tabulating the various behavioral categories into a matrix, thus providing a descriptive analysis of the results based upon the sequential nature of the observations.[1]

Studies based upon questionnaires distributed to colleges and universities throughout the United States[2,3] indicate that the major strengths of the Flanders system are:

1. It provides objective feedback
2. It helps make educational theory operational
3. Users gain insight into teaching behavior
4. It is easy to learn
5. As a measure of classroom climate it has both face and empirical validity.

These same studies listed the major limitations as:

1. The difficulty of training reliable observers, i.e., videotape or audiotape equipment is virtually essential to the training process
2. The nature of the categories in the matrix, i.e., they concentrate on verbal skills only, and they further require that distinctions be made between categories in accordance with fairly rigid guidelines which may not be satisfactory in all situations.
3. The reactions of teachers and students to the system, i.e., they very often fear it as an evaluative tool or become very defensive upon discovering that their actual classroom behavior belies their espoused philosophy.

The Flanders System of Interaction Analysis, as modified for physical education classes, consists of eleven categories which are classified as either direct or indirect according to the amount of freedom of response that they permit students. Direct teacher statements are of the type that tends to restrict the freedom of the student to respond, while indirect statements tend to maximize the freedom of student response. The eleven interaction categories can be divided into three major areas: (1) teacher talk, (2) student talk, and (3) nonverbal activity.

Teacher talk includes seven behavioral categories, which are grouped according to whether they are direct or indirect:

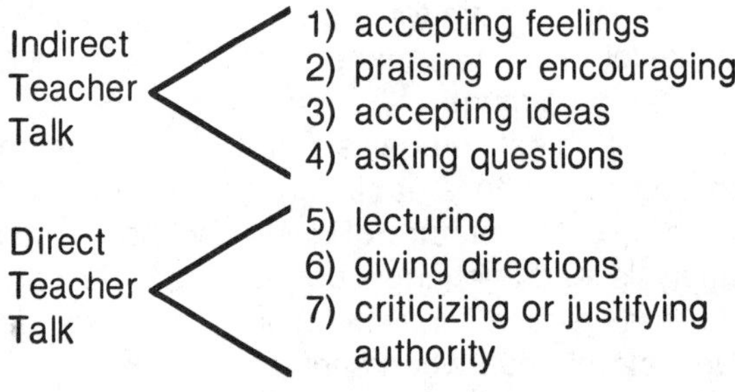

1. Philip Lambert, William L. Goodwin, and Richard Roberts, "A Note on the Use of Flanders' Interaction Analysis," *Journal of Education Research* 1008 (January 1965): pp. 222-24.

2. Edmund J. Amidon and Anita Simon, "Implications for Teaching Education of Interaction Analysis Research in Student Teaching" (Paper presented to the American Educational Research Association, Chicago, February 1965), ERIC #ED. 012 695.

3. Anita Simon, "The Effects of Training in Interaction Analysis on the Teaching Patterns of Student Teachers in Favored and Non-Favored Classes," Ph.D. diss., Temple University, 1970.

Student talk is divided into the following two observational categories: responding to the teacher (8), and student-initiated talk (9). Periods of nonverbal activity are classified in the final two categories: silence or confusion (10), and meaningful nonverbal behavior (11).

The observational technique employed in interaction analysis is basically quite simple. Every three seconds the observer records the category number of the interaction just observed. These numbers are sequentially recorded at the rate of one notation every three seconds unless more than one type of interaction occurs within the three-second interval, in which case all types of interaction noted are recorded. Observations can be done in person during the lesson or after the fact by reviewing video or audio tapes. After the observation period, usually one complete lesson, the codings are placed in an eleven-row by eleven-column table called a matrix for interpretation (see Figure 6.1).

	1	2	3	4	5	6	7_b	7_p	8	9	10	11	T	%
1														
2														
3														
4														
5														
6														
7_b														
7_p														
8														
9														
10														
11														
T														
%														

FIGURE 6.1. Matrix for Interpretation.

When completed, the matrix allows a multitude of analyses and descriptive observations to be made. The simplest of these is an examination of the percentage of tallies in each category. Other areas of examination provide a wealth of objective information concerning the amount, type, and sequence of teacher/pupil interactive events in the classroom.

Learning to Use the Flanders System in Physical Education Classes

The first and most important step in learning to use the Flanders system is to commit the categories to memory and to learn, at least in general terms, the types of behaviors which are included in each category. A list of the categories and their behavioral components is found in Table 6.1.

Table 6.1. Categories for Interaction Analysis.

Teacher Talk	Indirect	1. *Accepts Feeling*: Accepts and clarifies the feeling tone of the students in a nonthreatening manner. Feelings may be positive or negative. Predicting or recording failings included.
		2. *Praises or Encourages*: Praises or encourages student action or behavior, jokes that release tension, but not at the expense of another individual; nodding head or saying "um hum?" or "go on" are included.
		3. *Accepts or Uses Ideas of Students*: Clarifying, building, or developing ideas suggested by a student; as teacher brings more of his own ideas into play, shift to category 5.
		4. *Asks Questions*: Asking a question about content or procedure with the intent that the student answer.
	Direct	5. *Lecturing*: Giving facts or opinions about content or procedures; expressing his or her own ideas, asking rhetorical questions.
		6. *Giving Directions*: Directions, commands, or orders with which a student is expected to comply.
		7. *Criticizing or Justifying Authority*: Statements intended to change student behavior from nonacceptable to acceptable pattern; bawling someone out; stating why the teacher is doing what he or she is doing; extreme self-reference.
		* The subscript "p" is used for criticizing behavior which refers specifically to performance or attempts at physical performance.
		* The subscript "b" is used for criticizing behavior which refers specifically to student behavior or deportment.

Table 6.1 (cont'd).

Student Talk	8. *Student Talk—Response*: Talk by students in response to teacher. Teacher initiates contact or solicits student's statement. 9. *Student Talk—Initiation*: Talk by students which they initiate. If "calling on" student is only to indicate who may talk next, observer must decide whether student wanted to talk. If he or she did, use this category.
Silence	10. *Silence or Confusion*: Pauses, short periods of silence, and periods of confusion in which communication cannot be understood by the observer. *11. *Meaningful Nonverbal Activity*: Periods of silence in which the student is engaged in meaningful productive activity.
	*i. Place an *i* behind any of the teacher-talk category numbers when the teacher is addressing statements to an individual rather than to the entire group.

SOURCE: Edmund J. Amidon and Ned A. Flanders, *The Role of the Teacher in the Classroom* (Minneapolis: Association for Productive Teaching, Inc., 1967), p. 14.

*These items were added by the author and are not included in the original reference.

Having memorized the behavioral categories, one may then proceed to develop one's coding skills. This is best accomplished with the aid of videotapes or audiotapes of actual teaching situations. Select a tape or a series of tapes with good audio clarity and a fairly broad representation of interactive behaviors. Having chosen a tape for practice, work on only a few selected behaviors at a time. Let the matter of applying the entire system remain until after the individual categories have been mastered. While there is no set order in which the categories must be practiced, the following format has proven effective:

1. *General Coding Guidelines*
   a. A coding should be made every three seconds unless the behavior changes more rapidly. If, therefore, a teacher lectures for one minute, twenty category 5 codes would be entered. If, on the other hand, the following interchange took place:

      Teacher: "How many points are needed to win a volleyball game?"
      Student: "Five."
      Teacher: "Now Jimmy, you know that can't be right."

      the codings would be 4—8—7, regardless of the fact that the entire episode probably took place in little more than three seconds. In the latter case, the behavior changed, and, therefore, so did the coding.
   b. All codings should be made on the basis of what the behavior meant to the pupils. The really important question is not how the coder felt about a behavior, or how the teacher intended it, but how the student perceived it.

c. In each of the practice situations outlined, the coder should listen to the practice tape or tapes and encode only those specific categories of behavior called for in the exercise.

2. *The Use of Category 5 (Lecture) and Category 6 (Directions)*

Since, in most physical education classes, these two categories represent the predominant forms of teacher behavior, they provide an excellent starting point for the development of coding skills. The most frequently used of all the categories is category 5 (lecture). It is used whenever the teacher is attempting to communicate personal ideas or opinions. Category 6, on the other hand, is used when the teacher is giving directions which can be expected to result in an observable behavioral response on the part of the student.

All incidences of the occurrence of categories 5 and 6 in the practice tapes should be coded. Particular attention should be paid to the timing of those behavioral intervals which last longer than three seconds. Code the same tape several times and compare results, looking particularly for consistency of number choice and timing. Follow the same general procedure until all the categories have been learned.

3. *The Use of Category 4 (Asks Questions) Category 8 (Student-Talk Response) and Category 9 (Student-Talk Initiation)*

Any time the teacher asks a question about lesson content or procedure, the observer should use the category 4. Talk by students in response to teacher initiation or solicitation should be coded as number 8. The number 9 is used to identify talk by students which they themselves have initiated.

In general, the student's reply to code number 4 will always be categorized as an 8 (student response). If, on the other hand, a second student adds his or her own ideas to the ideas of the first student, the second student's statement would be coded as a 9 (student-talk initiation). Unsolicited student comments are almost always coded as a 9.

4. *The Use of Category 2 (Praise) and Category 7 (Criticism)*

Category 2 is used to code those teacher comments which serve to praise or encourage student behaviors. A comment that encourages a student to continue with an answer, such as "Please continue," tends to reinforce the student behavior and is, therefore, coded as a 2. Jokes and other forms of tension release are coded with a 2 as long as they do not come about at the expense of a student.

Category 7 is used for all statements which are designed to correct or modify student behavior from nonacceptable to acceptable standards. This category is also used to code statements designed to justify the teacher's authority or explain the reasons for his or her actions. Comments such as "You'll do it because I said so" or "I know what is best, after all, I've been through all this before" would both be coded as a 7 because of extreme self-reference and authority justification.

In physical education classes, category 7 should be subdivided into two different types of criticism: The code 7b should be used whenever the teacher is criticizing student behaviors. These critical comments would be directed primarily at discipline and control problems. The code 7p should be used when the teacher is criticizing student performance. These comments would be aimed at correcting the performance of some motor skill. When used, these subcodes may be entered in the matrix as two distinct categories.

5. *The Use of Category 1 (Accepts Student Feelings) and Category 3 (Accepts Student Ideas)*

   Category 1 is used to classify those teacher comments which accept or amplify the feelings of the student in a nonthreatening manner. Teacher comments which anticipate or restate student feelings are also categorized as 1.

   All statements which amplify or develop ideas initiated by a student are categorized as a 3. A restatement or rewording of the student's ideas would be included in this category, as would questions designed to further develop a student's idea. If, however, the teacher begins to include his own ideas in the comments, then code number 5 should be used.

6. *The Use of Category 10 (Silence or Confusion) and Category 11 (Meaningful Nonverbal Behavior)*

   All periods of silence in which no productive behavior occurs and all periods of confusion during which the verbal comments cannot be understood by the observer are coded with a 10.

   Category 11 is used to code those periods of silence during which the student is engaged in meaningful, productive activity. Periods of time during which the student is engaged in the practice of motor skills or other meaningful activity without verbal interaction are also coded in this category.

7. *The Use of the Subscript i*

   The teacher-talk categories (1-7) should be subdivided whenever the teacher is speaking to an individual rather than to the entire group by placing an *i* behind the number of the category observed when it is recorded on the observation sheet. This subdivision, while not entered in the matrix, does, through the simple quantification of the amount of individual attention given to students, provide a wealth of valuable information.

The coding of teaching behavior which is directed at individuals can only be practiced either by using videotape or by coding the actual lesson as it occurs, and it should be used in conjunction with the practice of the entire category system. In practicing the complete category system, there are a number of established ground rules which will prove particularly useful in differentiating among certain categories and which will help prevent many needless errors.[4]

Ground Rules

1. When not certain in which of two or more categories a statement belongs, choose the category that is numerically farthest from category 5.
2. If the primary tone of the teacher's behavior has been consistently indirect, do not shift into the opposite classification unless a clear indication of shift is given by the teacher.
3. As an observer do not be overly concerned with your own biases or with the teacher's intent. Rather, you must ask yourself the question, What does this behavior mean to the pupils as far as restriction or expansion of their freedom is concerned?

4. Ground rules 1-15 are taken directly from Edmund J. Amidon and Ned A. Flanders, *The Role of the Teacher in the Classroom* (Minneapolis: Association for Productive Teaching, Inc., 1967), pp. 24-29. Ground rules 16 and 17 were added by the author and do not appear in the original reference.

4. If more than one category occurs during the three-second interval, then all categories used in that interval are recorded; therefore, record each change in category. If no change occurs within three seconds, repeat the category number.
5. Directions are statements that result (or are expected to result) in observable behavior on the part of children.
6. When the teacher calls on a child by name, the observer ordinarily records a 4.
7. If there is a discernible period of silence (at least three seconds), record one 10 for every three seconds of silence, laughter, etc.
8. When the teacher repeats a student answer, and the answer is a correct answer, this is recorded as a 2.
9. When the teacher repeats a student idea and communicates only that the idea will be considered or accepted as something to be discussed, a 3 is used.
10. If a student begins talking after another student (without the teacher's talking), a 10 is inserted between the 9's or 8's to indicate the change of student.
11. Statements such as "uh-huh," "yes," "yeah," "all right," "okay," which occur between two 9's are recorded as 2 (encouragement).
12. A teacher joke which is not made at the expense of the children is a 2.
13. Rhetorical questions are not really questions; they are merely part of lecturing techniques and should be characterized as 5's.
14. A narrow question is a signal to expect an 8.
15. An 8 is recorded when several students respond in unison to a narrow question.

*16. Code an *i* behind the appropriate teacher-talk category only if the teacher's statement was directed to a single student and unheard by the majority of the class.

*17. Productive physical activity performed at the direction of the teacher is always coded as an 11. If the students are involved in physical activities which were not initiated by the teacher, code a 10. This is true even if the activity itself is productive in nature, i.e., pre-class basketball shooting or forward rolls practiced by an individual after the teacher has called for everyone's attention.

Developing the Matrix

Once a lesson has been coded, the observer is ready to record the tallies in the eleven-row by eleven-column form for interpretation, which is called a matrix. Before making any entries in the matrix, the observer must place a 10 before the first tally and after the last. The numbers are then entered into the matrix in pairs so that each number (with the exception of the first and last 10) is used twice. If the extra 10's were not added, two tallies would be lost. An example of the coding procedure follows:

Suppose an observer had just recorded the following series of tallies:

8 4 8 2 5 5 4 8 2

Place a 10 before and after the group of numbers.

Now enter the numbers in the matrix in pairs (the second example has brackets to denote the pairs). The first pair (10-8) would be entered in row 10 column 8, the second pair (8-4) in row 8 column 4, and so on until each number, with the exception of the first and the last 10, has been used twice. The completed matrix for the above figures is shown in Figure 6.2.

	1	2	3	4	5	6	7_b	7_p	8	9	10	11	T	%
1													0	
2					/						/		2	
3													0	
4									//				2	
5				/	/								2	
6													0	
7_b													0	
7_p													0	
8		//		/									3	
9													0	
10									/				1	
11													0	
T	0	2	0	2	2	0	0	0	3	0	1	0	10	
%	0	20	0	20	20	0	0	0	30	0	10	0		

FIGURE 6.2. Completed Matrix.

To check the tabulations for accuracy, add up the numbers in each row and each column. The total of row 1 should equal the total of column 1, the total of row 2 should equal that of column 2, and so on. Further, the total number of tallies in the matrix should be one less than the total amount of observation numbers on the original record. Ordinarily, a separate matrix is made for each separate lesson or classroom activity.

As mentioned previously, the completed matrix permits a multitude of analyses and descriptive observations to be made, the simplest of which is an examination of the percentage of tallies in each category. For example, in the earlier illustration there were ten tallies, and three of them were in row 8. Dividing the number of tallies in row 8 (three) by the total number of tallies (ten), we find that 30 percent of the classroom interaction took the form of student-talk response.

Another simple analysis can be made by totalling the number of *i*'s recorded and then dividing that number by the total number of tallies in categories 1-7. This will provide an accurate account of the percentage of teacher talk that was directed at individuals. The percentage of silence that took the form of meaningful nonverbal behavior can be found by dividing the number of tallies in category 11 by the total number of tallies in categories 10 and 11.

There are many other areas of the matrix which can be examined to provide a wealth of objective information concerning the teacher/student interaction in the classroom. The following descriptions cover seven areas of major concern in physical education. The definitions given here are taken directly from *Teacher Influence, Pupil Attitudes, and Achievement*, by Ned A. Flanders,[5] and our due indebtedness to the author is hereby acknowledged.

Extended indirect influence. This area of the matrix, located in the area of intersection of columns 1-3 and rows 1-3, represents the emphasis that the teacher gives to using student ideas, extending and amplifying student statements, and accepting and enlarging upon student feelings.

Extended direct influence. The area of extended direct influence is located at the intersection of columns 6 and 7 and rows 6 and 7. It indicates the teacher's emphasis on criticism and giving lengthy directions. Tabulations in this area suggest heavy focus on the teacher's use of authority.

Sustained student talk. Sustained student talk would be indicated by a build-up in the matrix cell located at the intersection of row 9 and column 9. This would indicate student-to-student communication.

I/D ratio. The I/D ratio provides an indication of the relative number of indirect and direct teacher statements recorded. It is found by dividing the total number of tallies in columns 1, 2, 3, and 4 by the total number of tallies in columns 5, 6, and 7 plus the total of columns 1, 2, 3, and 4.

Revised I/D ratio. A revised I/D ratio is used in order to find out the kind of emphasis given to motivation and control in the classroom. The number of tallies in columns 1, 2, and 3 is divided by the number of tallies in columns 1, 2, 3, 6, and 7 to find this revised ratio. This provides information about whether the teacher is direct or indirect in his or her approach to motivation and control.

Percentage of teacher talk. The percentage of teacher talk represents the amount of the total class time during which the teacher is speaking. To find the percentage of teacher talk, the total number of tallies in columns 1 through 7 is divided by the total number of tallies in the matrix.

Percentage of student talk. The percentage of student talk represents the amount of total class time during which a student is speaking. The percentage of student talk is found by dividing the total number of tallies in columns 8 and 9 by the total number of tallies in the matrix.

Once the categories have been learned, the Flanders system can be used for observational purposes. As long as the information obtained is compared only with one's own observations made on other occasions, minor differences in rate or accuracy of coding will be of little consequence, therefore, one need not be an expert in order to use the Flanders system productively. It has been found that with a moderate amount of practice, differentiating among behaviors becomes much easier and timing becomes far more consistent.

5. Ned A. Flanders, *Teacher Influence, Pupil Attitudes, and Achievement*, U.S. Department of Health, Education, and Welfare, Cooperative Research Monograph No. 12 (Washington, D.C.: Government Printing Office, 1965).

A further application of the Flanders system, which is of particular value to beginning teachers and those who wish to spot-check their performance, is the use of selected categories only. If, for instance, one wishes to observe the relative quantities of praise and criticism which were provided to one's students, it would be necessary only to record each separate occurrence of a 2 or a 7. Subsequent quantification would give an indication of the information desired and, more importantly, would heighten the teacher's awareness of these factors as they occur.

Although most analytical systems, due to their reliance on verbal behavior, are restrictive in their application to physical education and athletics, in recent years several tools have been designed specifically for the purpose of describing and analyzing selected aspects of physical education classes. While there is a great variety among the various tools in both the breadth and the depth of the analysis possible, each provides objective, reliable data concerning the actual teaching/learning process. The following summary descriptions cover a few of the new and interesting tools for descriptive analysis.

CAFIAS

The Cheffers Adaptation of the Flanders Interaction Analysis System, CAFIAS, differs from its predecessor primarily in that it recognizes the impact of factors other than the teacher on the learning process.[6] If a student learns, then teaching must be taking place. The source of that teaching, according to Cheffers, can be either the traditional class teacher, the environment, or other students. The CAFIAS system, therefore, uses a subscript *s* or *e* to indicate those instances when the teaching agency is either another student or some environmental factor. CAFIAS further expands the Flanders system by adding the dimension of nonverbal activity. All nonverbal categories are simply coded as the "ten" equivalent of their verbal categories. For example, a 2 (praise or encouragement), when presented nonverbally, becomes a 12 (nonverbal praise or encouragement).

CAFIAS also records the amount of time which a class spends working as a group (*W*) or in more individualized situations (*P*), so that a temporal analysis of class structure is possible in addition to the usual variety of analyses possible through a matrix presentation.

This system, while more cumbersome than Flanders', does offer a great deal more data and insight into the teaching/learning process as broadly defined. A summary of the categories in CAFIAS is found in appendix 1, on pp. 207-210.

THE FISHMAN SYSTEM

The Fishman system is designed specifically to analyze the type and amount of feedback which a teacher provides the students in a physical education class.[7] A checklist format is used to encode only those instances in which feedback is being provided to the student. Each instance of feedback can be classified according to its form, direction, time, intent, general referent, and specific referent. The operational definitions of the various subcategories are shown in appendix 2, on p. 211.

6. John T. Cheffers, Edmund J. Amidon, and Ken D. Rodgers, *Interaction Analysis: An Application to Nonverbal Activity* (Minneapolis: Association for Productive Teaching, Inc., 1974).

7. Sylvia Ellen Fishman, "A Procedure for Recording Augmented Feedback in Physical Education Classes," Ph.D. diss. (microfilm), Columbia University, 1974.

While this system, by its very design, looks at only a limited portion of the teaching act, it provides a wealth of information about specific events involving feedback. Furthermore, the system is simple enough that it can be effectively employed with minimal training. Given the substantial body of research supporting the importance of feedback in motor-skill acquisition and the ease with which the Fishman system can be employed, there appears to be a great deal of value to be gained by analyzing the feedback which we provide in our teaching.

A SYSTEM FOR ANALYZING SUPERVISOR/STUDENT-TEACHER INTERACTION

This system, designed by Blumberg and reported by Kraft, is included in this section because it clearly demonstrates the manner in which minor modifications can produce a major shift in the focus of an existing system.[8]

By making slight modifications in the existing category system and by adding five new categories, Blumberg has developed a tool for analyzing the interaction between a supervising teacher and a student teacher during a supervisory conference. The coding and matrix-development processes are essentially identical to the Flanders system; the data derived, however, is directly reflective of the type of interaction between the student teacher and the supervisor. The matrix analysis is aimed at demonstrating such factors as the degree to which interpersonal relationships are built and maintained, the degree to which the student teacher's ideas are used, and the amount of control which the supervising teacher exerts over the behavior of the student teacher.

The categories used in this system are:

Supervisor Behavior

1. Support-Inducing Communications Behavior
2. Praise
3. Accepts or Uses Teacher's Ideas
4. Asks for Information
5. Gives Information
6. Asks for Opinions
7. Asks for Suggestions
8. Gives Opinions
9. Gives Suggestions
10. Criticism

Teacher Behavior

11. Asks for Information, Opinions, or Suggestions
12. Gives Information, Opinions, or Suggestions
13. Positive Social Emotional Behavior
14. Negative Social Emotional Behavior
15. Silence or Confusion

DESIGNING YOUR OWN DESCRIPTIVE SYSTEM

As was previously mentioned, there is, at present, no simple descriptive tool for analyzing the total teaching/learning process in physical education. Furthermore, while there are several tools for viewing certain specific types of behavior, each teacher will, at some time,

8. Robert E. Kraft, "An Analysis of Supervisor/Student-Teacher Interaction," *JOHPER* 45, No. 3 (March 1974): pp. 37-38.

probably think of several facets of the teaching process that are of greater immediate concern. Fortunately, by following a few simple guidelines, teachers can design a descriptive tool for analyzing selected components of their behavior which will have face validity and a sufficiently high degree of objectivity to make it a very useful tool for self-analysis.

Before starting, one must remember the purpose of a descriptive system and the criteria by which it is identified. The primary reason for using any descriptive tool is to gather objective information about actual instructional occurrences. In so doing, it is usually necessary to 1) avoid qualitative or evaluative judgments, 2) select only a limited portion of the teaching/learning process for observation, and 3) classify behaviors into mutually exclusive categories. The following steps provide a framework for logically developing an individualized tool for the description of teaching behavior:

1. *Select and Specify the Conceptual Framework*

   Since the entire teaching/learning process is too broad to deal with efficiently, one must select the portion or portions of it which one considers of primary interest. Try to select an area which can be clearly defined and segmented into component parts. The area of discipline, for example, can be broken down into a variety of subcategories and thus offers a variety of observable factors. The time spent lining up, on the other hand, is essentially a single item. It may be a component of a larger area which would encompass all organizational factors, but as a primary focus for analysis it is rather limited.

2. *Define a Set of Categories Based on the Conceptual Framework*

   The set of categories designed should consist of all behaviors or events which comprise the area of study. The categories must be mutually exclusive, that is, each behavior or event observed must be assignable to one, and only one, category. The categories must also be broad enough to encompass every observable behavior within the conceptual framework.

   Carefully define each category and the set of observable behaviors or events which comprise it. Each category should be listed along with its definitions, the examples of the behaviors which comprise it, and any behavioral cues which would help an observer determine whether a particular action was ascribable to that category. Given the previously mentioned area of discipline, one might develop categories such as: 1) teacher comments aimed at criticizing inappropriate behavior, 2) teacher comments which prescribe more appropriate behaviors, and 3) teacher ignores inappropriate behavior.

3. *Design a Set of Guidelines by Which the Categories Can Be Recorded as They Are Observed*

   Determine the coding system used to identify the various categories which have been defined. Determine whether coding can be done during the class or whether videotaping or audiotaping procedures will be necessary. If a checklist is to be used, rather than a running tally system, the checklist should be designed so that the observer can, without any difficulty, make the desired notations on the appropriate section of the list. To code for discipline, one can simply make a notation denoting the type of unacceptable behavior, record the teacher-response category, and the time lag between teacher response and compliance.

4. *Develop a Systematic Method for Summarizing the Coded Data*

   In practically all cases, the data coded for an entire lesson will be cumbersome in length and excessive in detail. Some procedures for summarizing and analyzing the coded data must be developed. Minimally, one should be able to quantitatively analyze the codes in each category and make comparisons among them. Techniques for cross-referencing and comparing specific aspects of the coded material are also helpful in understanding the lesson. Finally, some means of providing a quick visual analysis of the coded material is immensely helpful, not just for self-analysis but especially for explaining the data to others. Various types of graphs, charts, and summary sheets have been proven successful, and any which suit the data and the purpose of the system should prove satisfactory.

The data on discipline might be summarized in the following ways: 1) total number of disciplinary actions; 2) percentage of successful teacher actions; 3) percentage of times each separate category of teacher behavior was successful; and 4) average time lag between teacher response and compliance, total and by separate categories.

5. *Field Test the System and Make Modifications*

No matter how carefully one designs a descriptive system, there are always behaviors which have been overlooked, categories which overlap, or coding circumstances which have not been planned for. A field test will permit one to systematically modify coding procedures where necessary, to develop additional ground rules, and, in some cases, to add or delete categories and thereby provide a better description of the desired behaviors.

By carefully following the systems outlined in this chapter, the interested teacher or student can develop a tool which will allow the analysis of selected aspects of the teaching/learning process in an objective, systematic manner. The analytical process, however, does not stop here. The really important question is how does one apply the data thus developed. If the main goal of behavior analysis is to provide data that will dazzle administrators, cooperating teachers, or research-oriented college professors, then the process will be a tedious, time-consuming chore that is better left unattempted. If, on the other hand, one harbors a sincere interest in developing the ability to teach in a manner that is consonant with one's personal philosophy, and if one is sincere in the desire to become the best possible teacher, then behavioral analysis is an opportunity which should not be missed. It is a technique which is well within the capabilities of any interested professional.

Remember, the system designed need not be a large-scale research tool. In fact, for actual self-analysis it is better that the categories and coding techniques be kept rather simple. The really important question is the degree of objectivity with which the desired data can be gathered and the personal interest which one has in the data thus derived. Appendices 3 and 4 contain two descriptive systems developed by undergraduate students. While not as sophisticated as the research tools previously summarized, they, nevertheless, have proven valuable in viewing selected aspects of the teaching/learning process.

REFERENCES

Cheffers, John T. F., Edmund J. Amidon, and Ken D. Rodgers, *Interaction Analysis: An Application to Nonverbal Activity* (Minneapolis: Association for Productive Teaching, 1974). Describes the use of CAFIAS. Particularly noteworthy is the provision of a computer program for matrix development and analysis.

Flanders, Ned A., *Teaching Influence, Pupil Attitudes, and Achievement*, U.S. Department of Health, Education, and Welfare, Office of Education, Cooperative Research Monograph No. 12 (Washington, D.C.: Government Printing Office, 1965). Provides an in-depth look at the Flanders System, its background, development, and some of the research which has developed from it.

Kryspin, William J., and John F. Feldhusen, *Analyzing Verbal Classroom Interaction* (Minneapolis: Burgess Publishing Co., 1974). An excellent, simple, how-to text for use of the Flanders System of Interaction Analysis.

Siedentop, Daryl, *Developing Teaching Skills in Physical Education* (Boston: Houghton Mifflin Co., 1976). Includes several interesting tools for analyzing classroom management, interpersonal relations, and other forms of teaching skills.

Simon, Anita, and E. Gill Boyer, eds., *Mirrors for Behavior I & II,* Classroom Interaction Newsletter (Philadelphia: Research for Better Schools, Inc., 1970). This is a two-volume anthology of instruments for the observation and analysis of the teaching/learning process. In all, seventy-nine systems are described.

chapter seven

Planning for Teaching

One of the most important factors in successful teaching is good planning. Good planning should be a deliberate attempt to insure that the instructional activities and the stated objectives of the program are well suited to the course being taught and are presented in an educationally efficient manner. Good planning constitutes the primary distinction between physical education and recess.

There are three basic levels of planning; curriculum planning, unit planning, and lesson planning. Overriding all three phases, however, is the need to develop clear objectives at all instructional levels.

DEVELOPING OBJECTIVES

An objective, according to *Webster's New Collegiate Dictionary*, is defined as "something toward which effort is directed: an aim or end of action." Objectives are necessary at all levels of the educational experience because they provide a clear description of the goals to be achieved. As one progresses from curriculum planning through unit planning to the development of lesson plans, one's objectives must, of necessity, become increasingly more specific in nature as the subject matter becomes more specific. The relationship of one set of objectives to another at each level can best be summarized in the following manner:

the sum of all lesson objectives = unit objectives
the sum of all unit objectives = curricular objectives
the sum of all curricular objectives = total school objectives
the sum of all school objectives = school board objectives

One can see, therefore, that objectives are necessary and interdependent at all levels, and that they must become more general as the level gets higher or the list would simply become insurmountable. A single lesson objective, for instance, might involve a forward roll, while the curricular objective might include all rotary movements, and the school board policy might simply call for the development of motor skills. In each case, however, it is necessary that instructional planning and program development be based upon a clearly defined set of objectives which leaves no doubt concerning the end result that is sought.

INSTRUCTIONAL DOMAINS

When writing objectives, one must be concerned with the total development of the student. Because instruction can have an impact on the attitudes and interests of students, as well as on their physical and intellectual development, it is important that objectives used in the planning of educational programs be reflective of these areas.

Although several investigators have attempted to classify objectives in various ways, the most widely accepted and frequently used technique is the taxonomic system developed by Bloom, Krathwohl, and their associates. They recognize three separate divisions or domains into which all objectives may be classified. The *cognitive domain* deals exclusively with the development of intellectual skills and abilities.[1] Factors associated with the development and display of knowledge, such as recall, recognition, and synthesis, form the basis of the cognitive domain. The *affective domain* is the most difficult of all to objectively measure in that it is comprised of interests, attitudes, and values.[2] The *psychomotor domain* was the last to be classified and the least commonly used of all the domains, despite its paramount importance in fields such as physical education.[3] Objectives in the psychomotor domain are concerned with the development of motor or manipulative skills.

INSTRUCTIONAL VERSUS BEHAVIORAL OBJECTIVES

It is important at this point to distinguish between two classes of objectives: Instructional (or process) objectives and behavioral (or product) objectives. Instructional objectives are those which describe the *process* which the teacher will follow in developing a given lesson or unit. Such objectives as those shown below are all instructional or process objectives:

The teacher will demonstrate the backward roll.
The fast-break offense will be diagrammed on the blackboard.
The steps of the Virginia reel will be described using verbal cues without music.

They tell what the teacher or coach will do during the lesson, and in some cases how it will be done. They do not, however, tell what the student will learn or how he or she will be required to demonstrate this knowledge. Process objectives could, in fact, be accomplished without students. The teacher could demonstrate, diagram, and describe them in an empty gymnasium.

Product objectives on the other hand, or behavioral objectives as they are commonly called, tell what the student is expected to do or *produce* as a result of the instruction provided. Product objectives stated in behavioral terms would include:

The student will diagram three separate defenses for the fast-break offense.
The student will successfully complete a layup from the right, left, and center of the key.
The student will run 1.5 miles in 12 minutes or less.

In each of these cases, the teacher and the student are both well aware of the requirements

1. Benjamin S. Bloom, ed., *Taxonomy of Educational Objectives, Handbook I: Cognitive Domain* (New York: David McKay Co., Inc., 1956).

2. David R. Krathwohl, Benjamin S. Bloom, and Bertram B. Masia, *Taxonomy of Educational Objectives, Handbook II: Affective Domain* (New York: David McKay Co., Inc., 1964).

3. Anita J. Harrow, *A Taxonomy of the Psychomotor Domain* (New York: David McKay Co., Inc., 1972).

for satisfactory achievement of the objectives, because the outcomes of the instruction have been specified.

Both instructional and behavioral objectives are valuable parts of the planning process. Behavioral objectives tell what the student is expected to do or accomplish, and the instructional objectives tell how the teacher will guide the students to the accomplishment of the behavioral objectives. With good behavioral objectives to describe the product which is sought, the selection of teaching styles, instructional aids, and testing procedures is greatly simplified. One does not select a ball without knowing the type of game for which it is to be used, or a tool without knowing the type of work to be done. How, then, can one hope to effectively select teaching styles, instructional aids, testing procedures, etc., without knowing the specific outcomes which they are to help achieve or evaluate? Obviously, one cannot. In fact, as a general rule, the more explicitly stated the objective is, the more easily the teacher can plan for its achievement and, therefore, the higher the probability that students will attain it.

Objectives, either process or product, must be specific if they are to be of value. This is particularly true in the field of physical education, where we have traditionally attempted to justify our programs by producing objectives which promise such things as an appreciation for physical fitness or a belief in the value of fair play, and any number of other nebulous concepts that cannot even be uniformly defined, let alone systematically developed and evaluated. Since finances are always an important consideration in education, the public demands that teachers produce evidence to verify the achievement of their stated objectives and to justify the continuation of their programs. If such evidence is to be forthcoming, it is essential that objectives be stated in such a manner that their intent is clear and that their achievement can be observed and evaluated. If the objectives of a program can be agreed upon, and their achievement can be verified, then accountability, far from being a threat, becomes an effective tool for program development.

PROCESS OR INSTRUCTIONAL OBJECTIVES

As previously stated, instructional objectives define the process which the teacher will follow in the development of a lesson or unit. Curriculum guides, unit plans, and lesson plans in all fields are replete with examples of instructional objectives such as these:

The proper putting stance will be demonstrated.

The impact of industrialization on the small truck farmer will be explained.

The teacher will summarize the events leading to the Louisiana Purchase.

These are useful and productive items because they allow teachers to see at a glance what type of behavior is expected of them. Lessons, therefore, can be planned to guarantee that the necessary topics are demonstrated, discussed, or explained. Furthermore, the teacher can, without too much imagination, surmise some kind of terminal behavior which the student should show and some means of testing for it. As long as the instructional objectives have been specifically stated and leave no doubt regarding the type of behavior expected, they present no major problem. Most teachers would find them equally easy to implement.

Problems arise, however, when one attempts to develop a reasonable means of evaluating students entirely on the basis of instructional objectives. In terms of the earlier examples, just what type of terminal behavior should a student show after the proper putting stance has been demonstrated? How will the teacher know what has been learned? Some of the possible alternative student behaviors which could be applied to the previously stated objectives are given in the following examples:

Objective: The proper putting stance will be demonstrated.
Possible Terminal Behaviors:
Demonstrate the proper putting stance.
Describe the proper putting stance.
Using the correct putting stance, sink 5 of 8 putts.

Objective: The impact of industrialization on the small truck farmer will be explained.
Possible Terminal Behaviors:
List 5 effects of industrialization on small truck farmers.
Write an essay on the effects of industrialization on small truck farmers.
Develop a model plan for the future of truck farms reflective of new industrial trends.

Objective: The teacher will summarize the events leading to the Louisiana Purchase.
Possible Terminal Behaviors:
Describe the events leading to the Louisiana Purchase.
List those individuals most involved in the Louisiana Purchase and describe their roles.
List the major reasons for and against the Louisiana Purchase.

Clearly one can see that a wide variety of terminal behaviors can be developed for any given instructional objective. While this range of choice may, in some ways, be construed as a valuable preservation of the freedom of academic choice which is afforded the teacher, this may not, in fact, be the case.

There is no way of predicting, based upon the instructional objective, exactly what the student should learn or how he or she should display this knowledge. The student, therefore, is unable to prepare or plan for a test until it is announced and explained. Even more important, however, is the fact that if three teachers are following the same instructional objectives in the same or different schools, they could all choose different behaviors for their tests. Any comparison among classes or groups would be impossible. The associated inability to compare and contrast the outcomes of the instructional objectives makes it virtually impossible to determine whether or not they are, in fact, having the desired impact upon student development. The only thing which can be uniformly controlled is the instructional behavior, and that behavior is, therefore, no longer readily adaptable to individual student needs and abilities.

PRODUCT OR BEHAVIORAL OBJECTIVES

A solution to the ambiguity encountered in the development of terminal behaviors which correspond to stated instructional objectives is found in the use of behavioral objectives. Behavioral objectives specify what the student should be expected to do or produce as a result of the instruction provided. The question of how a lesson will be taught is not specified, merely the expected outcome. The process is, therefore, essentially the reverse of that used in instructional objectives. Given an expected outcome, the teacher must select an appropriate instructional format. As an example, consider the following objective:

Students will attain an average score of at least 6.5 on four side-horse vaults of their choice.

There is little question regarding the terminal behavior which is expected of the student, but the teacher has a great deal of latitude in the planning and development of teaching and practice sessions. Virtually any instructional format which resulted in the specified terminal behavior would be regarded as acceptable.

One can readily see that, with behavioral objectives, the teacher and the student can each have a clear idea of the goals to be accomplished from the very outset of instruction. Furthermore, test results can easily be compared across groups if desired because all groups are working toward the same narrowly defined ends. Finally, behavioral objectives, while standardizing the educational outcomes, do not restrict the freedom of the teacher to choose the instructional format which is best suited to each individual class, group, or student.

Developing Behavioral Objectives

Most authorities agree that there are three major steps in the process of writing behavioral objectives:

1. Identification of the terminal behavior or the product that is expected
2. Description of the conditions under which the terminal behavior is to be demonstrated
3. Specification of the level of performance that must be attained

Some authors[4,5,6] also identify an additional step which precedes these; the identification of the group for whom the objectives are intended. This step is necessary, however, only when the students may vary. If, for instance, a set of objectives is intended for a very diverse group of people, it may be wise to specify the specific portion of the group for which each objective is intended. For example, a gymnastics class composed of boys and girls ranging in age from 7 to 15 years might need such objectives as:

The 10-year-old girls will perform three mounts of their choice on the balance beam with an average score of 5.

All 14- and 15-year-olds will correctly execute forward and backward somersaults on the trampoline.

All 7-year-olds will correctly execute consecutive forward and backward rolls.

If, on the other hand, a set of objectives has been designed for a particular third-grade class, there is little value in beginning each separate objective with "The third-grade students." Even when there is a variety of student groups included in a set of objectives, it is usually clearer and requires less space and effort to organize the objectives according to groups and label the groups thus formed rather than naming the group each time an objective is written. For the purposes of this text, therefore, primary attention will be given to the steps of identification, description, and specification.

4. R. J. Kibler, L. L. Barker, and D. T. Miles, *Behavioral Objectives and Instruction* (Boston: Allyn & Bacon, Inc., 1970).

5. C. F. Paulson and F. G. Nelson, "Behavioral Objectives," in *CORD National Research Training Manual*, ed. Jack Crawford (Oregon State System of Higher Education, Teaching Research Division, 1969).

6. William J. Kryspin and John F. Feldhusen, *Analyzing Verbal Classroom Interaction* (Minneapolis: Burgess Publishing Co., 1974).

Identification of the Terminal Behavior

Identifying the acceptable terminal behavior is the first and foremost step in developing well-written behavioral objectives. If the objective is to be observable and measurable, it is imperative that the writer clearly identify the type of behavior that is acceptable. The behavior must be stated in such a manner that one can see exactly how the student will be required to demonstrate that the objective has been accomplished. Verbs, such as *solve, demonstrate, write,* and *complete* denote behaviors which can readily be observed and therefore are useful in the development of well-stated objectives. Verbs such as *understand, appreciate, like,* and *value*, on the other hand, are very broad and leave a great deal to the imagination if used in objectives. How does a student graphically demonstrate his or her appreciation of a skill, or understanding of a concept? Certainly there are ways, but these alternative behaviors must clearly be described if the objective is to be of value.

Objectives which require the student to perform a forward roll, demonstrate the proper putting technique, or list the defensive positions on a baseball team are very specific in their identification of terminal behaviors and, as a result, provide a good basis for the development of behavioral objectives. The clarity and immediate visibility of the designated terminal behaviors makes them easily understood and readily assessable.

How, then, does one handle such goals as appreciation, sportsmanship, and other specific values? There are two choices: either one can simply declare that they are unobservable and, therefore, inappropriate for use in behavioral objectives, or, one can determine those visible behaviors which indicate appreciation or certain values and then write an objective which calls for their demonstration. If, for instance, one believes that congratulating one's opponents after an athletic contest is an indication of good sportsmanship, then an objective can be developed which calls for this specific observable behavior. It is possible, if one desires, to subdivide the broad area of sportsmanship into one or more observable behaviors which can be incorporated into meaningful objectives. In this manner, broad verbs which denote a wide range of behavioral possibilities can be made specific and thus more adaptable to use in behavioral objectives. A partial list of verbs appropriate to use in preparing behavioral objectives is provided in appendix 5.

Equally as important as the clarity of the verb used, is the specificity of the subject matter to which it refers. Too often, behavioral objectives are written in such a manner that they can be tested only through a single test item. An objective such as "The student will explain, in writing, the infield fly rule," can only be evaluated by asking the student to explain the infield fly rule in some written form. The content is restricted to a single piece of subject matter — the infield fly rule. While this may pose no serious problem when the objectives are being designed for a single lesson, the number of such objectives necessary to satisfactorily describe the goals of an entire unit would be monumental. An alternative to developing such incongruous lists of objectives is to provide more generalized content specification while maintaining explicit conditions. A reasonable objective for an entire unit on baseball might be one which required the student to explain, in writing, any of the rules of play. While such an objective would include in its scope the previously stated infield fly rule, it would also require a knowledge of balks, player substitution, and all other rules of the game. The teacher would be free to select from a wide range of potential test items, all of which required a written description of some rule.

By using a more generalized content portion of the objective, teachers can include a broader range of subject matter in their plans without becoming bogged down in an endless list of overly specific objectives. The type of behavior remains explicit, while the subject matter is broadened to allow a more practical set of written objectives. Ideally, the breadth of the content portion will vary in direct relationship to the period of time over which the objective is to apply. An objective for a single half-hour lesson can, and usually should be, quite specific. Unit objectives, on the other hand, will be applied over several lessons and should therefore refer to a broader content base.

Description of the Conditions

Having described the terminal behavior which is to be expected of the student, the teacher must then describe the specific conditions under which that behavior must be exhibited. These conditions are directly related to testing procedures because they clearly spell out the manner in which the attainment of the objective will be demonstrated. For instance:

1. List the defensive positions on a baseball team *orally, in writing,* or *orally and in numerical order.*
2. *Given a list of seven side-horse vaults*, demonstrate any three of them.
3. *After each tennis match*, the student will shake hands with his or her opponent.

It is important that the instruction provided be closely tied to the condition element specified in the objective. It is unfair to the student and educationally unsound to teach students to respond by rote and then test them on their ability to apply information. Similarly, where instruction has stressed application and choice, a test of memorized facts will not be indicative of how much the students have learned.

Since any instruction should have at least some potential of transfer, one should try to avoid statements of condition which are so restrictive that they can apply only in a single, narrowly defined instance. The following objective, which concerns the design of a game that would develop flexibility, has sufficient breadth to allow a wide variety of solutions:

> *Given any seven free or inexpensive pieces of equipment,* the students, *in groups of four*, can design a unique game to develop flexibility.

Written in a more restrictive form, however, the potential for transfer is virtually eliminated:

> *Given two jump-ropes, two tires, a wand, and two paper-towel rolls*, each group of four students, *two male and two female,* shall design a unique game to develop flexibility.

One can clearly see that the conditions called for in the second example are highly restrictive. There is no guarantee that a student could develop a unique game with any equipment other than that which was stated. In fact, if the instruction is specifically geared to the attainment of the objective, the student will probably never get the opportunity to practice with any other equipment; unless, of course, there are other equally specific objectives to cover all the other possible types of equipment. Herein lies one of the potentially major problems in the use of behavioral objectives; overspecificity. This is a two-fold problem in that it locks students into a very narrowly restricted set of behaviors which offers little potential for transfer. Furthermore, it forces the teacher to compose an inordinately large number of objectives in order to attain the goals of even a single lesson.

Specification of the Level of Performance

Having identified the terminal behavior desired and the conditions under which it is to be demonstrated, it is now necessary to specify the level of performance that must be attained. If, for example, an objective required students to demonstrate ten foul shots under game conditions, the question arises as to the percentage of shots that must go into the basket, as well as to the perfection of form required. A properly written objective would clearly state the level of performance required for its successful completion.

Objectives such as the following have clearly specified performance levels with varying degrees of content specificity.

1. The student will *attain a score of 85 percent or better* on a multiple-choice test of the rules of field hockey.
2. The student will attain *an aggregate score of at least 15 points* on any three long-horse vaults of his or her choice.
3. The student will *successfully* serve a tennis ball to each of three designated targets on the court *in eight out of ten attempts.*
4. The student will verbally describe the correct method of making *every spare* during a regulation bowling game.
5. The student will demonstrate *correct* body position while *successfully* fielding *seven out of ten* batted balls.

It should be clear that, regardless of the specificity of the content, the level of performance must still be explicitly identified. In the fourth example, for instance, the student may be called upon to describe the method of making any of a wide variety of possible spares. Regardless of which spares are described, however, the answer must be correct *every* time in order to successfully achieve the objective.

The specification of performance levels is necessary because both the teacher and the student must be able to ascertain when an objective has been successfully accomplished. If only 50 percent accuracy is required, additional concentration beyond that level does nothing for the attainment elsewhere. If, on the other hand, 100 percent success is required, stopping the instruction and/or practice before that level is reached virtually guarantees failure.

The following examples should help eliminate any confusion which may remain concerning the terminal behavior, condition, and performance criteria phases of behavioral objectives.

1. In a game situation, the student will successfully complete four of ten attempted spares.

Terminal Behavior:	Completing spares
Conditions:	Game situation
Criteria:	Successful completion of four out of ten

2. During the in-class tournament, the student will maintain at least a .225 batting average.

Terminal Behavior:	Maintain batting average
Conditions:	During in-class tournament
Criteria:	At least .225

3. Given any four pieces of equipment, the student teacher can develop an innovative game for any grade level specified by the professor.

Terminal Behavior:	Develop an innovative game
Conditions:	Given any four pieces of equipment for any grade level specified by the professor
Criteria:	Every time (implied)

The Use and Abuse of Behavioral Objectives

By now it should be clear that behavioral objectives can be applied to any level of the curriculum. They can, and should, be applied to everything from general school objectives to specific lesson plans. The very act of developing objectives of this type forces the teacher to think in terms of the expected outcomes of the educational process and the manner in which students will be expected to demonstrate the attainment of these end products. This may very well be the major value of behavioral objectives. It is difficult to imagine how any conscientious teacher could describe the expected outcomes of the teaching process but not modify the instructional format to guarantee the attainment of those outcomes. Since the objectives are stated in behavioral terms, they are easy to assess and can, in many cases, be informally evaluated during the instructional process. This is particularly true if the instruction is individualized and self-testing situations are included in it. If planning and writing behavioral objectives leads teachers to view their teaching more analytically and to be more conscious of the end products they seek, then the process can be of tremendous value.

If, on the other hand, the process results in a situation wherein teachers slavishly prepare their students to take specific tests, or worse yet, spend more of their teaching time testing than instructing, then the use of behavioral objectives becomes a very limiting and counterproductive exercise. Under such circumstances it would be far better for the teacher to design the objectives, think about how they might affect the teaching/learning process, and then discard them and teach according to whatever modified plan evolved from this exercise. At least in this manner the instruction would be based upon behavioral outcomes, and, while there would be no assessment of their accomplishment, neither would there be the overemphasis upon testing that too often accompanies the use of behaviorally stated objectives.

Finally, it should be noted that behavioral objectives offer an ideal vehicle for the individualization of instruction. If students are provided with a list of behaviorally stated goals at the beginning of a unit, and are allowed the opportunity for individualized practice and instruction, they can monitor their own progress and improvement any time they wish. They are, therefore, constantly in touch with their abilities and shortcomings and can adapt their expectations to those of the teacher. Furthermore, by varying those portions of the objective that deal with conditions and/or criteria, a range of objectives can be developed which will allow for individualized goal setting within uniform terminal behaviors. The conditions involved in foul shooting, for instance, would vary from practice situations, to class tournaments, to intramural contests. Obviously the varying degrees of pressure present in each situation affect the difficulty of the objective. Similarly, the criteria for successful achievement could vary anywhere from 0 to 100 percent, thus allowing a tremendous range of difficulty. The same process could be followed with any objective or group of objectives, thereby allowing the teacher, the student, or both to develop individualized learning packages which are geared specifically to the ability levels of each particular individual.

Like any other teaching tool, behavioral objectives are no better than the teachers and administrators who apply them. If the objectives are predicated upon a concrete assessment of the ability levels of the pupils and are applied by conscientious professionals who recognize the student as the most important link in the teaching/learning process, behavioral objectives offer great promise for the development of instructional techniques which are soundly predicated upon desired outcomes. Without such personnel, however, behavioral objectives become merely more busywork for the teacher and, in too many cases, a source of far too much testing for the students. Remember, the primary task of teachers is *instruction.* It is necessary to evaluate the outcomes of our instructional programs, but the testing process must never be allowed to become the predominant or controlling force within those programs.

THE CURRICULUM

Once the objectives for the physical education program within a school or school district have been set, it is then necessary to develop a curriculum which will provide for the accomplishment of those objectives. The curriculum should be instructional in nature, directed toward stated educational and societal goals, and should meet the needs of students of all grades and abilities.

Guidelines for Curriculum Development

Scope of the Curriculum

The scope or breadth of the physical education curriculum should encompass the needs of all students at all grade levels. The activities selected for inclusion should contribute not only to present developmental needs but to anticipated future needs of the students as well. Since virtually all program objectives include reference to the productive use of leisure time as an adult, it is essential that the physical education curriculum provide instruction in activities appropriate to this objective. Moreover, since it is impossible, or at least impractical, to teach *every* possible recreational activity, the curriculum must provide students with a frame of reference which will allow them to engage in and interpret new activities on their own and develop a positive attitude toward activity in general. Given a thorough background in and understanding of basic movement concepts and the factors involved in physical and motor-skill development, each individual student should be better equipped to approach the learning of new physical activities.

Sequence of Activities

In terms of the ease of learning, the safety of the participants, and the maintenance of student interest, it is critical that careful attention be given to the sequence of activities within the curriculum. Optimal learning is facilitated by the presence of sufficient background experiences in preparatory activities. It is wise, therefore, to provide experiences at lower grade levels which will provide a solid foundation for later learning. Too much repetition and overlap on the other hand, is likely to reduce or completely extinguish both student and teacher interest. It is, therefore, necessary to plan a careful balance of activities that will provide the necessary background and lead-up skills without becoming unduly repetitious. More will be made of this point in a later discussion of curricular forms.

Grade-Level Divisions

The curriculum should, as a general rule, be divided into sections appropriate to students at different grade levels. The most common pattern provides separate curriculum planning for the high school, the junior high or middle school, and for the elementary school. The elementary school curriculum is, in many cases, further subdivided for planning purposes into grades K-3 and 4-6. However one chooses to divide the curriculum for organizational purposes, or, indeed, whether or not one wishes to divide it at all, the question of continuity in program development remains paramount. The entire K-12 program must, when taken as a whole, present a unified sequence of activities which builds progressively toward the attainment of a single set of objectives. The planning must be coordinated at all grade levels to insure sufficient breadth to the activities, to provide for the development of skills which will be required for later activities, and to avoid unnecessary overlap and undue repetition of instruction.

Integration of Learning

The physical education curriculum cannot be viewed as an isolated factor within the school setting. The whole is more than merely the sum of its parts. If one is concerned with the development of the whole child, all facets of the total school curriculum must be interrelated and coordinated. There are innumerable opportunities for the reinforcement of academic skills within the physical education program. In the primary grades, for example, a game of "Simon Says" can become the starting point for an exciting discussion of gravitational force. Simply tell the children "Simon says jump up." When they come down, tell them they have all lost because Simon didn't say for them to come down. From that point, a guided-discovery lesson on gravitational force is almost self-sustaining. With older students, one can vividly illustrate the effects of axial length on the speed of rotation by having a student assume a straight hanging position by holding on to a single, still gymnastic ring with both hands. Then, spin the student and tell him or her to alternately open and close his or her legs. The resultant changes in speed will become immediately visible and provide an excellent illustration of an often misunderstood scientific principle. Classroom teachers can provide similar reinforcement of the concept being taught in the gym if they are made aware of them.

The key here is a coordinated effort on the part of the entire instructional staff to provide a program that will best develop the whole child. Such a program will not only provide better learning and reinforcement of skills, it will better prepare the student to cope with the complexities and interrelationships commonly found in everyday life as well.

One point, however, must be emphasized. Physical education is a distinct subject-matter area with a unique importance in the process of child development. While the program should be coordinated and integrated, one should never lose sight of the individual contribution which the physical education curriculum can and must make to the development of the whole child.

Extra Class Activities

Extra class activities, such as intramurals and interscholastic athletics, are an important aspect of the total school program and should, therefore, receive the same kind of careful planning as the regular instructional program. Opportunities for voluntary participation in physical activities should be provided at all grade levels. These opportunities should be consistent with the curriculum goals for each grade level and should be carefully tailored to the needs and abilities of the students. Under no circumstances should the extra class program at the elementary or junior-high levels be regarded as developmental or "feeder" programs for high school interscholastics. The most important consideration must be a conscientious attempt to meet the extra class needs of *all* students at *all* grade levels rather than developing more and bigger programs for a select few.

The End Versus the Means

A physical education program exists only because it is of value to the total educational experience and well-being of students. The focus of the program must, therefore, remain on the student. All teachers and administrators involved with curriculum development and implementation must realize that the outcomes of a curriculum, in terms of student behavioral change and development, are far more important than the curriculum itself. Physical education does not exist to perpetuate the game of football or to guarantee that every student experiences the thrill of participating in a wrestling tournament. Activities such as football and wrestling are activities which may very well aid in accomplishing a wide variety of meaningful and important objectives, such as developing a deeper understanding of selected motor patterns, providing a frame of reference from which to view spectator sports in later life, developing habits of good sportsmanship, or improving the physical fitness of the students. They are not, however, meaningful ends in and of themselves, and must not be construed as such. The means/ends relationship between physical activities and sports skills, on the one hand, and curricular objectives, on the other, must always be kept in the proper perspective.

Curricular Forms

Activity-Based or Traditional Curriculum

The traditional activity-based curriculum is still, unfortunately, the most common curricular pattern in many schools. The curriculum is based almost entirely upon established sports and physical activities which are presented as separate units organized in conjunction with their usual playing seasons. Traditionally, a unit on football is followed by one on soccer or speedball, which is in turn followed by basketball, gymnastics, wrestling, and so on.

This type of program has the advantage of capitalizing on the seasonal interests of the students and it does an excellent job of reinforcing established cultural patterns in terms of sports and physical activities. It is, however, virtually impossible to justify the educational value of such a curriculum solely on the grounds that it reinforces cultural patterns and existing interest areas. A major disadvantage of an activity-based organization is that it tends to become excessively repetitious. A student is, in many cases, exposed to the same sports activity at the same time of the year from elementary school through high school. Such extensive repetition is surely excessive, and tends to result in a quick review of skills followed by an in-class tournament in many grades. It is difficult, indeed, to justify the continued existence of an entire program of such activities and, unfortunately, physical educators in many states are presently learning this lesson the hard way. Parental demands for accountability, coupled with a budgetary situation where primary importance is placed upon the educational value gained for the dollars spent, have caused many administrators to seriously challenge the place of physical education in the total school curriculum. Activity-based curriculums have, in general, proven themselves to be inadequate tools with which to meet this challenge.

The Selective Curriculum

The development of selective or elective curriculums is a relatively recent form of physical education scheduling. Since the focus of a selective curriculum is activity based, the innovative features of such a program lie chiefly in the manner in which individual activities are chosen for inclusion. It is, therefore, more of an innovative scheduling technique than it is a totally new curriculum design.

Selective curriculums are designed for use at the secondary level and are based on the assumption that by the time students have reached secondary schools, they have developed a broad enough background in the field of physical education and are therefore prepared to exercise judgment concerning future activities and areas of concentration. As a general rule, students are periodically presented with a list of choices from which to select those activities in which they will participate during a given marking period or semester. Although the major thrust of most selective curriculums is in the area of recreational or carry-over activities, many school districts very wisely divide the choices into developmental activities, individual and dual sports, and team sports. The students are then required to select a certain number of activities from each area over the course of their secondary school careers.

There are several advantages to a selective curriculum:

1. It multiplies the opportunities for meeting individual needs and interests.
2. Because of the selection factor, it tends to produce classes with higher interest levels. This statement, of course, assumes that the selection possibilities are, indeed, rather broad and that students are not channelled into particular classes or subjects.
3. It allows administrators to make use of and develop faculty teaching strengths. Instead of teaching all the activities included in the curriculum to one class, teachers now teach only a certain number of activities to several classes. Where, because of student interest, new activities are called for, the teachers must be adaptable enough to develop the needed instructional expertise.
4. The curriculum can be designed to include introductory, intermediate, advanced, and independent-study courses. Students can, therefore, choose instructional levels which are more closely suited to their abilities and can, in some cases, specialize in selected areas.

The primary disadvantages of a selective curriculum are temporal and organizational. It is a difficult and time-consuming task to organize and administer the actual student selection process. First, second, and even third choices must be provided for; some equitable system must be devised to decide who chooses first, second, or last; and some means of balancing class size and instructor loads must be devised. Many larger schools presently employ a computer program to organize and regulate such registration data. Regardless of the manner in which individual classes are selected, there is a need for detailed record keeping and counseling so that all students are assured of a balanced program of activities geared to their individual needs and interests. The really important point here is that while the students are given a certain amount of freedom of choice in their selection of activities, we, as professionals, have a responsibility to assist them and guide them in such a manner that they learn to use those choices wisely both as students and in the future. Care must be exercised, however, lest this assistance and guidance effectively eliminate the student's freedom of choice. A modification of this principle is seen in the format where the first-year high school student is required to take a variety of activities in order to establish a firm introductory base. During the remaining high school years, however, the student is given *total* freedom of choice. The assumption behind this type of format is that after the foundation is properly laid during the first year, the student can and will make intelligent choices of activities without faculty assistance. An example of a selective curriculum is included in appendix 6.

Conceptual Curriculum

A conceptual curriculum, according to Good, is a "method of teaching which emphasizes the usefulness of learning through the formation of consistent, generalized symbolic ideas."[7] In the conceptual curriculum, basic concepts rather than activities become the focus. A unit of instruction, for instance, might focus on the concept of leverage and its application to physical activities, and any and all appropriate sports skills and examples would be used to illustrate the various specific principles involved. The goal of the conceptual curriculum is to develop the student's ability to understand, analyze, and evaluate physical activities in a manner which provides greater meaning. Since, in the conceptual curriculum, the focus is on the use of activities in order to learn and understand larger ideas or concepts, the quality of the curricular objective becomes of paramount importance. The objectives must be broad enough to permit illustration and instruction through a wide variety of media. The concepts, once learned, must be transferable to new skills and situations yet to be encountered, and they must be meaningful enough to justify the time and effort expended on their development.

A conceptual curriculum is, as a general rule, more easily justifiable than a traditional activity-based curriculum because it focusses on more than mere participation in an activity for its own sake. In a conceptual curriculum, an activity is a means to the accomplishment of a much wider variety of objectives. One shortcoming, however, is that a complete unit on a given sport or activity is usually not encountered. The overhand serve in volleyball may be encountered in a conceptual unit on leverage principles or one on summation of forces or, perhaps, not at all. There will not, however, be an entire unit on volleyball alone. An assumption is made that the student with a firm conceptual background will rapidly transfer and apply such concepts as the principles of leverage and summation of forces to the learning of the overhand serve or any other skill, whenever it is encountered. Research tends to show, however, that such transfer is most likely to occur when the relationships and applications are made clear to the student.[8] Therefore, unless, at some point in time, a unit on volleyball is taught in such a manner as to make clear the relationships between the concepts and their application in the sport, there is no guarantee that the student will perceive these relationships or make productive use of them.

This emphasis on conceptual theory to the exclusion of specific sports activities appears to be an overreaction to the shortcomings of an activity-based curriculum. This problem may be offset by limiting the conceptual approach to the elementary level and by applying the background thus developed to specific sports and activities at the secondary level.

Other Forms

While there are, obviously, any number of curriculum designs presently in use and still to be devised, the three discussed here are those that are primarily used today, and, in all probability, will remain in use for some time to come. And perhaps because of our own lack of imagination, they will provide the basis for most "new" curriculums developed in the immediate future. The student who is interested in further pursuing the topic of curriculum development will find some useful references at the conclusion of this chapter. Particular attention should be paid to the work of Taba,[9] whose spiral curriculum provides much of the basis for the conceptual organization and insures the kind of continuity of instruction, without excessive repetition, that is so necessary in any good curriculum. Attention is also

7. Carter V. Good, *Dictionary of Education*, 2nd ed. (New York: McGraw-Hill Book Co., 1973), p. 588.

8. Joseph B. Oxendine, *Psychology of Motor Learning* (New York: Appleton-Century-Crofts, 1968), pp. 82-90.

9. Hilda Taba and J. C. Hills, *Teacher Handbook for Contra Costa Social Studies; Grades 1-6* (San Francisco: San Francisco State College, 1965), p. 11.

directed to the inverted curriculum or curriculum based upon retroaction as presented by Miller, Cheffers, and Whitcomb.[10] This form of curriculum places the teacher in the role of advisor and facilitator, while allowing the student to decide what forms his or her learning experiences will take, and how and when he or she will participate. There is constant assessment and adjustment on the part of both teacher and student, as both will be providing input into the ongoing process of curriculum structuring and revision. While the inverted curriculum may be impractical in most situations at present, its theoretical foundation must be reckoned with in the development of curriculum models for the future.

THE K-12 CURRICULUM: A SUGGESTED APPROACH

While the presentation of any suggested approach to curriculum design without specific details regarding the philosophy, size, location, etc., of a particular school is a chancy business at best, the following general guidelines should have application in most situations.

General Philosophy

Because physical activity is an essential aspect of human life, a carefully planned program of physical education must be considered an integral part of the total school curriculum. The physical education program should guide the student toward the development of a sound body capable of efficiently and actively interpreting mental processes. The program should be designed to strengthen the bond between mental activity and its physical interpretation at the same time as it teaches physical skills and activities necessary for the effective utilization of adult leisure time.[11]

Since there is a wide diversity in the physical and mental needs of children at different developmental stages, the physical education program must be broad in scope and encompass a wide variety of activities. Planning must take into account not only present needs, but future needs as well. Learning activities should be designed which recognize the individuality of each student and provide an opportunity for personalized learning and development. Students should be led to a more complete understanding of their own bodies and physical development, and this knowledge should provide the basis for a lifetime of learning and improvement in a manner and at a pace consistent with their own abilities.

The physical education program, if it is to be a truly functional part of the total school curriculum, must stimulate the intellect of the student. No longer is it sufficient to know only *how* to perform an activity or skill. The emphasis in today's schools must be on a deeper understanding of the various component parts as well as on the "why" of the activity. The ultimate objective of the physical education curriculum must be the development of students who participate freely, actively, and with understanding. This means that a student must learn to think as well as to act. Thought is necessary to provide an aim and purpose for physical activity, and any activity performed without an understanding of this aim and purpose is simply mimicry. Furthermore, it is only through thoughtful practice and modification that motor skills can be perfected. The physical education curriculum must provide a con-

10. Arthur G. Miller, John T. F. Cheffers, and Virginia Whitcomb, *Physical Education: Teaching Human Movement in the Elementary Schools* (Englewood Cliffs, NJ: Prentice-Hall, Inc., 1974), pp. 63-4.

11. Adapted from the Physical Education Curriculum for Grades K-5 of the Highland Park Public Schools, Highland Park, New Jersey.

scious thinking/learning experience based on physical activity through which students can develop the concepts, skills, and attitudes necessary for a healthy and productive adult life.

The Elementary School Curriculum

The elementary school curriculum should be designed to develop in the student a thorough understanding of fundamental movement concepts and patterns, the ability to readily accommodate one's own physical responses to any new set of circumstances, and an understanding of one's body and its fitness potential.

Children of pre-school and primary ages need to develop their ability to control and manipulate gross body movements. This calls for the provision of successful experiences in generalized movement patterns. The truly important factor at this age is whether or not the child can exhibit complete conscious control over his or her gross body movements, rather than the relative style or the accuracy with which any given movement can be performed.

As the child develops both confidence and ability, the general skills learned in the primary grades may be developed and refined. At this time it is possible to place greater emphasis on accuracy and form in the refinement of previously learned motor patterns. Children can then learn to consciously manipulate and evaluate their own motor behavior in relationship to external models or to the movements of others.

These goals are best achieved through a conceptual curriculum with its basis in movement education and perceptual motor training. The elementary school is not the place to develop little athletes who attempt to duplicate adult games with immature bodies and insufficient skill in general body control. If the fundamental movement patterns are thoroughly learned at this level, specific sports skills can be far more readily learned at a more appropriate time. Furthermore, there is no educational excuse for teaching football, softball, or field hockey year after year from grades 3 through 12. It would be roughly the same as teaching the Pythagorean theorem in its complete and refined form in the third grade, continuing the instruction in roughly the same manner each year until students can apply the theorem, and then continuing in the same manner until high-school graduation, using progressively more practice drills and seatwork because the students no longer need the pure instructional format. How much wiser to develop background skills in the early years, teach the specifics when there is sufficient background for the students to cope with them, and then go on to further develop and adapt the skills according to individual needs and situations.

The elementary school, then, should provide a thorough background in fundamental movement skills and patterns organized according to a conceptual framework. Figure 7.1 provides an outline illustration of the concepts included in one elementary curriculum which offers particular promise for the development of a sound background in movement skills.

The Junior High or Middle School Curriculum

If a student comes to the junior high or middle school with a thorough background in fundamental motor skills and patterns, then the stage has been well set for the development of a wide variety of specific sports skills. It is at this stage that the student should be exposed to the total range of individual, dual, and team sports and activities. The goal at this level should be to provide a basic understanding and appreciation of as many skills and activities as possible, so that the students can make intelligent choices regarding their own preferences for areas of concentration.

FIGURE 7.1. Elementary Physical Education Curriculum Highland Park, N.J.

This curriculum is organized around three primary conceptual areas:

1. Human movement influences and is influenced by the individual's *state of fitness.*
2. Human movement influences and is influenced by *social processes.*
3. Human movement influences and is influenced by a variety of *mechanical principles.*

Schematically, these concepts and the various subconcepts within them, are represented as follows:

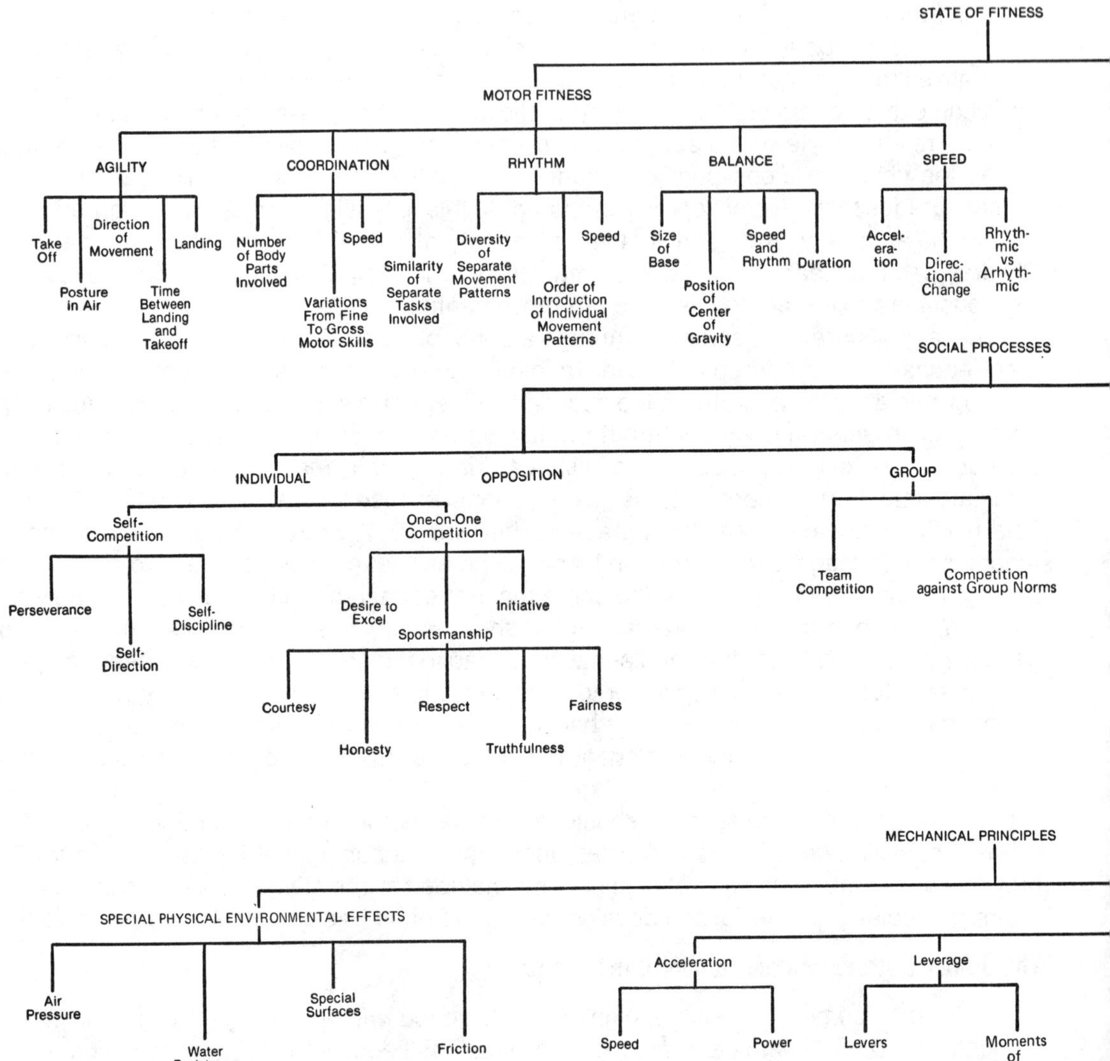

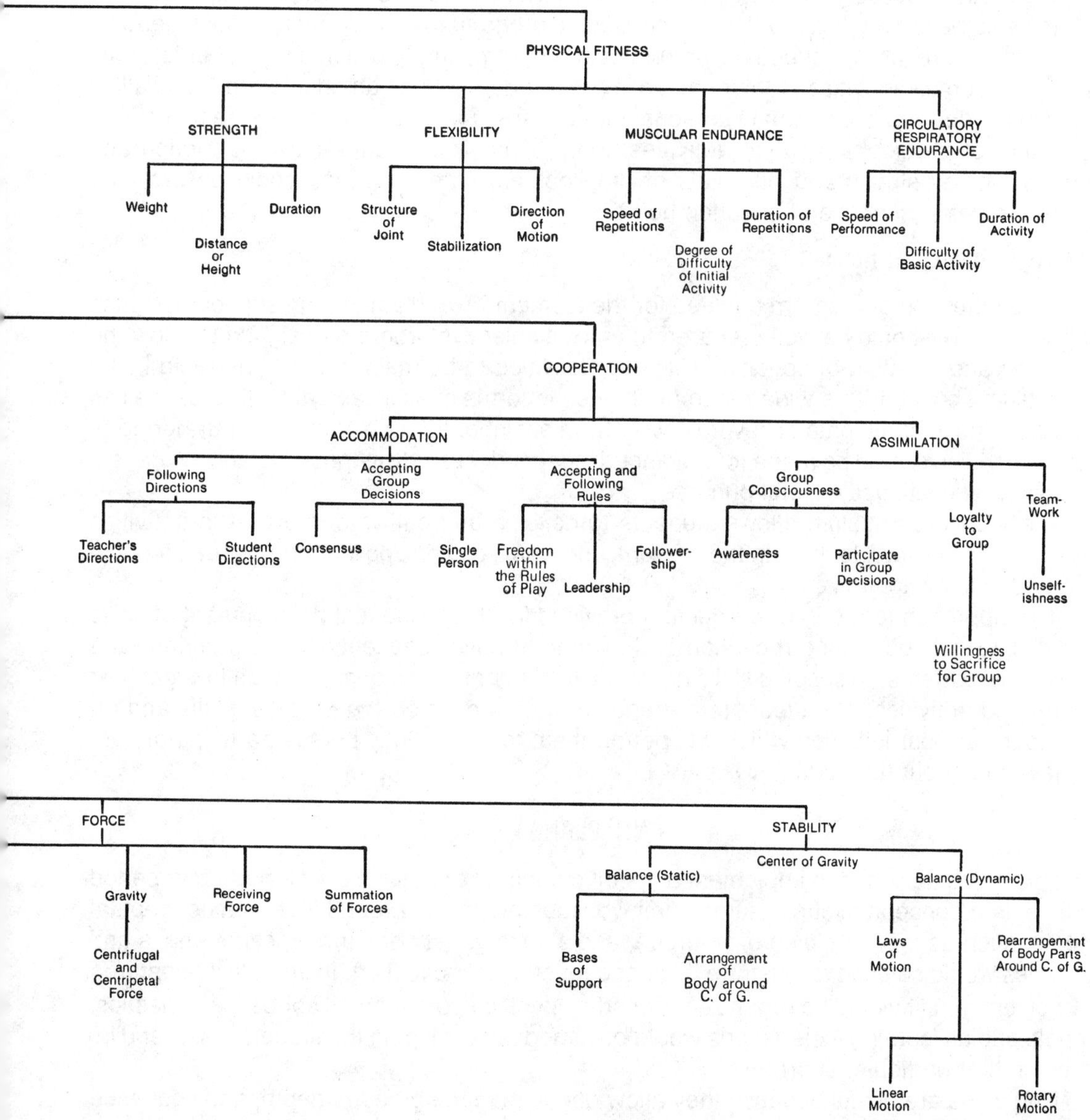

PHYSICAL FITNESS
STRENGTH
Weight
Distance or Height
Duration
FLEXIBILITY
Structure of Joint
Stabilization
Direction of Motion
MUSCULAR ENDURANCE
Speed of Repetitions
Degree of Difficulty of Initial Activity
Duration of Repetitions
CIRCULATORY RESPIRATORY ENDURANCE
Speed of Performance
Difficulty of Basic Activity
Duration of Activity
COOPERATION
ACCOMMODATION
Following Directions
Teacher's Directions
Student Directions
Accepting Group Decisions
Consensus
Single Person
Accepting and Following Rules
Freedom within the Rules of Play
Leadership
Followership
ASSIMILATION
Group Consciousness
Awareness
Participate in Group Decisions
Loyalty to Group
Willingness to Sacrifice for Group
Team-Work
Unselfishness
FORCE
Gravity
Centrifugal and Centripetal Force
Receiving Force
Summation of Forces
STABILITY
Center of Gravity
Balance (Static)
Bases of Support
Arrangement of Body around C. of G.
Balance (Dynamic)
Laws of Motion
Rearrangement of Body Parts Around C. of G.
Linear Motion
Rotary Motion

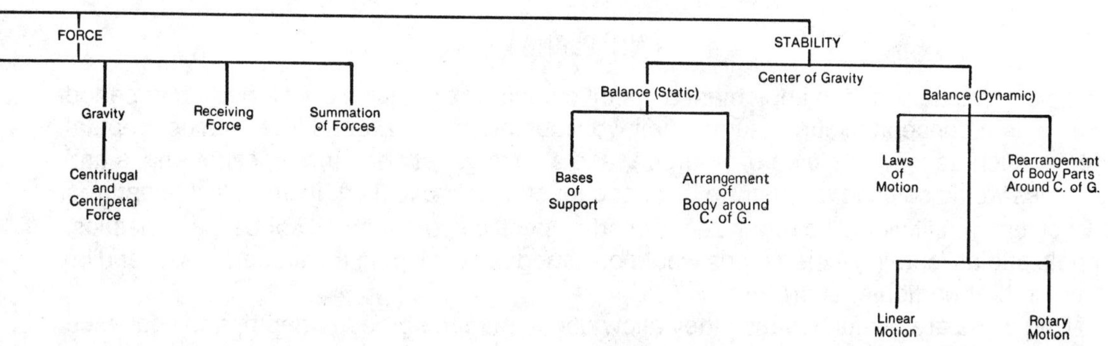

It would seem logical that, in the average three-year program, no activity should ever have to be encountered twice. Each separate sport or activity should, instead, be thoroughly covered once. The seventh-grade program, for instance, might concentrate on team sports, the eighth on individual and dual sports, and the ninth-grade curriculum might encompass a wide variety of outdoor recreation skills.

Such a program would avoid needless repetition, build upon previously learned skills and concepts, and provide a sound background for future participation and individual development. The teacher, in developing instructional plans, could capitalize on the students' background by making specific reference to those concepts and movement patterns directly necessary for the successful attainment of each new sports skill.

It would be wise in the development of such a program to provide regular open periods, other than the regularly scheduled instructional program, during which time students would be free to pursue activities of their choice in greater depth. Such an adaptation would allow students to develop and maintain personal-interest areas while gaining exposure to the total spectrum of physical education activities. Such a provision would allow instruction and practice for all students at all levels of development. These periods could be provided before and after school and on lunch hours.

The High School Curriculum

Given the type of program outlined for the elementary and junior high schools, the high school student should be well prepared to enter a selective program designed to allow the selection and isolation of specific skills and activities to be mastered and perfected. The curriculum should offer a wide range of choices in terms of skills and activities, as well as opportunities to participate at several levels from beginner through advanced. Furthermore, some provision should be made for advanced independent study in those instances where it serves an educationally useful purpose.

A selective curriculum allows students to develop and cultivate interests in activities which are meaningful to them in the present, and which can be applied throughout a productive and healthy adult life.

This approach to the K-12 curriculum provides for the sequential development of skills and abilities without undue repetition and overlap. It builds sequentially, from generalized movement patterns, to specific skills and activities, to principles of application in organized sports and activities. The students are encouraged to develop the physical skills and attitudes toward participation which will permit them to intelligently pursue participatory activities throughout their adult lives.

UNIT PLANS

Unit plans are designed to implement a specific concept or activity over a particular period of time. In a conceptual curriculum, a unit would be organized around a central conceptual theme, such as the principles of leverage, and a wide variety of learning experiences and activities would be used to illustrate this concept and its application. In an activity-centered curriculum, a unit would be organized around a specific sport such as softball, gymnastics, or golf, and all learning experiences would be aimed at developing the students' skill and interest in that particular sport.

Unit plans are useful because they allow one to plan the breadth, depth, and sequence of the instruction in a given concept or activity. They provide greater detail concerning the organization and development of learning experiences, resource materials, and evaluation techniques, and they provide a ready reference and resource for the development of sequential, unified daily lessons.

While there is a wide variety of approaches to the development of unit plans, the following format has proven valuable. This format provides necessary information and resource material without restricting or unduly limiting the freedom of the faculty to structure particular classes in the manner best suited to their individual needs.

Title and General Information:

Briefly and specifically name and define the activity or concept being taught. List particular phases of the unit which, for whatever reason, should be particularly emphasized or related to other units.

Objectives:

Provide a complete list of all the objectives for the unit. The objectives should be stated clearly, explicitly, and without undue verbiage.

Sequence:

Provide an outline of the material to be covered and the order in which it is to be presented.

Suggestions for Illustrative Activities:

This is particularly useful in a conceptual curriculum. Provide some means for demonstrating the practical application of the concept or activity covered by the unit. Illustrative activities are particularly useful in initiating a unit because they provide a frame of reference for ensuing instruction and they eliminate the possibility of teaching a skill or concept to which the students have no ready reference.

Suggested Learning Experiences:

Present examples of specific experiences designed to teach the main components of the unit. Include introductory, developmental, and culminating experiences.

Suggested Evaluative Activities:

Include suggestions for student self-evaluation as well as for teacher assessment.

Resources:

Provide a list of suggested resources for use in the unit. Include such things as:

1. Equipment and materials
2. Instructional aids
3. Community resources
4. Bibliography

While the above format has the advantage of specifying the objectives of the unit and the scope as well as the sequence of the material to be included, it allows the teacher to select specific learning experiences that can be used to attain these ends. Teachers are free to select illustrative, learning, and evaluative activities from the list provided or, if they prefer, to design activities of their own. The result is a unit with a unified subject-matter base for all students which, at the same time, allows the teacher to develop specific lessons according to individual needs, abilities, and interests.

LESSON PLANS

One of the most common criticisms leveled at student teachers is poor planning. They simply fail to adequately prepare themselves for their teaching experiences. Unfortunately, when they observe expert teachers in the hopes of finding a solution, they notice little if anything in the way of formal written planning. Why, then, should they be expected to develop extensive written plans? The answer is really quite simple. The experienced teacher has dealt with the subject matter for many years, and has developed the ability to mentally rehearse the lessons prior to execution. Through long years of experience and practice, the need for extensive written plans diminishes but the mental process by which they were developed remains. Experienced teachers have, in general, developed the ability to rapidly anticipate the variables involved in any given situation and adapt their behavior to them. The student teacher, on the other hand, rarely has sufficient background upon which to base such adaptations. They are apt to be nervous and somewhat unsure of themselves, and so, will probably forget several important aspects of their lessons if they are not firmly implanted in their minds. Written plans insure thought and preparation prior to teaching. They help to avoid the spur-of-the-moment type of decision making which can so frequently go awry, and they help to guarantee continuity from one lesson to the next. Perhaps the main value of lesson plans, however, is that they allow teachers to take a close critical look at their teaching plans before they are used. Many potential problems and pitfalls can be eliminated before they occur, and some form of instructional continuity can be established.

Lesson plans should emanate from a unit of instruction for use in a single class session. Unlike unit plans, they are usually intended for the exclusive use of the teacher who designed them. They should, therefore, be designed specifically for a given instructional situation, and application in any other situation must be viewed in terms of changes necessarily made in the original plan. Regardless of the format used in lesson planning, the following important considerations should always be made:

1. Good planning takes effort. In some cases, it may be necessary for a novice teacher to spend more time planning than actually teaching. The results, however, will more than justify the effort.
2. Thought must be given to:
   a. previous experiences of the students
   b. available time and equipment
   c. desired goals and outcomes
   d. efficient organization of students and equipment
   e. order of presentation of subject matter
   f. conformance to standard school procedures
3. All lessons should provide maximal opportunity for active participation and involvement on the part of the student.
4. Games and culminating activities should be clearly associated with the subject matter being taught.
5. Every lesson should provide some degree of instruction. Play periods are conducted at recess, not during the physical education class.
6. Each lesson should close with a summarizing statement from the teacher. Providing a very brief review and evaluation of the day's activities helps to impress students with the important points and prepare them for future lessons.
7. The continuity and interrelationships of subject matter should be considered in planning and explained to the students whenever appropriate.

Lesson Plan Format

While the exact form of the lesson plan is largely a matter of individual choice, the following format follows the pattern of the unit plan previously explained and allows one to carefully consider the important aspects of the lesson:

Content: ____________________

Date/Time: __________ Teaching Station: __________ Size of Class: __________

1. *Specific Objectives*
   These should be explicit statements about what the student will be able to do or say as a result of this particular lesson. They are best stated behaviorally, as was explained on p. 102.
2. *Sequence*
   Provide a brief outline of the material to be presented in the order of its presentation. This should include introductory or illustrative activities, specific learning experiences, and culminating or evaluative experiences. Include time estimates.
3. *Illustrative Activities*
   How can the main idea or focus of this lesson be made clear to the class? Can its practical application be demonstrated or explained?
4. *Learning Experiences*
   In-depth review and analysis of the major points of the lesson. Thorough development of this section will reinforce the teacher's understanding of the activity during the planning stage and serve as a reminder of the important teaching points immediately prior to and, if necessary, during the class session.
5. *Culminating Activities*
   These include activities which will culminate the lesson and summarize the material, as well as appropriate tools for teacher evaluation and student self-evaluation.
6. *Specific Procedures*
   a. How can the normal administrative details such as dressing, showering, and taking roll be most efficiently handled?
   b. How will the class be organized at all times?
   c. How will the class be moved from one organizational pattern to the next?
   d. What equipment is needed, where and when?
   e. What kinds of demonstrations or instructional aids are planned? Where and when are they needed?
7. *Personal Comments*
   This section, which should be completed after the lesson, calls for a self-evaluation on the part of the teacher. One should ask such questions as: How well did the lesson go? Where did it break down? What aspects were particularly valuable? What should be changed before the lesson is repeated? Were all the objectives achieved? Which of the objectives will need further explanation or emphasis? This is also a good place to consider some form of student assessment of the lesson.

While this is a lengthy and time-consuming format to apply to each individual lesson, it includes those factors which most directly influence the success or failure of a given class. It is, therefore, essential that each item be carefully developed prior to the start of the learning experience. With practice and experience, the amount of time spent in *writing* the plans can be greatly reduced. No teacher, however, regardless of their experience or ability, should fail to give *careful* thought and consideration to all aspects of lesson development.

One final point deserves to be emphasized here: the best written plans are only as good as a teacher's ability to implement them. Beautifully designed lessons, carefully typed to impress a principal or college supervisor are of no value if they cannot be implemented on the floor of the gymnasium. If the plans are not meaningful in terms of actual teaching, then they are an exercise in futility. Teachers should never put anything in their plans that they do not fully intend to carry out, and if subsequent evaluations show that certain aspects of the lesson are consistently omitted or bungled, one must ask why. Having once ascertained that a problem exists, the question becomes: Is the problem due to faulty planning or to some other factor? The following questions should assist the teacher in making that decision:

1. Are your goals realistic and attainable?
2. Have you considered:
   pupil background and ability levels?
   student interest?
   student attitudes toward the subject matter and you?
   your own interest and enthusiasm for the subject?
3. Do you know your subject matter well enough?
4. With regard to the subject matter:
   was it too easy or too difficult?
   did you make allowances for individual differences?
   was it made interesting and meaningful to the students?
   was there sufficient variety?
5. With regard to teaching style:
   were you comfortable with the teaching style?
   were your students ready to accept the relative degree of freedom or limits imposed upon them?
   did you modify unsuccessful techniques during the lesson?
   did you utilize a variety of styles?
   did you make provisions for variations in learning rates?
   did you provide sufficient feedback, both positive and negative, to the student?
6. With regard to organization and administration of the lesson:
   were your explanations and directions clear and concise?
   did the pupils understand exactly what was expected of them?
   were you well prepared?
   did you have emergency plans for rainy weather?
   did you know where the classes should be at all times and how they should get there? did they know this?
   were your classes ready to begin on time? If not, why?
   was all equipment ready and in good repair when needed?
   did you provide for the most efficient distribution of equipment and materials?
   how efficiently organized were such things as roll taking, locker room procedures, and post-class cleanup and return of equipment?
   have you analyzed each class in terms of discipline and your role in controlling it?

If the answers to any of these questions are unsatisfactory, then one should begin the process of self-improvement by planning the necessary adjustments and then diligently practicing their implementation.

REFERENCES

Bloom, Benjamin S., ed., *Taxonomy of Educational Objectives Handbook I: Cognitive Domain* (New York: David McKay Co., Inc., 1956).

Corbin, Charles B., *Becoming Physically Educated in the Elementary School* (Philadelphia: Lea & Febiger, 1976.)

Gilbaugh, John W., *How to Organize and Teach Units of Work in Elementary and Secondary Schools* (Palo Alto, CA: Fearon Publishers, Inc., 1957).

Goodlad, John I., *The Changing School Curriculum*, a report from the Fund for the Advancement of Education, August 1966.

Kibler, R. J., L. L. Barker and D. T. Miles, *Behavioral Objectives and Instruction* (Boston: Allyn & Bacon, Inc., 1970).

Krathwohl, David R., Benjamin S. Bloom and Bertram B. Masia, *Taxonomy of Educational Objectives Handbook II: Affective Domain* (New York: David McKay Co., Inc., 1964).

Kryspin, William J. and John F. Feldhusen, *Writing Behavioral Objectives: A Guide to Planning Instruction* (Minneapolis: Burgess Publishing Co., 1974).

LaPorte, William Ralph, *The Physical Education Curriculum* (Los Angeles: College Book Store, 1968).

Mager, Robert F., *Preparing Instructional Objectives* (Palo Alto, CA: Fearon Publishers, Inc., 1962).

Michaels, John V., Ruth Grossman, Lloyd F. Scott, *New Designs for Elementary Curriculum and Instruction* (New York: McGraw-Hill Book Co., Inc., 1975).

Nixon, John E. and Ann E. Jewett, *Physical Education Curriculum* (New York: The Ronald Press Co., 1964).

Oliver, Albert I., *Curriculum Improvement* (New York: Harper & Row Publishers, Inc., 1977).

Plowman, Paul D., *Behavioral Objectives: Teacher Success Through Student Performance* (Chicago: Scientific Research Associates, Inc., 1971).

Singer, Robert N., and Walter Dick, *Teaching Physical Education: A Systems Approach* (Boston: Houghton Mifflin Co., 1974).

Tanner, Daniel, *Using Behavioral Objectives in the Classroom* (New York: The Macmillan Co., 1972).

chapter eight

The Evaluative Process

Evaluation is an ever-present factor in the process of education. It is a continuous process which is carried out either formally or informally by every person who is even remotely connected with the school system. Students evaluate their teachers and the curriculum, parents evaluate the manner in which the schools affect their children, teachers evaluate the performance of their students, and administrators evaluate the effectiveness of their faculty and the curriculum. Whether the results of such evaluations are seen in enrollment figures, in the relative success of school-related questions at the ballot box, on report cards, or on teacher evaluation reports, one fact remains clear: the educational process, as a whole, is intimately intertwined with the process of evaluation. Since this evaluation can be used as an indication of anything from past achievement to present capabilities to future directions, there can be little doubt that evaluation must be carefully considered as part of the educational planning process.

There is a major link between evaluation and planning as seen in the relationship between goals and objectives, on the one hand, and evaluative criteria, on the other. Unless there is some predetermined set of standards or objectives to which one can refer, evaluation becomes simply a matter of personal opinion, and planning is no more than a subjective response to that opinion. Herein lies the greatest flaw in the informal evaluations presented earlier. Certainly students, parents, and administrators can and do evaluate teachers, but without some established set of evaluative criteria, factors ranging from knowledge of subject matter and style of teaching to voice modulation, color of eyes, and charisma are all likely to enter into the process. Color of eyes, voice modulation, and charisma, in fact, will probably be evaluated most often because they are more easily perceived. The crucial problem here, however, is that each evaluator will have a different set of standards by which to judge the criteria. If, on the other hand, the objectives are clearly stated and well defined; then evaluative criteria can be designed which will reflect the achievement of the stated objectives.

The second link which unites the processes of planning and evaluation is the function of the evaluative information once obtained. If the process of evaluation is to be based upon the stated objectives of the program, then the results should reflect the degree to which the objectives have been achieved. The information should serve not only as a commentary on the past efforts and present status of a program and its facilitators, but as a means of charting future directions as well. The planning process itself should be based, at least in part, on an objective knowledge of the present status of the program, the faculty, and the pupils. This chapter will, therefore, briefly examine the process of evaluation as it relates to those three areas of the curriculum.

EVALUATION OF THE PHYSICAL EDUCATION PROGRAM

Program evaluation has always been an important function of educational institutions. The current emphasis on accountability, however, has caused this function to be viewed from an entirely different perspective. No longer is the evaluation of educational programs conducted entirely by and for the school itself. The process has been redesigned to include input from virtually everyone with a vested interest in, or knowledge about, the growth and development of children. The result is that educational programs are no longer being evaluated solely in terms of the quality of the facilities or the breadth of the curriculum, but more specifically upon the degree to which the stated objectives of the program are achieved. Schools are now being held accountable for the product of their efforts: that is, whether and how much the students have learned. The intent of this form of accountability is threefold. First, it allows for the specific revision of the curriculum in order to better attain the stated objectives. Second, it allows for the identification and elimination of undesirable outcomes. Third, it serves as an effective means by which the administration and the public can monitor the schools.

The Development of an Accountability System

Regardless of the specific form taken by the accountability system in any given school, the following general steps must invariably be followed in its development:

1. *Determine the basic goals of the program*
   The development of basic program goals should be a joint effort conducted by representatives from the parents, the community, the professional staff, and, if necessary, an expert in the field. Goals for specific curriculums, when formulated separately, should always be consistent with those of the total school program.
2. *Secure the approval of the local board of education*
   As a governing body, the board has both the right and the responsibility to review and approve any and all matters pertaining to educational programs within their district. Any modifications to existing programs or procedures must have prior board approval.
3. *Reduce the stated goals to measurable objectives*
   Once the general goals have been approved, they should be broken down into specifically measurable objectives. (See the discussion on objectives in chapter 7.)
4. *Assess, as accurately as possible, the present level of the students with regard to the objectives*
   The information thus derived is essential to the development of meaningful teaching strategies and accurate post-instructional comparisons. Great care must be exercised here to guarantee that the test used is an accurate indicator of the specific objectives to be measured.

5. *Develop and implement instructional units*
   Based upon the objectives of the program and the present level of the students, instructional units should be developed and implemented by the professional staff.
6. *Assess the achievements of the pupils*
   The achievements of the pupils should be assessed in terms of the specific objectives of the program. The results of this assessment can then be compared to the pre-instructional data in order to determine the relative degree of change.
7. *Analyze the instructional program in light of the results*
   Having gathered data regarding the effects of the instructional program, a detailed analysis should be conducted to ascertain those areas in which improvement is needed. Weaknesses, when detected, should immediately be investigated and specific suggestions for improvement should be developed.
8. *Interpret the results to the school board and the community*
   One important aspect of an accountability system is the requirement for disclosure of results. This is usually carried out by some designated administrative representative, and the disclosure should always be presented with a clear, concise format which lists the process, results, strengths, weaknesses, and proposals for change.

Other Means of Program Evaluation

While accountability systems are rapidly becoming the dominant method of program evaluation, they are by no means the only option. Checklists and questionnaires, both locally developed and nationally standardized, have been widely utilized for many years.

The checklist or questionnaire format has the advantage of codifying those aspects of the program which are considered to be of importance and presenting standards for their attainment. The major disadvantage of such evaluative tools is that they tend to concentrate on the presence of more readily identifiable factors such as equipment, teaching stations, and specific subject-matter components. They do not, as a general rule, bring to light the outcomes of the programs or their identifiable effects upon students. An example of an established checklist for the evaluation of physical education and athletic programs is included in appendix 7.

A Suggested Approach

Because any evaluative system must be comprehensive in order to be fully successful, it is suggested that both of the preceding techniques be used in the evaluation of the physical education program. The accountability method, because of its emphasis on pupil achievement is absolutely indispensable. Pupil growth is, after all, the primary reason for the existence of the schools. The checklist format, on the other hand, focuses attention on important administrative aspects of the program. Questions that are raised and comparisons that are made may help identify the source of achievement deficiencies revealed through the accountability process, or they may point the way toward at least one means of buttressing the proposals developed in relation to student performance on the various achievement measures used.

EVALUATION OF TEACHERS

The evaluation of teaching is a matter of critical importance in education, and yet, it is usually the least effectively accomplished administrative task and the most feared by the faculty.

Teacher evaluation is an important link in the improvement of instruction. It offers the most educationally acceptable rationale for decisions regarding tenure, salary adjustments, and promotion. It provides, at least, one form of incentive for the continued professional development of the faculty, and it is, therefore, not at all surprising that most teachers view the process with some concern. The process is often poorly organized, highly subjective, and a source of embarrassment and discomfort to both the evaluator and the teacher being evaluated. In such a situation, normal concern understandably leads to outright fear and distrust.

Development of an Attitude of Acceptance

If the process of teacher evaluation is to be viewed as anything more than an onerous task that is to be tolerated only when necessary, then both teachers and supervisors must reach a common understanding of the philosophical and practical considerations which form its foundation. Such an understanding is based on an appreciation of the following points:

1. It should be recognized and accepted that members of the school board, as employers, have a *right* to evaluate their employees, and that school principals and department chairpersons, as their appointed representatives, are charged with the *responsibility* of carrying out this task.
2. It should be understood that the primary purpose of any evaluation is educational improvement. On-the-job growth and development should be a major outcome of any evaluative scheme.
3. Closely related with on-the-job growth is an abiding concern for the future improvement of the total program. If evaluation is to have an effect on the educational process, then it must focus not only on the activities of today, but on the manner in which they affect or fail to affect the problems which may arise tomorrow and the ability of the student to relate to them.
4. The process should be performance centered. Too often in our attempts at evaluation, we tend to focus attention on those things which are missing with comments such as "You didn't summarize the lesson" or "You forgot to demonstrate the overhand serve." While there is, of course, always a need to point out such items, it is essential that feedback provided be of a form that recognizes things which *did* happen whether positive or negative, e.g., "You provided individual feedback to practically every student in the class" or "Your class was left unattended for five minutes while you gathered equipment."
5. The behaviors to be measured and the criteria by which they will be judged must be carefully developed and clearly understood by all. Nothing is more difficult to prepare for than an evaluation based on unknown criteria. The more aware the teacher is of the evaluative criteria, the greater the likelihood of self-improvement and, therefore, the higher the probability of a positive formal evaluation.
6. The process of evaluation should involve the teachers themselves. Teachers should be involved in the development of the criteria against which they will be measured. They should be assisted in developing self-evaluative processes which will enable them to assess their own progress toward meeting these criteria, and they should be encouraged and assisted in their efforts at improvement based upon the results of both the formal and self-applied evaluations.

7 Whatever form the formal evaluation process takes, it must be very well developed and administered with diligence and fairness. Because teacher evaluation is such an explosive issue, and because it affects job security, salary, and, probably most importantly, the professional ego of the teacher, anything less than complete attention by all parties to the organizational and administrative factors involved will almost certainly lead to serious problems.

Common Forms of Teacher Evaluation

Teacher Self-Evaluation

The ability to systematically evaluate oneself with some reasonable degree of objectivity is probably one of the most important factors in teaching success. The use of descriptive analytical tools, such as those described in chapter 6, or checklists like the one shown in Figure 8.1 are all very useful for the teacher interested in self-improvement. The most effective technique of self-evaluation, however, is probably a careful enumeration of the objectives of a given lesson or unit and a systematic assessment, done with as much frankness as possible, of the degree to which they were achieved.

FIGURE 8.1. Rutgers College Student Teacher Self-Appraisal Checklist.

Planning	Yes	No	Notes
1. Have you prepared written lesson plans for all classes which describe at the minimum, the purpose, procedures, and evaluation techniques?			
2. Have you familiarized yourself with the school, school policies, community resources, etc.?			
3. Does your planning reflect an understanding of the students and the community?			
4. Do your lessons provide for individualized skill progression?			
5. Have you planned for instructional aids?			
6. Are you thoroughly familiar with the subject matter?			
Execution			
1 Are supplies and equipment distributed quickly and efficiently?			
2. Have you checked the facilities and equipment for safety?			
3. Is all available space and equipment efficiently used?			
4. Are you alert for safety hazards during the class?			
5. Is your speech grammatically correct?			
6. Are your verbal instructions heard and understood by all?			

FIGURE 8.1 (cont'd).

Execution (cont'd)	Yes	No	Notes
7. Are your instructions and demonstrations accurate?			
8. Do you stimulate the creativity of the students?			
9. Do you know and use your students' names?			
10. Do you actively interact with students by instructing, advising, or providing feedback throughout the lesson?			
11. Do you adapt your teaching style to suit the situation?			
12. Are you able to recognize and effectively deal with discipline problems?			
13. Do you ask questions and make use of student ideas?			
14. Do you use sarcasm?			
15. Do you show favoritism or a greater amount of attention to any student or group of students?			
16. Do your classes change activities quickly and efficiently?			
17. Do you personally supervise your classes throughout the assigned period?			
Evaluation			
1. Do you use evaluation as a teaching tool?			
2. Do you modify your lessons to reflect the results of evaluation?			
3. Do you provide ample feedback during the lesson?			
4. Do you keep records to reflect student progress?			
5. Do you evaluate your own teaching in terms of specific goals and outcomes?			

NOTE: This checklist was adapted from *Performance Evaluation Project, June 1973,* a report by the Physical Education Task Force, State of New Jersey, Department of Education, Division of Field Services, Bureau of Teacher Education and Academic Credentials.

In order to be truly effective, the enumeration of both the successes and the failures must be accompanied by "why" and "how" questions. Why did this technique work or fail to work? How can that objective be better accomplished? These are the kinds of self-evaluative questions that should be asked daily. They should be applied to every lesson, regardless of the type of subject matter. If one honestly attempts to apply in subsequent lessons the answers to questions such as these, eventual self-improvement is virtually guaranteed.

Class Visitations

Class visitation is one of the oldest and most common forms of teacher evaluation. In most school districts, supervisors are required to make a minimum number of supervisory visits to each teacher's classroom annually. The greatest problems with these visits are the difficulty of providing systematically objective feedback and the possibility that a visit will take place on an unusually good or bad day. For this reason, most supervisors maintain a list of specific reference points to look for during their visits, and they attempt to spread their visits over a variety of times and classes during the school year.

Evaluation of Course Materials

A great deal of information regarding the level of preparation and effort put forth by a teacher, as well as the learning rate of the pupils, can be gleaned from a careful examination of course materials. Such things as lesson plans, handouts prepared for student use, and test materials provide an index of the quantity, quality, and relevancy of a teacher's out-of-class preparation. Furthermore, an analysis of test performance and grade distributions can, over time, provide insight into the area of student achievement.

Student Opinion Polls

In an age when more and more physical education programs are being provided on an elective basis and student involvement in program planning and development is increasing rapidly, it is not at all surprising to see that greater importance is being attached to students' evaluations of their teachers. While there is a very real concern for the objectivity of such ratings and the degree to which personality factors and student success in the course are controlling variables, a carefully prepared questionnaire like the form shown in Figure 8.2 can greatly reduce the subjectivity and provide a source of valuable and informative feedback regarding both the program and the instruction.

FIGURE 8.2. Rutgers College Professor and Course Evaluation Questionnaire.

Please fill in blanks with information provided by the instructor, *and* then mark the mark-sense form on lines as directed.

	mark lines			mark lines
Subject Index______	(1,2,3)	Course No.____ (4,5,6)	Section No.____	(7,8)
Lab. Sec. No.______	(lines 9,10)	Name of Teacher __________		(lines 11,12,13)

Mark line

14 Class: 1.Freshman 2.Sophomore 3.Junior 4.Senior 5.Graduate

15 Approximate cumulative average. 0. no cumulative average yet established 1. 1.0-1.5 2. 1.6-2.0 3. 2.1-2.5 4. 2.6-3.0 5. more than 3.0

16 Is this course required? 1. Yes 2. No

17 Is this a course offered by your major department? 1. Yes 2. No

I. Evaluation of Instructor

18 Does the teacher generate enthusiasm for the subject?
1. very much 2. a good deal 3. moderately 4. a little 5. unenthusiastic

FIGURE 8.2 (cont'd).

Mark line

19 How consistently does your teacher stimulate intellectual curiosity?
1. always 2. most of the time 3. sometimes 4. rarely 5. never

20 To what degree does the teacher appear to be in command of course material?
1. completely 2. very well 3. sufficiently 4. poorly 5. does not know it.

21 Rate the teacher's ability to make the material understandable.
1. excellent 2. good 3. average 4. poor 5. very poor

22 Rate the teacher's ability to speak.
1. excellent 2. good 3. average 4. poor 5. very poor

23 Rate the teacher's interest in his or her students.
1. very interested 2. generally 3. moderately 4. rarely 5. indifferent

24 Is the teacher accessible when you seek assistance?
1. always 2. usually 3. occasionally 4. rarely 5. never

25 How fair is the teacher in evaluating the students?
1. very fair 2. usually fair 3. fair 4. unfair 5. very unfair

26 Without regard to your likes and dislikes of the course material, compare this teacher with others you have had in college.
1. one of the best 2. good 3. average 4. below average 5. one of the worst

II. Evaluation of Course

27 Rate the subject matter in this course.
1. fascinating 2. very interesting 3. interesting 4. of little interest 5. boring

28 Rate the reading material. (Leave blank if no required readings.)
1. excellent 2. good 3. average 4. poor 5. very poor

29 How heavy is the course workload?
1. very heavy 2. heavy 3. about average 4. light 5. minimal

30 Approximately what percentage of classes did you attend in this course?
1. 100-80 2. 80-60 3. 60-40 4. 40-20 5. 20-0

31 What percentage of classes in this course do you feel was worth attending?
1. 100-80 2. 80-60 3. 60-40 4. 40-20 5. 20-0

32 To what extent do you believe this course has general educational value to you as an individual?
1. a great deal 2. well above average 3. average 4. not much 5. not at all

FIGURE 8.2 (cont'd).

Mark line

33 To what degree was the general "atmosphere" in the classroom conducive to an exchange of ideas and to learning?

1. very high 2. high 3. average 4. low 5. minimal

34 Was it your impression that cheating was:

1. non-existent 2. almost none 3. no serious problem 4. fairly common 5. widespread

35 In a general appraisal, how would you compare this course to others you have had?

1. one of the best 2. good 3. average 4. below average 5. one of the worst

III. Comments

1. On the teacher, his methods, or any problems not covered above and suggestions for improving teaching effectiveness.
2. On the course and suggestions as to how it could be improved.
3. On the questionnaire and suggestions for its improvement.

Student Progress

The primary thrust of educational accountability systems is to hold teachers responsible for the learning and development of their students. Whether measured in terms of national norms and standards or the relative growth from pre-test to post-test situations, the analysis of the effects of instruction in terms of student progress will, most certainly, continue to be an important aspect of teacher and program evaluation. The evaluation of student progress, however, must never become the governing factor in program development and instructional planning. The temptation to "teach to the test" is ever present, and such teaching will produce unquestionably the desired outcome in terms of test scores. Unfortunately, teaching to the test can deprive the students of a wealth of information necessary to develop interest, insight, and understanding. In the long run, therefore, the process becomes counterproductive in that it achieves only short-term goals.

The Technology of Teacher Assessment

Probably the greatest single asset to the evaluation and improvement of teaching has been the development of videotape replay systems. Most school systems have at least one of these units, and the simplicity of their operation and relatively low cost of tapes has led to their increased use in the recording of teaching performances.

From a supervisory standpoint, videotapes provide an accurate record of an actual situation which can be preserved, studied, discussed, and compared with other lessons given by the same or different teachers. The supervisor and the teacher can view the lesson jointly, noting exactly what did or did not occur. Suggestions for change can be related to specific occurrences, the clarity of which will not suffer from lapses of memory or emotional response. If the supervisor is truly interested in the improvement of teaching, as opposed to the accumulation of documentary evidence upon which to base the retention or termination of teachers, then videotape analysis is an invaluable asset which all teachers can and should accept.

From the standpoint of self-improvement, the videotape system is equally useful. The accuracy of information can be preserved and one's performance can be viewed privately without the intervention of an evaluative third party. Portions of the lesson can be replayed by a teacher who wishes to fully understand certain circumstances and develop alternatives, and, in addition, student reaction to the lesson can also be assessed at that time in order to develop the best possible plans for future lessons.

The Total Evaluation Package

No single evaluative technique is totally satisfactory in and of itself. The more data available to both the teacher and the supervisor, the greater the likelihood of an accurate assessment of teaching success. If a teacher is truly concerned with self-improvement and earnestly seeks the best possible learning situation, then every assessment tool should be applied at one time or another. Techniques which are not routinely employed by the supervisory staff for the purpose of formal evaluation should be informally applied by the teacher for self-improvement purposes. While it might seem like the overall process could consume a great deal of one's free time, it is precisely this willingness to expend one's personal time in search of professional excellence that most clearly distinguishes an excellent teacher from the mediocre ones; and what with the present surplus of teachers, administrators are no longer willing to recommend tenure for teachers who are incapable of demonstrating excellence.

STUDENT EVALUATION

Evaluation of student performance and progress is becoming more and more an integral part of all physical education programs and is, therefore, an essential responsibility of the teacher. If one wishes to illustrate the benefits of a positive program of physical education, then it is necessary to pinpoint the amount and type of developmental changes that it has brought about in students. Given the broad diversity of skills and abilities present in any given class, some form of pre-testing is necessary in order to assign pupils to instructional groups and to plan meaningful learning experiences. Testing can be a strong motivational factor in teaching as well. Even if one removes the obvious threat of a grade, most children will try to do their best on any form of test, whether it is supervised by the teacher or self-administered. As a form of motivation, testing can stimulate learning and development and can assist the teacher and/or pupil in pinpointing areas of weakness for future concentration. Testing is also necessary in order to provide some objective, reliable means of assessing pupil progress and presenting this information to parents in meaningful form.

Teacher-Administered Evaluation Techniques

Observation

The use of teacher observations in assessing student performance is very common and, indeed, very valuable in the field of physical education. An observant teacher can readily pinpoint the strengths and weaknesses of pupils by viewing their classroom behavior and performance. By observing the student during a normal class period, the teacher is able to view the child in relation to others of the same age and grade, thus providing some form of comparative analysis.

There is, however, one major problem with teacher observation; it is very difficult to eliminate the high degree of subjectivity which inevitably comes into play. The "halo" effect, the personal feelings of the teacher, and the relative performance of the remainder of the class all enter into this form of evaluation.

A great deal of this subjectivity can be eliminated by the use of score cards or checklists during observation. A simple list of the important items one wishes to look for reduces the subjectivity, standardizes the qualities observed throughout the entire class, and, in general, makes for more complete and useful observation. The likelihood of observing and evaluating different types of behaviors among the students in a single class is eliminated, and the teacher is provided with a constant reference for observation of those behaviors which, in terms of the stated instructional objectives, are of primary importance. Examples of observation tools are included in Figures 8.3 and 8.4.

FIGURE 8.3. Checklist Format for Student Observation.

Note: Each student should be observed several times during the term to determine whether improvement has occurred.

Examples of behaviors to be observed	Names of Students						
1. Assists classmates in learning situations							
2. Arrives promptly for class							
3. Follows problems through to completion							
4. Willingly attempts new skills							
5. Achieves creative solutions to problems							
6. Accepts criticism							
7. Corrects observed performance errors							
8. Accepts others							
9. Applies skills in game situation a. Level swing b. Proper body position for fielding ground balls							

NOTE: Behavioral examples are for illustrative purposes only. Specific behaviors should be derived for each individual situation.

FIGURE 8.4. Individual Response Scale (Cheffers, 1973).

Instructions:
1. Select one individual.
2. Watch him or her exclusively.
3. Fill in the rating scale *after* the class has finished.
4. Where you think the child/youth/adult evidences contrary behaviors, show the behavior most consistently observed.

Details:

School ______________________

Class ______________________ Boys

Numbers ______________________ Girls

Setting ______________________ Coed

Type of lesson ______________________

Scale

1. How does the child participate?

Actively eager	1	2	3	4	5	Actively reluctant

2. Is he or she dependent upon friends?

Always crowds together with friends	1	2	3	4	5	Never notices others

3. Does he or she laugh, smile, and frequently get excited?

Excited	1	2	3	4	5	Bored

4. Where does he or she most often fasten his or her gaze?

On the teacher	1	2	3	4	5	Away from the teacher

5. How does he or she react to teacher's criticism?

a. Emotional dimension appears hurt	1	2	3	4	5	Shrugs off criticism
b. Behavioral dimension changes behavior	1	2	3	4	5	Does not change behavior

FIGURE 8.4 Individual Response Scale (cont'd).

6. When the teacher is giving directions, his or her response is:

	1	2	3	4	5	
Attentive: with the teacher						Inattentive: not with the teacher

7. How does he or she respond to teacher's praise?

	1	2	3	4	5	
Loves it						Resents it

8. Did he or she function better during teacher-directed (whole class) activities or in group/individual activities?

	1	2	3	4	5	
whole class						Group/ Individual

9. Is he or she verbal?

	1	2	3	4	5	
Talks a lot						Never says a word

10. Does he or she have a long attention span?

	1	2	3	4	5	
Hangs on every word from the teacher						Frequently distracted

11. Is he or she in conflict with other children in the class?

	1	2	3	4	5	
Quarrels, fights						Friendly, liked by everyone

12. Is he or she a leader in both actions and words?

	1	2	3	4	5	
When he or she does something he or she attracts attention						Never even noticed by anyone

Observable Teacher Effect

In general you would say, from the observable behavior of the student, that the teacher's influence on the child was:

	1	2	3	4	5	
Very obviously positive			No observable influence			Very obviously negative

SOURCE: Arthur G. Miller, John T. F. Cheffers, Virginia Whitcomb, *Physical Education Teaching Human Movement in the Elementary Schools* (Englewood Cliffs, N.J.: Prentice-Hall, Inc., 1974), pp. 46-47. Reprinted with permission of the publisher.

Student Interviews

While very time consuming, the student interview provides a wealth of information that can be gathered in no other way. Besides assessing a student's knowledge of factual material and ability to perform a given motor task, the perceptive teacher can develop a great deal of insight into the areas of student understanding and feelings. By questioning beyond simple memorization, for instance, the teacher can begin to assess the degree to which a student understands and can apply a concept. Furthermore, in an interview situation, removed from the pressure of peer observation, a student will often be much more forthright in expressing feelings and attitudes about the program, specific aspects of it, or physical activity in general. Such information is of tremendous value both in evaluating and restructuring a program and in understanding and relating to each student.

An interview, like an observation, tends to be subjective in nature, and one of its chief assets is its flexibility to allow for individual differences and to promote freedom of communication. This subjectivity and flexibility, however, make consistently reliable data regarding a large student population very difficult to obtain. For this reason, it is wise to develop a list of specific topics and questions to be covered, thus insuring a certain degree of consistency among interviews. It is, however, important to allow sufficient time to investigate unspecified areas of concern or interest to the student, which, while not on the checklist, may become evident during the course of the interview.

Tests

Written tests and tests of performance have always formed the cornerstone of all educational assessment. Tests can be locally developed or standardized for large-scale usage and comparison among similar groups. A test, however, no matter how good or highly regarded, should never be administered for its own sake. Tests should be selected and administered according to their ability to complement the objectives of the unit or lesson. Unless a test accurately assesses the degree to which the students have attained the stated objectives, there is little justification for taking the time to administer it.

Good test selection and development is essential to a productive testing program. Some of the generally accepted criteria for evaluating tests are reliability, objectivity, validity, and the availability of norms. *Reliability* is the term used to describe the consistency of the results produced by the test. Simply stated, a reliable test is one which would yield the same results when repeated by the same teacher to the same group under similar testing conditions. An *objective* test is one which is free from opinion or bias. If three different teachers gave the same test to the same group under similar conditions, the degree to which their results agreed would be a measure of objectivity. *Validity* is the degree to which a test measures what it is supposed to measure. If, for instance, two different tests are considered valid measures of tennis fundamentals, a student who scores the highest score in the class on one could be expected to do equally well on the other. *Norms* are test scores derived from large population samples which are used in making comparisons among groups. Most standardized tests have norms which can be used to compare any given class with a standard for its grade level. Great care should be exercised in the use of norms. It is important to know the size of the group from which the norms were derived. Obviously, the smaller the original group, the less faith one can put in the degree to which the norms are representative of the total population. One must know the age and sex of the normative group.

Certainly norms derived from groups of fifth-grade boys could bear little relationship to those of eighth-grade girls. Finally, it is wise to examine the geographical areas from which the norms were developed. Norms for swimming skills developed in southern California might prove an unrealistic yardstick by which to measure the performance of students in Idaho.

Procedures for Administering Student Evaluations

No evaluation program can succeed without a great deal of planning, preparation and followup. The time spent actually administering the test or tests is, in a very real sense, only one small part of the entire evaluative process. Testing, like teaching, can be viewed in terms of three phases. The pre-class or planning phase; the execution phase, wherein the test is actually administered; and the evaluation phase, during which time results are analyzed and feedback is provided to the students.

The Planning Phase

The first and most important part of the planning phase is the selection or development of the actual evaluation instrument. Before selecting an appropriate instrument, the following factors should be considered:

1. How suitable is the test for administration to the specific group in question? In ascertaining suitability, the teacher should particularly consider the skill level of the participants in relation to the requirements of the test. Will the students perceive the test as being challenging and meaningful?
2. How easily can the test be administered? Is there sufficient equipment, space, time, and assistance available to efficiently administer the test in question?
3. Can the test be used as a practice or learning tool? A test which serves no function other than assessing performance at a given point in time is severely limited in its usefulness and educational value.
4. How easily can the test be scored and interpreted? This question is asked, not merely to reduce the workload of the teacher, but far more importantly, to reduce the time between administering a test and providing feedback to the students.

Once test selection has been completed, it becomes necessary to plan for its administration. The testing site should be surveyed and a testing plan developed. All necessary equipment must be checked for defects and reserved for the appropriate time and place. The floor plan should be designed to insure smooth movement of groups between stations and permit sufficient space at all stations to minimize distractions and safety hazards. Instructions for administering the test should be developed and any assistants and/or scorers should be selected and trained.

Finally, the test should be announced and explained to the students so that they can come to class prepared to comply with whatever changes may have been made in the normal organizational routine. It is important that the class be arranged in the most efficient and effective manner possible. The actual administration of the test will be greatly facilitated if the students have knowledge beforehand of exactly where they will be expected to be and when and how they should get there.

The Execution Phase

The teacher must arrive at the testing site early, in order to set up all necessary equipment and give a final check for safety hazards or potential sources of confusion. When the students arrive, they should receive any written materials which may be necessary, as well as a brief review of the guidelines for their participation.

While students should be encouraged to do their best on the test, it is important that this encouragement be provided in an objective, factual manner rather than an emotional one. Remember, the goal of the test is to provide specific data concerning the ability levels of the students. The more emotionally charged one allows the testing situation to become, the more inefficient and less accurate the entire process is likely to be.

Supervise the entire testing operation. Be sure all assistants and scorers are carrying out their duties properly, and provide whatever additional information and guidance may be needed. Even the best of plans have been known to go awry, so be prepared to make adjustments and changes wherever necessary. Under no circumstances should the teacher utilize testing periods to catch up on reading or to plan strategies for Saturday's game. Testing is a very important aspect of teaching and deserves one's full supervisory attention.

The Evaluation Phase

Once the test has been administered and the results have been compiled, analysis must begin. The individual results must be interpreted and compared with the results of the test groups. Group results can then be compared against the scores of other similar groups if available. One very important analytical step, is the comparison of the results to the designated objectives of the program. How well did the students achieve the objectives? How well did the test discriminate among the various levels of achievement? What are the strengths and weaknesses of the students as reflected in the test? What instructional changes must be made as a result of the abilities demonstrated by the students? Were there signs of any common areas of weakness which might indicate an instructional breakdown and a need for remediation? These and many other similar questions can and should be considered after the administration of a test.

Finally, the students should receive feedback regarding the test. This should be provided at the earliest possible opportunity and should be done in a thorough, factual manner. It is far more important that students understand where their performance did or did not measure up to the expectations of the teacher, and how they can go about remedying the problem, than it is for them to hear an emotional denunciation of any and all poor test performances. Without accurate feedback and concrete proposals for remediation, a test is merely a technique for making comparisons and assigning grades. With feedback and followup, it is a learning experience; it is an opportunity for individual diagnosis and prescription which allows both the student and the teacher to gain greater insight into the realm of individual needs and abilities.

Student Self-Evaluation

Practically any evaluative tool can, with some degree of modification, be used in student self-evaluation. Self-evaluation is a very useful process because it allows the students to periodically assess their own abilities without the pressure of attaining a grade or meeting a norm. They can, with some assistance and instruction from the teacher, carefully assess and monitor their own progress and gauge their preparedness for the more formalized teacher-administered tests.

Besides the obvious educational advantages involved in monitoring one's own progress and receiving feedback in a totally personal and private manner, there is another value to be derived from self-testing which may, in the long run, be of even greater importance. The students can learn how to assess themselves and develop an appreciation and understanding of the values and applications of the technique. Throughout life, in virtually every field and discipline, there are opportunities for self-assessment. The more one is able to objectively analyze and evaluate one's own performance, the better that performance is likely to become. It is, therefore, quite reasonable that we, as teachers, should help our students develop an understanding of self-evaluation techniques.

Several factors must be present in order for student self-evaluation to be successful:

1. *The student must be familiar with the criteria for successful performance.* Regardless of what is being measured, one must have some form of yardstick against which to compare it. Objectives stated in behavioral terms are very helpful here in that they provide specific guidelines regarding acceptable performance and how it will be measured (see chapter 7).
2. *Students need to understand general testing procedures.* The need for accuracy and objective judgment is of prime importance in any testing procedure. The problems caused when one attempts to interpret carelessly gathered data should be made clear to the students.
3. *Sufficient time and encouragement must be provided for student self-assessment.* A teacher who merely suggests that students may wish to check their own progress during their free time will meet with very little success in most cases. If, on the other hand, class time is provided for the purpose, the reasons are stressed, and the techniques clearly outlined, the experience is far more likely to be a successful one.
4. *Teacher feedback is necessary during the self-evaluation process.* The nature of the feedback, however, should be somewhat different from that which many teachers most commonly employ. Comments such as "Let me show you," "Do it this way," "No, Johnny, that wasn't a 'good' vault, I'd only call it 'fair,'" and "Is that all you did?" are clearly out of place here. All teacher feedback should be aimed at strengthening the evaluative process and the students' impressions of themselves as evaluators. Questioning techniques are particularly appropriate. Comments such as "How are you doing, Margaret?" "Were you able to meet all of the criteria?" "Which ones are giving you difficulty?" "Where do you feel you still need work?" and "That is a good job of evaluating yourself" are all designed to center the student's attention on the task at hand and reinforce the idea that self-assessment is important.
5. *Student self-evaluation should not be used as a criteria for the assignment of grades.* The whole idea of self-evaluation is to provide personalized feedback without the pressure of grading. Do not negate the entire process by using data derived from student self-evaluations to assign grades. This should not be taken to imply that students cannot or should not assist in the administration of teacher-administered evaluation techniques. There should, however, be a clear distinction between those techniques which are used in testing for grades or in teacher evaluation and those which are used by the students for self-evaluation. Grades should never be assigned on the basis of the latter.
6. *Students should be assisted in developing follow-up action based upon their evaluation.* Knowing where they stand is only half the battle. The students must then be given the opportunity to do something about it. This involves counseling to develop courses of action, provision of classtime for self-directed work, teacher encourage-

ment to seek alternative avenues for developing the skills in question, and the provision of time for follow-up testing.

While the process of student self-evaluation may seem to require a particularly mature level of independent performance and judgment, and in one sense this is definitely true, such behavior is well within the realm of the average elementary school child. The key to success lies in careful and gradual preparation on the part of the teacher. Students who have never experienced independent decision making in the classroom cannot be expected to function in a fully independent manner without a great deal of preparation (see the discussion of style modifications in chapter 2). If, however, preparation is provided and the teacher is careful to develop the process properly, student self-evaluation is a tremendously enlightening and rewarding educational tool for student and teacher alike.

REFERENCES

Haskins, Mary Jane, *Evaluation in Physical Education* (Dubuque, IA: William C. Brown Co. Publishers, 1971).

Magnussen, Henry W., Melvin W. Gype and Thomas A. Shellhammer, *Evaluating Pupil Progress* (Sacramento: California State Department of Education, 1960).

Sax, Gilbert, *Principles of Educational Measurement and Evaluation* (Belmont, CA: Wadsworth Publishing Co., Inc., 1974).

chapter nine
Discipline and Class Control

One of the greatest problems faced by beginning teachers is discipline and class control. Often, student behaviors do less to disrupt the learning process than do the teacher's reactions to them. Teachers frequently *react* to student behaviors rather than evaluating them and acting in a manner designed to affect them. Their actions are, in many cases, characterized by short-term goals and spur-of-the-moment decisions that lead to greater problems than those which the actions were intended to correct. While there is no single best method of approaching disciplinary problems, there are a number of principles which, when properly applied, can have a positive influence on the effectiveness of one's teaching.

The best way to deal with disciplinary problems is to prevent their occurrence. While it is not always possible to avoid disciplinary problems, a teacher who plans carefully, develops and enforces reasonable rules of conduct, and pays attention to many of the organizational details that are frequently taken for granted should be able to greatly reduce the incidence of classroom disruptions.

PLANNING AND CONTROL

The curriculum, itself, is a major factor in the development and maintenance of a good learning environment. The more interesting and meaningful the subject matter is to the students, the less likely it is that disciplinary problems will arise. Individual lessons should be geared to pupil needs and interests, and the level of presentation should be appropriate to the ability levels of the students. If the tasks presented to a given class are either too easy or too difficult, the resultant boredom or frustration on the part of the students will, in all probability, lead to behavioral problems. In most cases, the solution to such problems lies in the development of stimulating and meaningful learning tasks rather than in some form of disciplinary action.

One should exercise particular care in the planning of those aspects of the lesson that pertain to the movement of groups and the distribution of equipment (see chapter 11). An increase in organizational efficiency usually results in a decrease in potential discipline problems.

If a behavior problem appears to be generalized throughout the entire class, the best solution could very well be a change in plans. Sometimes the mood and concentration level of an entire class can be altered as a result of unpredictable circumstances. A surprise quiz given the period before, the first snow of the season, or an assembly program before or after class can all have adverse effects on student behavior. If such problems cannot be anticipated, one must be flexible enough to accommodate the varied behaviors exhibited by the class. If such generalized problems seem to be occurring with great frequency, however, there is a strong possibility that the interests, abilities, and personalities of the students have not been properly assessed and that more in-depth analysis is called for in one's planning.

If a single individual or a relatively small number of students are consistent sources of disruption, try to determine whether they may be experiencing frustration due to their inability to achieve success or because it comes so easily that there is no challenge. Remember, it is usually easier for a child to say he or she struck out because he or she was fooling around than to admit to being a poor hitter. If the student cannot be helped to achieve success quickly, it may be wise to reduce the frustration of the situation while a solution is worked out. This will necessitate a certain amount of pre-planning for individualization within the class, but the results will more than justify the effort. An example of just such a situation involved an eighth-grade boy who was six feet tall and weighed almost two hundred pounds. His behavioral problems started the day his class began a gymnastics unit. By taking the boy aside and giving him extra instruction in spotting techniques, and by making his exceptional abilities in this area known to his classmates, who gladly took full advantage of his skill, his teacher helped him become a highly functional member of the group. Certainly his learning experiences could not center entirely around spotting, but the successful experiences thus derived helped him absorb the frustration of many unsuccessful attempts at learning simple tumbling stunts. While he did not become a highly skilled gymnast, he did maintain both a positive self-image and a productive class role while learning most of the basic stunts. Modifying the planned organization and content of the class to better meet the needs of a particular individual resulted, in this case, in a better learning situation for all.

TEACHING STYLE AND ATTITUDE

Given a carefully developed curriculum and well-planned, meaningful lessons, why is it that some teachers still seem to have more discipline problems than others? The answer, as often as not, lies in the interaction between the teacher and the students and in the teacher's attitude toward self and students.

The best teachers tend to feel comfortable and confident in the classroom. They view their students as being basically good and capable of productive learning so long as their energies and interests are properly channelled. They select and develop teaching styles which meet the needs of the students within the constraints imposed by their own personalities and preferences.

A good teacher sets limits and recognizes that positive control and discipline enhance rather than detract from a learning situation. Positive class control also tends to increase the stature and respect of the teacher in the eyes of the students. In such a situation, behavioral deviations are viewed in the context in which they occur and are more easily dealt with in a thoughtful, learning-directed manner. In short, a good teacher *acts* rather than *reacts*. Teachers whose initial reaction to a disciplinary problem is "How can they do this to me?" are already well on their way to disaster. Discipline problems are rarely directed at the teacher in a personal manner. They can usually be traced to some remediable factor or circumstance.

Keeping in mind that the teacher is the primary role model for the students, one must therefore be sure that the example set is one of dignity and control. Remember too, warmth and compassion are important factors in interpersonal relationships that need not interfere with one's ability to remain an authority figure who is capable of saying no and having students respond appropriately. This matter of social distance is critical to the development of a good classroom atmosphere. Perhaps this can best be summarized by saying that 1) students are individuals, worthy of respect and consideration, 2) instructional programs are run *for* students *by* teachers, and 3) in general, those teachers who consider student needs and desires in arriving at their decisions achieve greater success.

Another simple aspect of one's daily teaching behavior which can have a great impact on student behavior is the rapidity with which a teacher can learn and use the names of all students. This allows students who exhibit behavioral deviations to be treated as individuals rather than anonymous offenders. The relative safety provided by such anonymity is one of the reasons that substitute teachers frequently experience discipline problems. The use of students' names allows the teacher to direct needed commentary in such a manner as to insure an immediate and specific effect.

There are, of course, a great variety of factors in one's teaching style and attitude which can either singly or in combination exert a great effect on the behavior of a class and the individuals within it. Among them are:

1. The pitch, modification, and clarity of one's voice.
2. The personal interest and enthusiasm shown for the subject matter.
3. The presence of distracting mannerisms.
4. The evidence of teacher prejudice or favoritism.
5. The diversity of teaching styles and learning tasks.
6. The use of eye contact when speaking.
7. The ability to conduct oneself with confidence and composure, even if the situation has caused inward upset.
8. While the expression of honest annoyance is acceptable, allowing one's judgment to become clouded by personal emotions greatly increases the likelihood of failure.

Above all, relax, smile, and enjoy the students and teaching. If the teacher is unhappy, chances are very good that the students will share the same feelings. The more that students perceive the teacher as caring about and enjoying both them and the subject matter, the more likely it is that they will strive to please. Remember, respect cannot be demanded, it must be earned on the basis of total behavior, knowledge, warmth, and consistency.

Environmental Effects

The general condition and appearance of the gymnasium, locker rooms and equipment can have a great effect on the behavior of the students who use them. Gloomy, messy, or disarranged rooms are not conducive to good work habits and desirable behavioral patterns. Broken equipment should be immediately replaced or repaired to discourage vandalism and encourage a sense of pride among the students in the quality of the environment. Rooms which are well lighted, neatly arranged, and have interesting displays on the walls tend to encourage more productive task-oriented behavior.

The relative speed and ease with which the teacher is able to take attendance and distribute equipment, the amount of time which the pupil must spend waiting a turn or moving from one task to another, and the degree to which the teacher is able to visually supervise the entire class are all important variables affecting discipline and class control, and they should receive careful attention in planning.

Another environmental factor which has a major effect upon student behavior is the teacher's proximity to students in the gymnasium. Many problems can be corrected or entirely avoided by simply adjusting one's physical location. Moving closer to students whose attention seems to be wandering often helps refocus their attention on the desired learning task. Teachers should always try to position themselves in such a manner that the entire class is within their field of vision. If for some unavoidable reason one's attention must be directed away from some portion of the class, one should be aware of the dangers involved, and be sure to make frequent spot checks on that portion of the group which is otherwise unobserved. As was mentioned previously, maintaining an atmosphere of control and careful supervision is one of the most effective methods of avoiding classroom misbehavior. (For a further discussion of adequate class supervision, see chapter 10.)

ESTABLISHING RULES

In the final analysis, the teacher is responsible for the learning environment in the classroom; the teacher is the final source of authority within that class. Most good teachers will permit as much self-direction and sharing of authority as their students can effectively handle, but they still maintain the balance of power and the final right of approval.

Rules are necessary in all learning situations because they delimit the boundaries of acceptable behavior. The exact number and type of rules will vary with the class and the subject matter. One point, however, is crucial: the rules that are established must be clear and concise, and they should enhance rather than detract from productive learning.

It is wise to involve the students in the development and enforcement of rules of classroom behavior and management. This involvement is essential because students should be taught to accept responsibility for self-direction and sharing authority, and furthermore, because students tend to respond better to rules which they have helped formulate. Whether the rules are arrived at democratically or autocratically, they should above all be simple and be clearly understood by everyone involved. There should be no more rules than are absolutely necessary for the maintenance of a productive learning environment, and all of the rules should be fairly and consistently enforced.

The manner in which the rules are conveyed to the student is as important as the manner in which they were developed. While all rules should be explained verbally, student recollection of such explanations tends to dim with time. It is wise, therefore, to provide regular verbal reinforcement and to post written reminders as well. The rules of conduct in the locker room, for instance, should be prominently and permanently posted near the entrance. Rules pertaining to other aspects of the program can be posted as the need arises and removed when they no longer serve a useful purpose.

Rules should, whenever possible, be written in positive terms. A rule which simply states "Dressing time: five minutes" is clearer and more concise than one which states "Do not take longer than 5 minutes to dress." Listing all the *don'ts* tends to create a feeling of oppression and restrictiveness, while listing the *dos* merely provides the security of knowing what is expected. It is, therefore, far wiser to post those things which the students are expected to *do* before class, for example, than to enumerate those things which they *may not* do. The latter gives no concrete guidance as to what *is* acceptable.

AN OUNCE OF PREVENTION . . . DOESN'T ALWAYS WORK

Despite concerted efforts to prevent discipline problems, some students will, on occasion, misbehave. When this occurs, the teacher is usually faced with two distinct problems. First, order must be restored to the learning environment, and then the cause of the problem must be eliminated in order to prevent a recurrence of the same or similar types of misbehavior. While teachers usually assume that a single action on their part can solve both the long- and short-term problems, such is not always the case. Some actions which temporarily curtail student misbehaviors may, in the long run, actually encourage the offender to repeat the inappropriate behavior at some future date.

Analyzing the Problem

One means of avoiding a situation where the punishment encourages or, at best, fails to sufficiently discourage the offense is to view the situation analytically. In essence, there are only two forms of misbehavior. An individual either does something that has been prohibited or fails to do something that has been required. In either case, the alternative solutions must be based upon the probable causes of the problem.

One must first ask the question, "Is the desired behavior within the capability of the child?" If the answer to this question is no, then all the punishment and haranguing in the world will not solve the problem. All that is required in this case is for the student to be taught how to do whatever is expected. It is, of course, far more likely that the student could perform the desired task given the necessary interest or confidence. Again, the solution is relatively simple; one must help the student develop the desire and willingness to attempt the task. There are several factors to be considered at this juncture that could point the way to alternative solutions.[1]

Is Nonperformance Rewarding?

In some cases, students may find the attention they receive for misbehaving to be so satisfying that they are willing to tolerate whatever punishment may be imposed. If this seems to be the case, the solution is simple; remove the rewarding factors. If a student is seeking attention, be sure that attention is given more frequently and more warmly for constructive behavior. Another possibility is the presence of a situation where the class itself is rewarding the negative behavior. When inappropriate behavior results in an increased social status, punishment is usually ineffective. The solution lies in modifying the attitude of the class so that they, as a group, tend to discourage rather than reward behavioral problems. Occasional class discussions and involvement in the development and implementa-

1. For an excellent technique in dissecting problems of performance and nonperformance, see Robert F. Mager, *Analyzing Performance Problems* (Belmont, CA: Fearon Publishers, Education Division of Lear Siegler, Inc., 1970).

tion of rules and regulations as well as a high interest in the productive tasks of the day tend to develop desirable attitudes towards classroom discipline. A final possibility is that the teacher's own reaction to the misbehavior is perhaps making it rewarding. If teachers get flustered and become involved in bickering sessions or exchange sarcasms with students, there is a strong likelihood that they are unknowingly rewarding the misbehavior.

Probably the greatest single reward a teacher can offer for misbehavior is to attempt to correct it and fail. Teachers who set out to correct a situation, should not stop until they have succeeded. Teachers who say "Stop that" but fail to follow through until the behavior ceases, are, in effect, telling students that they don't approve of their behavior but are powerless to stop it. Students will, therefore, continue to search for the *enforceable* behavioral limits since they are obviously different from the *desired* limits.

Does the Performance Really Matter?

The really important point here is not whether the teacher thinks that a particular form of behavior matters, but whether the students feel the same way about it. Do they recognize some favorable outcome as being likely to occur if they uphold stated standards? Conversely, do they anticipate any negative consequences associated with noncompliance? In short, how will the student benefit? Is there a consistent system of reward and punishment?

Rewards

The giving of rewards constitutes one of the most effective tools at the teacher's disposal. Rewarded behaviors tend to persist whereas unrewarded behaviors tend to be extinguished. It is, therefore, only logical that the rewarding of acceptable behavior is one excellent means of improving the discipline and control within the class. To have the greatest impact, rewards should be meaningful to the student and closely follow the acceptable behavior. While the exact type of reward which serves as the best motivation will vary with the age and interest of the class, non-material inducements are generally favored. Such things as affection, approval, personal praise, leadership responsibility, and increased opportunities for decision making have often proved to be highly effective. The effect of such nonmaterial rewards, however, is strongly dependent upon the respect and personal feelings which the students have for the teacher. Unless the students like and respect their teacher, they are not likely to be favorably affected by an increased show of affection or approval. In such a case, one must seek out other things which will be viewed by the student as meaningful.

Punishment

Punishment is a common form of teacher reaction to student misbehavior. As a general rule, punishment tends to bring about an immediate cessation of the unwanted behavior, but it fails to eliminate or reduce the factors which prompted it. While punishment tends to stop unacceptable behaviors, it does not, in and of itself, give guidance concerning the type of behavior that *is* appropriate. In order to be most effective, punishment should, therefore, be accompanied by some explanation of why it is being imposed and what type of behavior is expected in the future.

Too much punishment tends to result in a general restriction of behavior, increased anxiety levels, and a lack of warmth and respect in the class. A teacher can avoid much unpleasantness by clearly delineating between punishable offenses and those which can be handled effectively in other ways; and by making it clear that it is the particular *behaviors* that are the source of displeasure, and not the person responsible for them.

On the other hand, one can greatly increase the effectivenss of punishment if the following guidelines are kept in mind:

1. Punishment is most effective when it interrupts or immediately follows the undesirable behavior.
2. Punishment should be applied with firmness and consistency.
3. Threats that cannot or will not be carried out should never be made. They tend to be ineffective, as are vague references to some unspecified punishment.
4. Unless one can be sure that the entire class is really to blame, mass punishment should never be meted out. It tends to be unfair, offers no real educational advantage, and often forces the teacher and the class into adverse roles.
5. Exercise or extra work should never be used as punishment. Avoidance responses brought on by such punishment are frequently generalized to an entire activity or subject, thereby defeating the entire purpose of physical education. It is essential therefore, that the punishment fit the misbehavior and be specific to it.
6. Do not force students to rebel. The more public the censure, the more likely it is that the student will respond adversely. Embarrassment is the worst form of punishment and virtually guarantees resentment and/or rebellion. Consider students' feelings carefully before imposing punishment.
7. Above all, never impose unnecessary punishments. If, for instance, in a basketball unit, the students habitually bounce balls during the instruction phase, punishment, while initially effective, is probably unnecessary. It would be simpler and more considerate to give instruction before they get the balls, or have them sit on the balls while the teacher speaks, or sit with the balls in their laps, or any number of other less threatening solutions.

Is There an Obstacle?

When students fail to meet the teacher's expectations in terms of their behavior, it may be wise to investigate the possibility that some factor or factors beyond their control are causing or contributing to the problem.

In many cases, for instance, the problem can be traced to the fact that the students do not know what is expected of them. Have the rules of conduct been clearly defined? Have they been explained to the entire class and reinforced? When was the last time the teacher followed up behavioral criticism with some statement regarding the type of behaviors that are expected? Are some of the more important rules posted anywhere to serve as a reminder to the students? The answers to these and other similar questions could very well provide a simpler solution to a great many discipline problems.

Another possible obstacle that should be considered is the possible presence of distractions within the environment. Many times one must teach in less than perfect situations. Frequently gymnasiums must be shared by classes. Even under the best of circumstances, the presence of such classes, or the noise levels which they create, and students' natural inclination to "see what the other kids are doing" present serious obstacles to the smooth functioning of a class. While these obstacles cannot be completely removed, many of their effects can be minimized. The higher the interest level of the students in a particular class, the less likely it is that they will waste their time by watching other activities. If the difficulty seems to be associated with moving the group from one place to another, changing organizational patterns, or holding pupil attention during group instruction, the cause may be noise levels. Two facts must be accepted at the outset. First, there is very little that one can do to change the noise created by other classes, and second, it is virtually impossible to scream constantly above those noise levels. Practical alternatives include:

1. Giving group instructions in written form and supplementing these with individual instruction.
2. Listing all organizational changes and the times for each in some prominent place, such as on a locker room door.
3. Making all group changes on a single signal.

It has also been found that if the organizational patterns and the times at which changes must be made are known by the students, and if sound reinforcement techniques are used, classes can change patterns at predetermined times without need of a signal from the teacher. In such cases, procedural guidelines can be presented in written form and posted in some prominent place before class. Additional instructions and guidelines for performance can be provided at each teaching station. The teacher, in such a situation, is freed from the role of traffic controller and can concentrate on providing individual instruction and feedback. While such an organizational procedure is both successful and considerate of the students' feelings, it cannot be accomplished without a great deal of planning and preparation on the part of the teacher. All decisions regarding the organization of the class must be made well in advance, and guidelines must be formulated, published, and consistently reinforced. See chapter 11 for a more detailed discussion of class management.

The Ripple Effect

The effect of any given disciplinary situation goes beyond the particular student involved and affects the entire class. The manner in which a teacher handles a particular disciplinary situation can have a profound influence on the ensuing behavior of both the parties involved and any spectators. If, for instance, a teacher becomes agitated and upset, and ends up bickering or exchanging sarcasms with the misbehaving student, the entire class is likely to become upset. The students' estimation of the teacher's ability to control the group will probably decrease, and the learning environment will, at least temporarily, be lost. When unsuitable behavior occurs, it should be dealt with quickly and simply. The offending student should be made aware of what was wrong and what is expected in the future. Care must be taken that students understand it is the inappropriate behaviors that are disapproved of and not them. If a student feels publicly embarrassed or challenged, in all likelihood an argument or sarcastic answer will be utilized as a face-saving device. In such circumstances a ripple effect is set in motion, and the manner in which the teacher deals with the problem will affect the entire class.[2] Never argue or respond to students on an immature level, and above all, do not attempt to match sarcasms with them. The key here is to keep ones' own dignity and poise and to allow students the security of maintaining their self-respect. If an argument appears unavoidable, get the rest of the class involved with the activity, and deal with the situation quietly, off to the side.

2. William J. Gnagey, *Discipline: A Maintenance of a Learning Environment* (Washington, D.C.: National Education Association, 1975).

When a misbehaving student submits to discipline, when the teacher is clear about who was misbehaving and what that person should have been doing, and when the teacher is firm without becoming overbearing and focuses attention upon the effect of the disturbance on the rights of others; then the class is more likely to consider that the infraction warranted the action taken and that the disciplinary technique was justified.

The more interested the students are in learning and the greater their respect is for the teacher, the more the ripple effect tends to work in the teacher's favor. Students will tend to assume that the teacher is fair and interested in their welfare and will, therefore, submit more readily to the teacher's judgment and control. This kind of respect cannot be demanded, it must be earned, and once earned, it should be carefully cultivated and nurtured. Without it, teaching can degenerate into a constant battle for situational control. In this regard, it should be mentioned that on those occasions when one overreacts to a situation or is unduly abrupt or unfair to a student, one should admit the error. Do not attempt to hide the obvious, or cover it up with a show of power. Admit the error and try to avoid it in the future. Far from diminishing the respect which the students feel, such honesty and sincerity tend to increase it and, more importantly, prevent the ripple of bad feelings that sweeps through a class when one member is unjustly or too harshly treated.

Behavioristic Approaches to Class Control

No discussion of control techniques would be complete without some mention of the behavioristic approach. Teachers who espouse this approach believe that behavior modification techniques can change unacceptable behavior patterns into more acceptable ones.

Behavior modification is based upon three concepts that are fundamental to social psychology: punishment, extinction, and reinforcement. Certain behaviors result in reinforcement. These behaviors are, therefore, more likely to be repeated in the future. Certain other behaviors result in punishment and are, therefore, less likely to be repeated in the future. A third category of behaviors includes those behaviors that meet with no response at all. These will undergo gradual extinction; they will simply be exhibited less frequently as time passes. Practically all behavior is influenced by its consequences, particularly those consequences which are interpreted as being either reinforcing or punishing.

The application of behavior modification techniques in an educational setting calls for a careful delineation of the desired behavioral forms, the setting of perfomance objectives, and the application of immediate and consistent reward procedures. Disruptive or otherwise unacceptable behavior is constantly met with punishment until it ceases to be exhibited.

This approach makes the assumption that the cause of the problem is irrelevant. The goal is simply to mold the student to meet the situation created within the environment. Some would seriously question the morality of such molding as well as the long-term effects on the value system of those students whose behavior is manipulated through a system of external rewards.

No one, however, questions the fact that people can be trained through the use of positive and negative reinforcement, and that the behavioral modification approach has met with success in some situations.

Is There a Best Way?

Unfortunately, there simply is no single best way to approach the problems of discipline and class control. Like teaching styles, disciplinary approaches are subject to a wide range of variables, and any given course of action or combination of approaches is likely to work at some time for some teachers and fail miserably at other times in the hands of a different teacher.

In order to achieve the highest probability of success, one should attempt to become comfortable and familiar with a variety of alternative techniques for controlling and modifying student behaviors. One factor, however, takes precedence over all others: teachers must be comfortable and confident in dealing with students. Teachers who are unable to relax and think in the midst of disruptions, or teachers who habitually react to behavior problems and become personally upset rather than carefully choosing solutions will most assuredly feel as though they are constantly plagued with control problems. If, on the other hand, a teacher maintains an atmosphere of mutual respect in the classroom, provides challenging and meaningful lessons, and presents a poised, confident image, most problems will never occur.

When first meeting a new class, the same general guidelines apply with regard to control as applied in the selection of a teaching style. It is best to begin with a more teacher-centered approach and gradually increase the involvement of students as they demonstrate the ability to cope with it. The old maxim is quite true. It is easier to loosen controls than to tighten them. Furthermore, increased responsibility tends to be interpreted as a privilege to be enjoyed within definable limits. This is a comfortable experience for most students and one to which they will usually respond favorably. Many new teachers fear that if they are strict in their approach to control they will not be liked. This is simply not true. Students will, in fact, often interpret the absence of sufficient class control as the simple failure of the teacher to cope with the situation. This forces the students to seek the limits of their behavioral freedom on their own, which can be a very trying experience for teachers and students alike.

Here are a few simple guides to personal presentation which should prove helpful:

1. Get to know all of the students by name and develop an understanding of their individual and collective personalities as quickly as possible. The best teacher behaviors are those that are clearly directed at specific individuals.
2. Avoid screaming. A firm, confident request or statement is usually far more effective than violent, threatening demands.
3. Use corrective behaviors which are different from the ordinary. The greatest impact is usually achieved by such behaviors. Silence, a sharp command, a scowl, or a simple clap of the hands are all effective means of correcting misbehavior in the proper circumstance.
4. Try to view the problem from the student's frame of reference and always keep in mind the possibility that something you are doing may be the cause.
5. Avoid public criticism. Although public praise can be very effective, public censure is usually a poor choice of action. It frequently forces the student to react defensively, which creates a worse problem than the one the teacher originally sought to correct.
6. Develop a direct and sincere approach to praise. If a student is told what is good and why, there is a greater likelihood that the approved behavior will be repeated. However, a mere "okay" or "good" really says nothing and soon has little or no effect on the students.

Whatever control techniques one may choose to employ, each new occurrence should be viewed as a separate instance with its own peculiar set of variables. Most of all, remember that while the mistakes made by the teacher may be at the heart of the problem, disruptive behavior is rarely, if ever, directed at the teacher personally. Treat the situation for what is is — a symptom of some problem which must be corrected and controlled if the best possible learning situation is to be maintained.

REFERENCES

Claryio, Harvey F., *Toward Positive Classroom Discipline* (New York: John Wiley & Sons, Inc., 1971).

Davis, Jean E., *Coping with Disruptive Behavior* (Washington, D.C.: National Education Association, 1975).

Discipline and Learning: An Inquiry into Student-Teacher Relationships (Washington, D.C.: National Education Association, 1975).

Discipline in the Classroom (Washington, D.C.: National Education Association, 1975).

Gnagey, William J., *Discipline: A Maintenance of a Learning Environment* (Washington, D.C.: National Education Association, 19759).

Howard, Alvin W., "Discipline Is Caring," *Today's Education,* March 1972.

Mager, Robert F. and Peter Pipe, *Analyzing Performance Problems* (Belmont, CA: Fearon Publishers, Education Division of Lear Siegler, Inc., 1970).

chapter ten

Legal Liability and Safety in Physical Education and Sports

While estimates vary, it is obvious that approximately one-third of all school children will sustain some type of injury each year. More important, at least from the standpoint of the physical education profession, is the fact that over half of these injuries will involve activities related to physical education. One study of accidents occurring in public junior high schools revealed that of 1,626 accidents in 207 schools, three-fifths of them involved physical education or closely related activities.[1] This number, while large, does not include a substantial number of cases which involve outside agencies such as recreation departments, fitness spas, private camps and schools, and the like.

The above figures are not intended to frighten or intimidate the teacher, but to make clear the absolute need for every physical educator to be thoroughly familiar with basic safety precautions as well as with the legal implications of pupil injuries. The careful exercise of one's rights and responsibilities serves both as a means of preventing pupil injuries through improved teaching practices and as a safeguard against unnecessary legal action resulting from reasonable pupil injuries.

In this chapter, the topic of safety shall be approached from a legalistic point of view. The process of litigation shall be explored and special emphasis will be placed on the sequence of events which transpire when a pupil or parent alleges that reasonable safety precautions were not followed. It is hoped that teachers will be able to reduce the likelihood of injury and injury-related litigation if they apply the general guidelines and precautions outlined in the following discussion of the situations that commonly give rise to student injuries and subsequent negligence claims.

THE TEACHER AS DEFENDANT: FROM CLAIM TO JUDGMENT

> Ladies and gentlemen of the jury: we are here today because a student has suffered severe and permanent injury as a result of a teacher's failure to exercise the degree of care which she owed to her students. The teacher was negligent. Due to this negligence a student has been made to suffer physical and mental discomfort, extensive medical bills, and finally, severe and permanent injury. Only you, the jury,

1. J.K. Dissinger, "Accidents in Junior High School Physical Education Programs," *Research Quarterly* 37 (December 1966): p. 495.

can compensate this student for the inexcusable and avoidable damage caused by the negligence of her teacher.

How do experienced teachers find themselves in a court of law, labeled as negligent by an attorney in an opening statement?

Approximately two years ago, Sally Evans was an average ninth-grade student in a physical education class conducted by Ms. Jane Armstrong. The activity on the day in question was tumbling. A twelfth-grade student demonstrated a forward roll to the thirty girls in Sally's class. The class was then divided into six equal groups and each group was lined up behind a standard six-by-twelve-foot mat. Ms. Armstrong instructed each student to perform consecutive forward rolls down the entire length of the mat and to cease the rolls when they reached the floor. Sally took her turn and performed obediently and conscientiously, rolling off the end of the mat onto the hardwood gym floor. A serious back injury resulted.

Sally's injury initiated a legal process which continued until the penetrating "Ladies and gentlemen of the jury." This incident will be carefully examined through the eyes of the student, the physical educator, and the attorney.

When the student, Sally Evans, sustained her injury in Ms. Armstrong's class, she had several legal or quasi-legal alternatives:

1. Obviously, she could have chosen to do nothing. Sally could have concluded that no negligence was involved, or she could have been unwilling to get involved with the legal system, or she could have misunderstood her rights. Until recently, these three positions allowed physical education teachers to remain blissfully immune to the legal system. No longer is this the situation. The public has become much more willing to follow through on grievances, whether they be real or imagined.
2. Sally could have attempted to achieve redress without professional aid by writing to the school administrator, the teacher, or their insurers and setting forth her claim. In all of these instances, the matter would ultimately have been decided by an insurance company. A claims adjuster would have offered to settle with her or refused payment, depending on the company's determination of what the legal outcome of Sally's case would be if she pursued it.
3. Sally could have sought the services of an attorney, who upon interviewing her would have had three choices:
   a. The attorney could refuse the case.
   b. The attorney could act as an official intermediary between Sally and the insurance company in an effort to negotiate a settlement without initiating a lawsuit.
   c. The attorney could institute legal action on Sally's behalf.

Sally chose to consult an attorney, who instituted a lawsuit on her behalf. This made final settlement of the claim a matter for the civil courts.

It is important, in seeking to understand the judicial process, to trace the steps which led from the initiation of Sally's lawsuit up to the opening statement which, understandably, struck apprehension into Ms. Armstrong. The pre-trial and trial practice to which Ms. Armstrong was exposed varies from court to court and state to state. The variations, however, are minor, and should not be allowed to overshadow the similarities. Jane Armstrong gained most of her knowledge of the legal process from her lawyer, *after* the complaint or suit had been instituted against her. The many questions she asked at that time should have been answered years earlier. Had this been done, the lawsuit and perhaps even the accident might have been avoided.

The Complaint

As with any legal action, Sally began her lawsuit by filing a *complaint*. Anyone can file a complaint against anyone else for any reason, although recovery after filing is by no means guaranteed. A complaint sets forth the basic legal theories upon which the plaintiff (Sally) will rely, and also the damages demanded. Sally asked for $100,000 in damages. This, like most initial demands for damages, is an inflated figure bearing only slight relationship to the final value of the claim. Lawyers do not wish to have their ability to negotiate restricted by a narrow limit on the dollar value of the suit, and so they often ask for what would be the highest possible award for damages. In requesting that figure, they are maximizing their opportunity to win the fairest and most equitable settlement for their clients.

Complaint papers are served, either by mail or by a representative of the sheriff's office, on any defendants involved in the case. Ms. Armstrong, much to her surprise, first became aware of her involvement in a legal action when she received her copy of the complaint in the mail. Upon receipt of the complaint, she immediately notified the insurance company which would be responsible for her defense. If she had not been insured, she would have had to arrange directly with an attorney to handle her defense.

Answers

The insurance company assigned a lawyer to handle Ms. Armstrong's case, who immediately filed an *answer* on her behalf. This answer was very general in nature. It denied the allegations brought forth in the complaint by the plaintiff, Sally Evans, and raised various defenses which the lawyer planned to use on behalf of the defendant, Ms. Armstrong. The procedure followed by the defense attorney was the most accepted method of pleading in a case involving personal injury.

The Process of Discovery

After the initial pleadings were filed, the case began to shift into high gear. Actions are rarely decided on pleadings, and the legal system allows great latitude to each party so that they can discover the other's factual and legal positions. The United States' system of civil law is neither a poker game nor a Perry Mason TV show. If the lawyers have been diligent, there should be no surprise witnesses or surprise positions when a case reaches court. The process of discovery effectively precludes this.

The process of discovery in Ms. Armstrong's case began when each lawyer exchanged *interrogatories* with the other. Interrogatories are written questions sent by one party to another to be answered within a given period of time. They are usually answered by the recipient with the aid of an attorney, and there is no adverse party present. Once completed, the answers to the interrogatories must be sworn to and returned to the lawyer sending or propounding them.

Another form of pre-trial discovery is the *deposition.* After completing her interrogatories, Ms. Armstrong received notification that she would have to go to her lawyer's office for further questioning. On arrival at the office she met Sally, Sally's attorney, and her own lawyer. All of them went into a large room where a certified shorthand reporter was present. She and Sally took oaths, which were administered by the reporter, wherein they both swore to tell the truth. The lawyers then proceeded to question them on the facts surrounding Sally's accident. Ms. Armstrong was advised that the questions asked of her and all of her answers would be typed and placed in a book. She was further told that, when her case was tried, this material could be read to the jury and used for a great variety of purposes. After the completion of these two most important discovery techniques, both sides knew a great deal about the position their opponents were going to take.

The lawyers did not stop at this point, but continued to pursue other methods of obtaining needed information. Sally's lawyer made a demand for a copy of Ms. Armstrong's lesson plans and Ms. Armstrong's attorney advised that, indeed, she must make one available to the opposition. Her attorney told her that a method of discovery called *production of documents* was being employed and that other documents which they could have requested, but which were not required in this case, included attendance records, accident reports, and virtually any written material that Ms. Armstrong might have had concerning Sally.

At this point, Ms. Armstrong assumed that discovery was complete. However, she received still another group of statements which she was asked to admit or deny. These statements included the following assertions:

1. Sally was your student on the day of the accident.
2. You employed no spotter at the end of the mat on which Sally was performing her forward roll.
3. Sally rolled off the mat and injured her back.

Ms. Armstrong was told that this form of discovery is known as a *request for admissions* and that it is often used to narrow the disputed issues at trial time. Some of these statements she agreed with, others she denied, and to still a third group she replied that she did not have sufficient information to make either an admission or denial. As far as discovery was concerned, the lawyers had now collected enough information to intelligently commence trial.

Legal conferences were the next order of business for each party. The facts were by now available to everyone, and the problem of evaluating the strengths and weaknesses of each case was up to both of the lawyers. Their evalutions would depend on the law, the facts, and even on the respective demeanors of the parties involved. Each was now ready to place a dollar value on the case which would satisfactorily conclude the litigation for their client. Unfortunately, there was no meeting of the minds on the dollar value of the case, and the case of *Sally Evans* v. *Jane Armstrong* proceeded to the court of the Honorable William W. Lindsay.

Requirements for the Plaintiff's Case

It must be reemphasized that Sally's case against Jane Armstrong was a civil case. Sally charged Ms. Armstrong with the commission of a *tort*, or a civil wrong. If Sally were to win her suit, she would collect damages which would have to be paid by Ms. Armstrong or by her insurance carrier. Unlike a criminal case, the loser in a civil case will have no recora nor are they accused of having any wrongful intent or motive, in most situations. As the lawyer said in the opening statement, the charge, here, was negligence.

What then is *negligence*? Negligence is the basis for almost every lawsuit which is brought against a physical education teacher or a coach. Very simply, negligence is the failure to do something that a reasonable, prudent person would have done under the circumstances, or the doing of something that a reasonable, prudent person would not have done. In determining Ms. Armstrong's negligence with regard to Sally, many questions must be answered, among them are:

1. Would the reasonable teacher have allowed Sally to tumble at all?
2. Would the reasonable teacher have provided more detailed instruction?
3. Would the reasonable teacher have provided a spotter?
4. Would the reasonable teacher require consecutive forward rolls before determining the student's skill with a single roll?

The establishment of negligence would, by no means, win Sally's case. In an early conference Ms. Armstrong inadvertently raised this point when she said to her lawyer, "Suppose I was negligent, what did I owe Sally?" If Ms. Armstrong did not owe Sally anything, her negligence would not be important. However, this is not the case. Physical educators owe a duty of care to their students. Every civil personal injury action must start with a duty owed. These duties are prescribed legally and it is left to the jury to determine from the facts if the duty has been violated. It is violation of this duty which constitutes negligence.

Having further established that Ms. Armstrong was responsible for Sally's well-being and, further, that negligent conduct would have breached this duty, Sally would have a good beginning towards an ultimate recovery. It would, however, only be a beginning and obstacles would still stand in her way. The negligence of the teacher would not be actionable unless it proximately caused Sally's injury. What is *proximate cause*? Volumes have been written concerning this concept, but for the purposes of this text it can be handled simply. Did the teacher's negligence cause Sally to injure her back? If the answer to this question is no, then no matter how negligent Ms. Armstrong might have been, Sally cannot recover damages. An example of negligence with damage but with no proximate cause between the negligence and the damage would be in the case of a vehicle that had been parked in a legal parking zone but was illegally facing in the wrong direction when struck by a second vehicle. The owner of the illegally parked vehicle would not have to respond in damages to the owner of the striking auto because the negligent parking did not *cause* the collision. In all probability if the car had been properly parked, the collision still would have occurred. However, if the headlights of the negligently parked car had been on and, because of the manner in which it was parked, they had blinded the driver of the second car, then proximate cause would have existed and the negligent parking would have been a proximate cause of the accident.

Several factors must be present before Sally can reasonably expect to win her suit. Ms. Armstrong must have 1) owed Sally a duty, 2) violated that duty, and 3) proximately caused her accident. Having shown that Ms. Armstrong's behavior satisfied these requirements, Sally next would have to show that her injury was *foreseeable* to Ms. Armstrong. Without foreseeability there would be no recovery of damages by Sally. It should be emphasized that foreseeability does not mean that Ms. Armstrong had to foresee precisely the damage which Sally suffered. If Ms. Armstrong could foresee that her actions could cause some damage, this requirement is satisfied, even though she was not able to foresee the particular damage-causing act which occurred. Imagine a car going down a street at 100 mph. It is foreseeable that this car could cause damage of some kind. The most obvious damage that could be caused would be the striking of another vehicle or a person. However, if the unlikely happens, this does not remove the element of foreseeability. For example, suppose the 100-mph vehicle badly frightens a child walking in a crosswalk and the child then runs at top speed across the street, striking a pedestrian who falls and breaks his leg. The negligent driver could not have foreseen this particular occurrence, but he certainly could have foreseen the probability of his actions resulting in damage to someone. For legal purposes, the pedestrian's fall to the sidewalk was foreseeable.

Duty, negligence, proximate cause, and foreseeability must be proven by the plaintiff and by the greater weight of evidence. This is because the plaintiff is legally charged with the burden of proof in regard to those elements which constitute his or her case.

How does one prove a case or a fact by the greater weight of the evidence? This is done by presenting physical evidence such as documents and exhibits and by presenting *testimony* from witnesses who appear in court. It is not done by means of an opening statement or a summation by a lawyer, because everything lawyers say is considered argument. Testimony can only come from duly sworn witnesses and from factual proofs such as documents and exhibits, which must be introduced into evidence during the trial. A lawyer's opening statement or final summation is not under oath and is never part of the evidence in a trial.

When Sally got to court, her lawyer made an opening statement to the jury and then called her to the stand. She was a *fact witness* and testified concerning what she saw, felt, and, to some extent, what she heard. She was followed by two classmates who corroborated her testimony and were also fact witnesses. Sally's lawyer then introduced some physical items into evidence. The lawyer then presented the mat which Sally was tumbling on at the time of the occurrence, as well as the attendance records and lesson plans which were received from Ms. Armstrong.

The next person called to the stand was Dr. Clyde Nixon, a gymnast of fifteen year's experience and presently the head gymnastics coach at a large university. Dr. Nixon was asked questions which qualified him as an *expert witness*, that is, one having greater knowledge, by virtue of experience and training, than the general populace in a specific field. Dr. Nixon had no first-hand knowledge of the facts, but based on a question put to him which incorporated all of the pertinent matters in evidence, he gave an opinion that Jane Armstrong had been negligent. The type of question put to him is known as a *hypothetical question* because it asks for acceptance of facts with which the witness is unfamiliar, but which are before the jury. In alleging that Ms. Armstrong was negligent, Dr. Nixon testified that she had not met the standard of care owed by a reasonably careful teacher to her pupils under the circumstances described in the hypothetical question.

Sally's medical problems were painful, costly, permanent, and severe, and considerable supportive medical testimony was, therefore, presented by her attorney. If, of course, Sally had suffered no injury, she would have been entitled to no damages, regardless of Ms. Arsmtrong's negligence.[2] After the doctors testified, the attorney rose and said, "The plaintiff rests."

At this point, Jane Armstrong's attorney rose to make a motion based on the law. The jury was dismissed and Judge Lindsay listened to legal argument. It should be emphasized that the sole arbiter of the law is the judge, while the jury retains complete jurisdiction over

2. A jury can actually award a nominal verdict, which is generally in the amount of six cents, if it finds a defendant negligent with no damages flowing from the negligence. It should also be pointed out that if an act is intentional or considered grossly or willfully and wantonly negligent, a jury may award punitive damages. Punitive damages bear no relationship to the injury; they are granted to punish the defendant. Therefore, in providing the amount of punitive damages that should be awarded, one must establish the defendant's financial worth. It takes greater damages, obviously, to punish a "prince" than to punish a "pauper."

the facts. Ms. Armstrong's lawyer recognized this principle and stated that if all the factual evidence thus far presented was accepted and believed, there existed no law which would allow Sally to recover or win her case. The acceptance or rejection of the claim was a legal issue then to be decided by the judge in Ms. Armstrong's favor. Naturally Sally's attorney disagreed and argued at great length. The judge considered both arguments and then ruled that the case should continue because factual issues were present. In other words, he stated that the law would allow Sally to win if the jury believed the facts that had been presented.

The Case for the Defense

Jane Armstrong now began her defense. In the beginning of the case, her lawyer had made an opening statement immediately following the plaintiff's opening statement. At that time, her attorney set forth Ms. Armstrong's position and said that she was not negligent, but that even if she had been negligent, Sally's own negligence had contributed to or solely caused the accident. Ms. Armstrong now took the stand to show that her actions were reasonable. Her primary defense was that she had exercised good teaching practices. In other words, she had acted as a reasonable and prudent teacher, and her actions in no way caused or contributed to Sally's injury. If the jury believed this, then Sally had not successfully carried her burden of proof and she would, of course, lose the case.

The next witness in Ms. Armstrong's behalf was one of Sally's classmates who testified that Sally did, in fact, have prior tumbling experience and knew that good practice called for a spotter. This raised the issue of whether Sally's own actions might have caused or contributed to her injury. Just as Sally had the obligation of proving that her teacher was negligent, so Ms. Armstrong was now obliged to leap all the legal hurdles previously placed in the plaintiff's path if she was to prove *contributory negligence* on Sally's behalf. Ms. Armstrong, thus, bore the burden of proof in this issue. She had to show a proximate cause between Sally's negligence and her injury and convince the jury that Sally should have foreseen that harm might come to her from her own actions. At the conclusion of the testimony by Ms. Armstrong and her witnesses, the defense rested and the factual case was completed.

Once again the jury was dismissed and each lawyer proceeded to make various legal arguments. At this juncture, both lawyers stated that if all the facts were taken in the light most favorable to their opponent, their client should prevail as a matter of law. Judge Lindsay quickly ruled against Sally's attorney but did listen to the defense lawyer's argument on two points. First, it was Ms. Armstrong's attorney's position that this injury, suffered by Sally, was "an act of God." The lawyer further contended that if the judge decided that it was not an act of God, Sally had assumed the risk of her injury by engaging in tumbling in a gym class.

In dealing with these issues, Judge Lindsay first handled the argument that Sally's injury had been an act of God. He stated that this, in reality, was not a separate defense, but that counsel was merely saying that Ms. Armstrong was not negligent. If, in fact, the accident was caused by something that no mortal could influence then, of course, the jury should find that Ms. Armstrong was not at fault. The judge stated that this determination was within the jury's province and the phrase "act of God" had no legal significance. The judge added that he would not charge the phrase "act of God" to the jury, because he felt it was encompassed within his negligence charge.

The judge then disposed of *assumption of risk* by stating that it was nothing more than either the absence of negligence by Ms. Armstrong, or a type of contributory negligence. He felt it was a technical defense with no real place in today's law; a defense which would only confuse and complicate a relatively simple case. The judge cited Chief Justice Weintraub's opinion in the case of *Meistrich* v. *Casino Arena Attractions*[3] as precedent for his statement.

The judge ruled that the witnesses presented by both sides made a factual case for the jury and that he would proceed to charge the jury as to the law involved. The judge also advised that he was going to charge the doctrine of *comparative negligence* because his jurisdiction had recently adopted his law. Up until a few weeks before this trial, had Sally been contributorially negligent to any degree which proximately caused her accident, she would have been totally disqualified from a verdict. Under the doctrine of comparative negligence, however, her negligence would only diminsh the amount she would recover. For example, if the jury decided that Sally was negligent to the degree of 20 percent, that Ms. Armstrong was negligent to the degree of 80 percent, and that Sally's damage award should be $50,000, Sally's $50,000 would then be reduced by 20 percent to $40,000. The amount of negligence of each party was, the judge said, solely within the jury's jurisdiction and was to be determined from the facts and, of course, the law as charged.

The Jury Verdict and Appeal Process

Judge Lindsay proceeded to instruct or charge the jury on those points that had been discussed throughout the trial: 1) the duty owed by Ms. Armstrong to Sally; 2) a definition of negligence; 3) a definition of proximate cause; 4) a definition of foreseeability; 5) the burden of proof which Sally had in establishing her case; and 6) comparative negligence and each party's burden in proving the degree their opponent was responsible for the injury. After explaining these items and, of course, going into the damages and the nature of damages, the judge then told the jury to return a verdict without sympathy, passion, or prejudice for any of the parties. He emphasized that this was a civil case and a unanimous verdict was not necessary; the agreement of any five of the six jurors would constitute an acceptable majority. The judge then dismissed the jury, telling them to deliberate and to let the court attendant know by a knock on the door when they had arrived at a verdict.

After deliberating for one hour and thirty-five minutes, the foreman of the jury notified the court that a verdict had been reached. Court was reconvened and the judge asked the jury to state their verdict. The foreman stated that they had found the defendant, Ms. Armstrong, 100 percent liable for Sally's injuries. The judge then asked the jury for their decision concerning the amount of the award made to Sally and was informed that Sally would be entitled to damages in the amount of $65,000.

The procedures outlined by the rules of court permit an attorney to make motions to the court within ten days of the entry of a jury's verdict. Accordingly, Ms. Armstrong's lawyer asked the court to set aside the findings of the jury, giving several reasons for this motion; particularly citing what the defense considered mistakes of law and improprieties in Judge Lindsay's charge to the jury. The attorney for the defense also took this opportunity to renew the arguments made at the completion of the trial.

After hearing arguments by both counsels, the judge stated that he was satisfied with his decisions on the law and that he believed his charge to have been correct. He went on to

3. Meistrich v. Casino Arena Attractions, Inc., 31 NJ 44, (1959).

state that although the defense had not exercised its right to assert that the verdict of the jury was against the weight of the evidence, he desired the court record to show that he considered the verdict of the jury to be a proper one. He noted that if, in fact, he believed that the verdict of the jury was not found on sufficient supportive evidence, he could have and would have reversed it. Thus, the trial-court phase of Sally's case against Ms. Armstrong was completed.

Still unsatisfied, Ms. Armstrong's counsel went to the appellate court of the state. This initial appeal was taken as a matter of right. That is; everyone has the right to one appeal. The appellate court also disagreed with Ms. Armstrong's position, and her attorney then applied for the right to go to the state supreme court. The supreme court refused to hear the case on the grounds that it did not involve an issue significant enough for their determination. The supreme courts of most states hear only a small percentage of those cases which they are petitioned to consider, and relatively few civil cases are heard at that level. Thus, after all the proceedings described, Jane Armstrong's insurance company made payment to Sally Evans and the case was laid to rest. Would it not have been better for Ms. Armstrong to have avoided this entire procedure by merely exercising sound teaching judgment and by observing some simple instructional and administrative guidelines?

In the following discussion, we will examine several of the specific problems which most commonly give rise to negligence claims and some of the instructional and administrative guidelines by which they can be prevented.

THE ADEQUACY OF SUPERVISION

The question of supervision involves both a quantitative and a qualitative judgment. Because competent supervision is the primary responsibility of every physical educator and because good supervision can prevent many needless accidents, the adequacy of the supervision provided is questioned in virtually every tort negligence case involving teachers. All teachers are expected to be competent in every activity which they teach or supervise. Moreover, they are required to provide constant supervision throughout the course of the instructional period.

The failure of a school board to provide supervisory personnel, for example, was held by the Minnesota Supreme Court as sufficient cause to award damages to a pupil who was injured when struck by a pebble while on an unsupervised playground.[4] In rendering its verdict, the court stated that it is necessary only to prove that a *general danger* was foreseeable, and that a competent supervisor, if present, would have prevented the accident. It was not necessary, therefore, to prove that the specific pebble-throwing incident was foreseeable, but only the general condition which, if left unsupervised, was likely to lead to an accident. In a similar finding that involved the accidental death of a 16-year-old student who had been engaged in "slap-boxing" during a noon recess in an unsupervised gymnasium, the Appellate Court of California held that:

> It is not necessary that exact injuries which occurred should have been foreseeable; it is enough that a reasonably prudent man would foresee that injuries of the same general type would be likely to occur in the absence of safeguards.[5]

4. Sheehan v. St. Peter's Catholic School, 188 NW 2d. 868, (1971).
5. Dailey v. Los Angeles Unified School District, 470 P 2d. 360, (1970).

Clearly, there is a responsibility incumbent upon all those who are involved in the educational process to supervise those areas of the school which are intended for student use, and to lock and maintain security over those areas which are not so intended. An unoccupied gymnasium should, as a general rule, never be left unlocked. The dangers are simply too great.

Another particularly interesting, though tragic, case which rested on both the presence and the adequacy of supervision is *Russell* v. *Morehouse College*.[6] This case involved the death of a college freshman who drowned during a required swimming course given by the physical education department of the college. It was alleged that the instructor introduced two upperclassmen who were members of the swim team to the class, organzied the class for instruction, and then left the upperclassmen in charge while he went elsewhere. In the course of the ensuing instruction, the Russell boy sank to the bottom and drowned, which was not realized until another student noticed the body approximately five minutes later. The evidence showed that neither of the assistants were trained instructors and that neither had seen the victim sink to the bottom of the pool. In its finding, the Georgia Court of Appeals supported the allegation by the plaintiff that:

> The fact of his sinking and the fact that his body was on the bottom of said pool should and would have been seen by a trained and experienced swimming instructor and that he would have been rescued by said instructor if said instructor had been present and watching from the proper location on the side of said pool . . . and that at least one of two trained and experienced instructors would have seen his sinking and his body on the bottom of said pool and rescued him, if at least two trained and experienced instructors had been in charge of said class at said time.[7]

It is particularly noteworthy that the Russell case clearly involves more than the mere presence of supervisory personnel. The adequacy of the supervision in terms of training, experience, and number is a decisive factor as well.

The following general guidelines should minimize the likelihood of accidents due to supervisory shortcomings;

1. Be sure that you are thoroughly familiar with the activity being taught. You must be the expert! Plan to minimize any and all dangers involved.
2. Establish safety rules for the gymnasium or athletic fields and insist that they be faithfully adhered to. Immediately note and correct any deviation from approved safety policies.
3. Always have thorough and written lesson plans. Not only does the act of planning tend to make the teacher more conscious of potential hazards, but the plans themselves can serve as legal evidence of your preparation and knowledge regarding the subject matter taught and the ability levels of your students.
4. Never leave your class unsupervised. Do not leave the class to answer telephone calls, to speak to other teachers or students, or for any reason. Even entering an equipment closet presents a period of supervisory absence which, regardless of its brevity, presents a hazardous condition.

6. Russell v. Morehouse College, et al., 136 SE 2d. 179, (1964).

7. Ibid., p. 183.

5. Take care to arrange your classes so that the entire group is within your field of view. If your back is turned to any part of your class, those students are not being supervised at that time.
6. If you are directed by your supervisor to teach a subject which is clearly beyond your capabilities, inform the supervisor of your present inadequacies and take every possible step to upgrade your own abilities.
7. Never leave an unsupervised gymnasium open to the public. The gymnasium is traditionally associated with a wide range of dangerous activities. It is reasonable to assume that students will participate in these activities in the absence of supervision, thereby exposing themselves to unreasonable risks. When the gymnasium is not in use, put away the equipment and lock the doors.

THE ABSENCE OF PROTECTIVE MEASURES

The teacher is expected to anticipate the hazards involved in any activity and to take whatever steps may be necessary to guarantee the safety of the student. This would include the provision of necessary safety equipment, such as catcher's masks, tumbling mats, and eyeglass guards, as well as sufficient provisions for the safety of spectators and nonparticipants.

A primary factor in cases involving the adequacy of protective measures, as in any liability case, is the foreseeability of the injury and the degree to which the dangers involved were known to those charged with supervisory responsibility. In a case involving an injury to a girl on a beach when she was struck by the discharge of a Roman candle ignited by boys in the park area, an appellate court held that:

> While the shooting off of firecrackers and Roman candles had been customary in celebrating the Fourth of July at a village park and the village had knowledge thereof and such acitvities were engaged in frequently, condition of the village park was unsafe so as to justify imposing liability on the village for injuries sustained by infant plaintiff when struck by a Roman candle ignited by a group of boys in the park.[8]

A similar finding of negligence on the part of the school board for an injury sustained by a 7-year-old boy when he fell to a wooden floor from a cargo net during a physical education class succinctly emphasizes the responsibility of the school district with regard to protective measures:

> A school district has a duty to anticipate reasonably foreseeable dangers and to take precautions protecting the children in its custody from such dangers. The child may sue the school district for injuries resulting from its failure to protect the child.[9]

The adequacy of the protective equipment provided for the participants was the issue in question in the case of *Diker* v. *City of St. Louis Park*.[10] The case involved an injury sustained

8. Caldwell, et al., v. Village of Island Park, 107 NE 2d. 441, (1952).
9. Tardiff v. Shoreline School District, 411 2d. 889, (1966).
10. Diker v. City of St. Louis Park, 130 NW 2d. 113, (1964).

by a boy during a practice hockey game in which he played the position of goalie. The court upheld a claim of negligence against the city in that they supplied goalie equipment to the boy but failed to supply a face mask, which would have prevented the injury he sustained when struck in the face by a puck.

In each of these cases, the primary question is whether or not the defendant should reasonably have been expected to anticipate the dangers, and whether the prudent application of protective measures would have prevented injury to the plaintiff.

There is a clear responsibility placed on all persons engaged in an instructional or supervisory capacity to take any and all precautions necessary to insure the safety and well-being of spectators and participants alike. Some guidelines for the prevention of injuries due to inadequate protective measures are as follows:

1. Be sure that all necessary safetv equipment is available and in good repair.
2. Insist that students use the proper safety equipment at all times. Never allow a student to assume the catcher's position, for example, without a mask, no matter how briefly. It only takes one swing of the bat to cause a painful and permanent injury.
3. Teach each student how to spot for gymnastic activities, and insist that spotters be employed at all times. People tend to get careless in the performance of simple skills which they have successfully performed many times over. Without proper spotting, such carelessness can and often does lead to serious injury.
4. If adequate protection cannot be provided for the student, then steps must be taken to modify the activity.
5. To sum up the question of protective measure, if there is a danger that cannot be eliminated, one must find and enforce some means by which the student can be protected from it.

SELECTION OF ACTIVITIES

Teachers are expected to select activities which are appropriate to the age, size, and skill level of their students. Failure to do so can and frequently does lead to serious injury, and therefore constitutes an act of negligence. All instruction should be carefully planned and should follow a sound developmental progression. Teachers who conscientiously develop unit and lesson plans on the basis of the needs and abilities of their students will probably never have to contest a negligence suit claiming poor selection of activities. If, however, a suit does arise, well-developed lesson and unit plans would provide the teacher with his strongest defense.

The case of *Bellman* v. *San Francisco School District* illustrates the problems which can arise when activities are found to be inappropriate for the students involved.[11] The evidence presented indicated that a high school girl was required to participate in a tumbling class against her will, despite her claims of an injured leg. The teacher did not directly give proper instruction, and the exercise assigned was beyond the expertise and physical ability of the student at the time. An appellate court held that these facts justified the awarding of damages to the pupil for injuries incurred when she failed to execute the tumbling exercise properly.

In another case, a school district and its agents were sued for injuries sustained by a 15-year-old high school freshman during a varsity football game. The court held that an alle-

11. Bellman v. San Francisco School District, 81 P 2d. 894, (1938).

gation of negligence was a proper cause of action against the district, due to the fact that the boy was allowed to participate in the game without having received proper instruction.[12]

Perhaps the legal importance of carefully selecting activities is most clearly illustrated in the case of *Govel* v. *Board of Education of the City of Albany*.[13] This was an action for injuries sustained by a student while attempting to perform gymnastic exercises in a physical education class. The liability was predicated upon evidence that the physical education instructor required the student, who was not exceptionally well skilled, to perform a task far beyond his ability despite the fact that several other students had been injured when attempting to perform the same task.

In finding the teacher negligent, the court asserted that a teacher of physical education has a duty to exercise reasonable care to prevent injury. This duty includes an obligation to assign pupils to activities which are within the limits of their ability and to properly supervise those activities. A breach of these duties constitutes negligence, and hence is grounds for legal action.

The following guidelines should be considered when developing and selecting activities for students of any age.

1. Always select activities which are within the reasonable ability limits of your students.
2. Classes are, as a general rule, made up of a heterogeneous mixture of students. Lessons must provide sufficient individualization so that each student can be challenged while none are endangered.
3. Good lesson plans and a comprehensive curriculum guide are indispensable items. They reflect not only the choice and planning of activities on a given day, they provide a record of the type and extent of the previous instruction that has been provided for each student.
4. Always have planned rainy-day activities that correspond to the unit under study. It is very difficult to justify an injury that occurred during an activity which was devised on the spur of the moment to adapt to foul weather and for which there were no adequate lesson plans.
5. Be sure you can provide a sound justification, consistent with the educational objectives of your school, for any and all activities selected. Too many children have been injured in activities which were selected "because the students enjoy it." Rarely does such justification impress conscientious professionals or aid in the satisfactory resolution of legal action.
6. A major factor to be considered in the choice of activities for any given program is the amount and type of available facilities. For example, some activities which are perfectly acceptable for a given class on a grassy field, would be very dangerous if performed on a paved surface.

THE CONDITION OF FACILITIES AND EQUIPMENT

Before using any instructional area, the teacher should always examine it carefully to be sure that it is free of hazards and obstructions. Such things as broken glass or holes in the

12. Vendrell v. School District No. 26C Malheur Co., 360 P2d. 282, (1961).

13. Govel v. Board of Education of City of Albany, 48 NYS 2d. 299, (1944).

playing field can often lead to serious injury. Furthermore, no child should be allowed to use a piece of equipment until the teacher has examined it to insure its safe operation and freedom from defect.

In the case of *Bush* v. *City of Norwalk*,[14] for example, the primary question to be resolved was whether or not a balance beam was in such an unsafe condition that it constituted a hazard to the students who used it. The evidence showed that the injury in question occurred when the beam slipped on the floor during the activity. It was further demonstrated that the base of the beam was smooth and had nothing to prevent it from sliding on the floor, which had been newly oiled and was rather slippery. The jury returned a verdict of negligence due to the condition of the equipment, which should have been noted and corrected by a prudent instructor.

The case of *Catalano* v. *Kansas City*,[15] involved an action by a minor to recover for personal injuries suffered when he stepped on broken glass on a city playground. The primary issue in this case was whether or not the plaintiff was required to prove, in order to collect damages, that the city had been aware of the specific broken bottle that had caused the injury. The court held that the city had notice of the generally unkempt and dangerous condition of the playground, and notice of the specific broken bottle was not necessary. The city was obligated to correct the general conditions in order to render the playground safe for use. Failure to meet this obligation constituted an act of negligence.

FIGURE 10.1. The end zone of the above intramural field extends onto a light traffic road. The potential hazards from vehicular traffic as well as from the surface irregularities created by the juncture of the grass and the pavement should be obvious. Note also the tire tracks above the goal line, which further add to the hazardous condition of this field.

14. Bush v. City of Norwalk, 189 Atl. 608, (1937).

15. Catalano v. Kansas City, 475 SW 2d. 426, (1971).

Too often teachers and coaches fail to provide a reasonable area of unobstructed space around playing fields and courts. In the case of *Stevens* v. *Central School District*,[16] the court held the school district responsible for injuries sustained by an adult plaintiff during a recreational basketball game that had been held in a high school gymnasium under the auspices of the recreation department. The plaintiff in this case was carried by the force of his own momentum through glass doors located directly behind the basket. The danger presented by the glass doors was found to have been foreseeable, and the failure to protect the participants from this danger, therefore, constituted grounds for negligence. It is of particular importance to note here that the plaintiff was an adult. The age of the participant did not substantially affect the responsibility of the school or the city to provide for his safety and well-being. If, however, it can be shown that the participant was well aware of the dangers involved in a given situation and knowingly ignored them, the liability of the supervisory body may be reduced or eliminated under the concept of contributory or comparative negligence. Such a situation is typified by the case of *Maltz, et al.*, v. *Board of Education of New York City*.[17] In this case, a 19-year-old collided with a door jamb in a brick wall located two feet behind a basketball backboard. The court denied his claim for damages on the ground that he had played on the same court several times, knew of the location of the basket and had, in fact, gone through the door or hit the wall on previous occasions. Since the plaintiff was a voluntary member of a recreational team and could have chosen not to play on the court that contained dangers of which he was fully aware, it was held that he assumed the risk of his own injury. It is important to note, however, that no person of any age can be considered to have assumed the risk of dangers of which he or she may reasonably be unaware.

FIGURE 10.2. The storage of matting immediately adjacent to the sidelines of the above volleyball court presents some very obvious hazards and liabilities. Since an out-of-bounds ball is playable in volleyball, the players on the right side of the net are particularly vulnerable to tripping on the obstacle and stumbling into the wall.

16. Stevens v. Central School District, 270 NYS 2d. 23 (1966).

17. Maltz, et al., v. Board of Education of New York City, 114 NYS 2d. 856, (1952).

Some guidelines for insuring the safety of facilities and equipment are:

1. Start every day with a walking tour of those areas of the buildings and grounds which will be used by your classes. Note any hazards, such as broken glass, holes in playing fields, loose locker benches, or unusual objects on or near the playing area, and take whatever steps may be necessary to eliminate them.
2. If a hazard cannot be removed, mark it clearly and keep students away from it until the problem can be corrected.
3. Inspect and *personally* test all equipment before students use it and periodically during its use. While students can, if properly instructed, set up equipment for class, the teacher should always perform the final inspection before its use.
4. Have gymnastic and climbing equipment installed and periodically inspected by professionals and obtain a certification of safety from the inspectors.
5. Replace worn or defective parts immediately. Under no circumstances should students be permitted to use any equipment which is in a state of disrepair.

INADEQUATE CONTROL MEASURES

Closely tied with the question of supervision is that of classroom control. Under no circumstances should the actions of one child or a group of children be allowed to create a hazardous situation for others. Horseplay not only impedes learning, it frequently leads to injury.

In the case of *Beck* v. *San Francisco Unified School District*,[18] where a 15-year-old student was injured by the sudden willful behavior of two 17-year-olds in a school yard during a carnival, a court of appeals affirmed a lower court finding of negligence. The evidence indicated that no teachers were present from some time before the accident until shortly afterwards. It was further alleged that rowdyism was a natural outgrowth of any such gathering of adolescents. In supporting the negligence finding, the court of appeals stated:

> It is not necessary to prove that the very injury which occurred must have been foreseeable by school authorities in order to establish that their failure to provide necessary safeguards constituted negligence, but negligence is established if a reasonably prudent person would foresee that injury of the same general type would be likely to happen in the absence of such safeguards.[19]

One important factor in cases involving control measures is the question of how long the disturbance in question had gone on before the injury, and how much previous notice the defendant had of the same or similar disturbances. In the case of *Aaser* v. *City of Charlotte*,[20] the Supreme Court of North Carolina held that the city was not liable for injuries suffered by a young girl when she was struck by a hockey puck in the hallways of the city coliseum. Although the accident was caused by the horseplay of a group of boys in a crowded hallway, there was no evidence to show that the same or similar disturbances had ever been observed, that the city had previously allowed dangerous activities to continue unchecked, or that the city had any reason to anticipate that the horseplay would occur. The

18. Beck v. San Francisco Unified School District, 37 Ca. Rptr. 471, (1964).

19. Ibid.

20. Aaser v. City of Charlotte, 144 SE 2d. 610, (1965).

injury, therefore, was the result of a sudden and unpredictable act that the city could not have reasonably been expected to prevent.

The California Court of Appeals summarized the matter of control measures by saying:

> The purpose of the law requiring supervision of pupils on the playgrounds and on the school property during school hours is to regulate their conduct so as to prevent disorderly and dangerous practices which are likely to result in physical injury to im-

FIGURE 10.3. There are several potential sources of liability in this picture. How many can you find? (The answers are printed upside down below the picture.)

(1) There are no floor markings to delineate the lifting and normal traffic areas; (2) weights strewn around the floor constitute an unsightly and unnecessary hazard; (3) broken and missing tiles on the floor present an opportunity for accidental falls and injury; (4) badly battered wood beams used in several types of exercise are inadequate for their use and expose participants to danger from slipping and splinters; (5) the bench on the left has lost its padded cover and now consists of a badly repaired board.

> mature scholars under their custody . . . when the omission to perform a duty, like that of being present to supervise the conduct of pupils during an intermission while they are eating their lunches in a school room, may reasonably be expected to result in rough and dangerous practices of wrestling and scuffling among the students, the wrongful absence of a supervisor may constitute negligence creating a liability on the part of the school district.[21]

Guidelines for the development and maintenance of appropriate control measures are:

1. At no time should the actions of one or more students be allowed to endanger the safety or interfere with the learning of others.
2. Establish and enforce rules of proper conduct for physical education classes and events.
3. The single best means of solving control problems is to anticipate and avoid them or to have a contingency plan for those occurrences which cannot be avoided. If particular students, groups of students, or teams pose a special control problem, take action to calm the situation before it erupts.
4. If a situation of horseplay, violence, or other improper activity develops in a class or an athletic event, take corrective action *immediately*. Such problems rarely solve themselves.
5. Never allow a control problem to so occupy your attention that you lose track of the rest of your class. If the problem is that serious, you have already allowed it to go too far and will probably need assistance to restore order.
6. Be sure that an adequate number of faculty supervisors and uniformed police personnel are present at all major athletic contests.
7. When control problems arise, your own ability to maintain a calm, confident attitude will be a major factor in reaching a satisfactory solution. You must look and act the part of the person in control.

POOR USE OF JUDGMENT

The area of teacher judgment is rather broad and encompasses a wide variety of situations where the teacher fails to apply common sense or prudent judgment and a student suffers harm as a result. Some examples are:

1. Asking a student to assume an unreasonable risk, i.e., take part in activities designed primarily to build "courage."
2. Failing to apply proper first aid when necessary, or exceeding the limits of first aid.
3. Knowingly allowing students to participate in activities which are unusually dangerous.
4. Allowing or devising a situation where a student is seriously mismatched in a situation requiring physical contact.

The quesiton of mismatching the abilities of pupils in games involving physical contact is a serious one, particularly in coeducational classes. The question, however, is basically one of height, weight, and ability, not sex. The Board of Education of the City of New York was held liable for damages suffered by a student when he was required to participate in a line-

21. Forgnone v. Salvadore Union Elementary School District, 106 P 2d. 932 (1941).

soccer type game where the instructor had made no attempt to match the students according to height or weight. An ensuing injury to a student was held to have been directly related to the considerable difference between his size and that of his opponent. It was, therefore, judged a preventable act of negligence.[22]

A wide variety of cases involving alleged judgmental errors focus on the area of first aid. In *Mogabgab* v. *Orleans Parish School Board*,[23] the court held that high school coaches who refused to allow a student athlete to receive treatment for approximately two hours after the symptoms of heat stroke and shock first appeared were guilty of negligence and liable for damages in the death of the student.

It should be noted, however, that while there is a clear obligation for a teacher or coach to apply proper first aid when necessary, there is no obligation to succeed in attempts to revive the victim. In the previously cited case of *Russell* v. *Morehouse College*, the plaintiffs charged that the instructors were negligent in that they failed to revive the victim after his body had been recovered from the pool. In responding to this charge, the Georgia Court of Appeals stated that, "While instructors had a duty to attempt to revive decedent by artificial respiration, there was no duty upon them to be successful in such attempt."[24]

While the notion of good judgment is tremendously broad, the following guidelines, based upon recurrent allegations in negligence cases, should provide a sound basis for avoiding many common errors in judgment.

1. Think before you act.
2. Never ask a student to perform any unreasonably dangerous task.
3. Be sure that you are well trained in the most current first-aid procedures.
4. Establish a list of written procedures to be followed in all accident cases and have emergency numbers handy.
5. While certain risks are often necessary in the interests of good teaching, be sure that any such risks are well thought out and any dangers to students have been minimized.
6. Never run a relay race or any other type of race to a wall or any other object that could cause injury.
7. Never hold running activities on an uneven or slippery surface.
8. Allow ample stopping space after finish lines.
9. Be sure the activities which you choose for your class are within the scope of the curriculum guide. It would be very difficult to explain why a child was injured in an activity which was not approved by the local board of education.
10. Take whatever steps may be necessary to avoid mismatch situations in activities where physical contact is likely. Students should be matched according to size and ability. Sex, in and of itself, is not a reasonable basis for matching students. In other words, a 100-pound boy attempting to block a 150-pound boy is no more or less mismatched than a 100-pound girl attempting to block a 150-pound boy. The importance of this factor is tempered considerably in interscholastic sports, due to the selectivity of the groups involved.

22. Brooks v. Board of Education of City of New York, 205 NYS 2d. 777, (1070).

23. Mogabgab v. Orleans Parish School Board, 239 S 2d. 456, (1970).

24. Russell v. Morehouse College, op. cit., p. 180.

There is little doubt that the field of physical education and athletics is fraught with a wide variety of risks and that we, as professionals, are more susceptible than any of our fellow teachers to legal action as a result of pupil injury. We cannot, however, accept dangerous situations, and the injuries which almost certainly accompany them, as inevitable. Certainly we must take risks. Of course it is impossible to avoid all potentially dangerous situations. We must, however, be prepared to accept full moral and legal responsibility for the welfare of those pupils charged to our care. Those risks which we do take must be carefully calculated to minimize the possibility of injury, and must be well justified on educational grounds. Such action will greatly reduce the likelihood of injury, and will effectively reduce the threat of legal action as a result of injuries that do occur.

REFERENCES

Appenzeller, Herb, *From the Gym to the Jury* (Charlottesville, VA: The Michie Co., 1970).

Bolmeier, E. C., *Legal Issues in Education*, abridged ed. (Charlottesville, VA: The Michie Co., 1970).

Hazard Analysis: Playground Equipment (Washington, D.C.: U.S. Consumer Product Safety Commission, Bureau of Epidemiology, April 1975).

Van Der Smissen, Betty, *Legal Liability of Cities and Schools for Injuries in Recreation and Parks* (Cincinnati: The W. H. Anderson Co., 1968).

chapter eleven
Classroom Management

A lesson plan can be divided into two operational components. The first, or instructional component, represents any strategy or activity which the teacher uses during the course of the lesson to achieve a predetermined goal. It is the core or the *content* component of the lesson (see chapter 7). The second, or managerial component, represents any mechanical aspect of the lesson which allows the teacher to make organizational changes or complete supervisory tasks. It is the support component of the lesson. A lesson plan that is devoid of or underdeveloped in either of these operational components, will prove useless and, in many cases, disastrous. However, many professionals, when planning lessons, concentrate their greatest efforts on selecting the strategies and devising the activities which they will use to create a positive learning environment, but completely neglect to provide for the mechanical details of the lesson. What they fail to realize is that a carefully chosen, well-thought-out set of activities, when finally presented to the class, can turn out to be a meaningless collection of isolated experiences if the teacher has not thought out smooth, efficient transitions from one activity in the sequence to the next. They also fail to realize that without well-thought-out traffic patterns, efficient equipment changes, or a multitude of other mechanical details, a lesson can be doomed to failure from the onset regardless of the quality and quantity of preparation done for the instructional phase.

In an area such as physical education, where lessons are supersaturated with movement of all kinds, a teacher must understand the importance of managerial procedures in relationship to instructional techniques. He or she must be able to carefully weave both components into the lesson plan such that the instructional phase of the actual lesson is complemented and supported in an unobtrusive manner by the managerial phase. A delicate balance of the two will increase the probability of presenting a successful lesson.

UNDERSTANDING THE ELEMENTS OF THE MANAGERIAL PHASE

The managerial phase of the lesson refers to all the mechanical operations that occur from the time a teacher arrives at school in the morning until he or she completes the last instructional responsibility of the afternoon or evening. This phase includes routine record-keeping such as roll call; organizational patterns such as squad formations; signaling techniques such as those used to begin or end an activity; procedures for assembly, dismissal, and emergencies; techniques for giving directions; and various other mechanical operations, such as distributing and collecting equipment.

Simply put, managerial procedures are the nuts and bolts of the lesson. When executed efficiently, they facilitate instruction and occur rather unobtrusively. When executed poorly, they can noticeably interrupt the flow and rhythm of the lesson, which contributes to classroom boredom, a number of discipline problems, and a rapid decline in class morale. In some cases, poor management can even serve to increase the number of safety hazards in the gymnasium.

If the managerial phase is to complement and support the instructional phase rather than conflict or compete with it, the teacher must learn to select appropriate procedures, foresee any inherent problems that may arise, establish an atmosphere for effective management, and, most importantly, be capable of executing the chosen procedures expeditiously.

SELECTING THE APPROPRIATE PROCEDURE

There are usually several available procedures by means of which a teacher can accomplish any managerial task encountered during the course of the lesson. The selection of the appropriate one for a given situation can be a simple matter if the circumstances which influence the conduct of a specific class are considered. Such consideration should focus on the following areas and raise the following questions:

The Students — Are the students self-motivated? Are they well disciplined? Do they have a positive attitude toward the activity? Do they relate well to each other and the teacher? Are they mature? Do they see an activity through to completion? How well do they follow instructions? What is their previous background?

The Situation — What are the circumstances under which a teacher must operate in relation to location, position, and time? Where is the activity being held? How long is the class? How large is the class? What stage of the unit has the class reached? How much equipment is available? What are the goals for the class? How long is the unit? What teaching style will be employed during the lesson?

The Delimiting Factors — What constraints are applied to each class? What boundaries must the teacher operate within? What school policies must be enforced in class? What departmental policies must be followed? What class policies have been established by teachers and students?

The Teacher — Who is the teacher? What kind of a personality does the teacher have? What teaching style does the teacher employ regularly? How positive is the teacher's rapport with the students? How long has the teacher worked with the students? How skillful is the teacher in assessing a situation? What is the likelihood of the teacher being able to gain control of a situation immediately?

By asking these and other similar questions, the teacher will gain an in-depth picture of the probable learning environment. Once this understanding is gained, the teacher is in a better position to select or devise a managerial procedure and evaluate its probable success. The answers to these questions will also help the teacher pinpoint potential managerial problems long before they can materialize.

This analytical process of procedure selection may occur each time the teacher develops a lesson plan, or it may occur only once over a specified span of time. For example, the teacher may choose to adopt, for purposes of expediency, one specific signal for beginning a class that will be used throughout the year. In this case, the teacher may select several alternatives via the analytical method and elect to experiment with all of them before arriving at a final decision. Once the decision is made, the analytical process then becomes a tool for the continuing evaluation of the managerial procedure. Selecting the appropriate activity is a paper-and-pencil exercise. Its effectiveness, however, depends upon the ability of the teacher to successfully execute his or her plans.

ESTABLISHING AN ATMOSPHERE FOR EFFECTIVE MANAGEMENT

Managing a classroom, especially one as large and lively as a gymnasium, can become a cumbersome task unless the atmosphere is flexible and responsive to change. Too militaristic an atmosphere will limit, if not completely eliminate the number of student self-management procedures which the teacher can employ to minimize managerial time and increase instructional time. At the same time, a laissez-faire atmosphere is not conducive to the routinization of certain procedures which are necessary if one is to expedite many supervisory chores. The perfect atmosphere is one in which the teacher is free to proceed in either direction or to allow both situations to occur simultaneously. It should be one that is carefully designed and administered by the teacher.

Establishing an atmosphere for effective management must begin on the first day of class. Students should be informed of the routines which will be employed daily and helped to understand the necessity of complying with them. Routines such as entering the locker room, obtaining an excuse, using equipment before class, assembling for roll call, or calling roll should be established during the first class period and enforced during the second class period. If necessary, signs should be posted reminding students of procedures which are extremely important, such as those which are used for emergency situations, or those which are frequently performed incorrectly. Remember, if the routine is worth instituting, it is worth the effort to properly enforce it. This means that the teacher should not only continually employ the routine but should do so with little deviation so that confusion can be avoided.

During the first class, the teacher should also begin laying the foundation for what might eventually become total student self-management. Wherever possible, the teacher should engage students in activities that permit them to experiment with various degrees of self-management. In certain situations, the teacher may even decide that the ultimate objective of the entire lesson should be to help the students develop self-management skills. In such a situation, all of the activities are constructed for the sole purpose of giving the students more and more responsibility for their own actions. Activities which require a student to follow a long list of instructions, complete a task in a specified manner, or meet at a designated location at a precise time are typical of the exercises employed in such a lesson. Lessons in self-management usually take place early in a semester in preparation for later work. In the case of young children, the teacher may conduct such lessons frequently throughout the year.

Because self-management activities are meant to assess the degree to which a student can assume responsibility for his or her own actions, as well as to give the student practice in conducting his or her own affairs, there should be an evaluation at the end of each session. In this way, the teacher can reward and reinforce positive behavior by publicly recognizing it and can emphasize the type of behavior which he or she values and considers appropriate.

If the teacher is successful in establishing an atmosphere where routinization of certain procedures and self-management of others can take place simultaneously, he or she will discover that very little time is wasted on managerial matters and that a greater amount of time is available for individual instruction. However, this type of an atmosphere can only be maintained by a skillful classroom manager.

THE SKILLFUL CLASSROOM MANAGER

The skillful classroom manager is one who can control and use time, space, and classroom climate to the best advantage. He or she is an individual who has the ability to:

1. Assess the potential of a given situation
2. Plan several plausible alternative procedures for any occasion
3. Decide on one best solution for the situation at hand
4. Execute any procedure smoothly and efficiently regardless of the circumstances
5. Gain control of any situation immediately
6. Assess a developing situation and quickly redesign a given plan if necessary

The skillful manager typically is adaptable, resourceful, logical, and confident. He or she is a master of both mechanical techniques and motivational devices, a person who is concerned with detail but not encumbered by it. In essence, the skillful manager is one who can bring order to any situation by putting everything to the best possible use.

Pre-planning is responsible, no doubt, for a great deal of a manager's success, but without a large repertoire of procedures to choose from, a manager's chances for repeated success in varied situations are probably diminished. For this reason, procedures should never be discarded, whatever their source. They should be collected and stored, without value judgments, because what may be unsuitable today may prove to be quite useful tomorrow.

LESSON MANAGEMENT PROCEDURES

On the following pages are several general headings which describe managerial episodes which take place regularly during the course of a lesson. Under each heading several alternatives have been listed to illustrate the various procedures which can be used to satisfy a given situation. In most cases the first listing is an illustration of the routinized form of a procedure while the last listing illustrates a self-management technique or one that allows greater latitude of movement for the student. While the teacher may prefer or agree with only one of the methods given, it should be remembered that all are correct. The degree of their usefulness or correctness is dependent upon the situation with which the teacher must deal.

Roll Call

Taking roll at the beginning of class is a standard procedure in most schools. This is usually accomplished by one of several methods. The determining factors for selection of the appropriate method are class size, class maturity, and the time period allotted for such a task. The teacher should try to select the method which appears most organized and proves most expedient. This is extremely important because roll call, being the first activity of the lesson, usually serves to set the tenor or tone of the lesson. If the procedure selected is tediously prolonged or terribly unorganized, the students will most often respond with some type of behavior that is counterproductive and unfavorable, usually in the form of boredom or alienation.

Counting Off by Numbers

Each student is assigned a specific number which he or she maintains throughout the year. This number indicates the position they will take at roll call and also the position of their name in the teacher's roll book. For example, if John Adams were number 1 in the teacher's roll book, he would also be number 1 in roll call line. When class begins the students either fall into a long line, shoulder to shoulder, facing the teacher, or form short files and commence counting upon the teacher's signal. If the count stops or a number is missed, the teacher places a mark next to the number (hence the student's name) and signals for the count to continue. This is a very militaristic form of taking attendance. Although it is somewhat impersonal, it can be accomplished quite rapidly after some practice.

Spot Formation

The student is assigned a specific spot on the gymnasium floor which corresponds to a seating chart that the teacher has prepared with the students' names. When class begins, the students sit in their assigned spot and the teacher scans the area for vacant positions. Finding a vacant position, the teacher records the date directly on the chart. At a later time the information can be transferred to the roll book.

Squad Formation

This method is similar to spot formation. Students are still assigned spots but the resultant files or rows are called squads. Each squad is assigned a squad leader, who may also be the captain of that particular squad when it forms a team. It is the responsibility of the squad leaders to record the absence of anyone in their respective squad. This method of roll call is probably most often used because it gives the teacher predetermined standard-size groups which can be used throughout the lesson for drills or team play.

Card Pick-Up

Using this method, the teacher never really has to formally take attendance. On the first day of class, each student is given an index card to which a safety pin has been attached. The students are instructed to first write their names on the card and then attach this card to their shirt. After class, the cards are collected. For each class thereafter, the teacher places the cards in an accessible position and, before the official signal to begin class, it becomes each student's responsibility to find his or her card and put it on. Any card left unclaimed at the beginning of class has the date marked on the back. In this way the teacher has an accurate account on each card of the student's absences. This can also be employed as a method for learning names.

Check In

The teacher waits at the locker room door and takes attendance as the students enter the locker room. (If the class is coed, the teacher stands at a particular gymnasium entrance instead.) In order for this method to be successful, the students must be given a specific time by which they must enter the gymnasium or locker room.

Sign In

A sign-in sheet is tacked to the door of the locker room or gymnasium. As the students enter, they write their name and the time of their arrival. This list is later checked by the teacher for absences or tardiness.

Hand In

This method is the least formal of all those listed and is usually not considered by the students to be a method for taking attendance. However, this method is very effective and allows the teacher to begin instructional activity at the earliest possible moment. The procedure is very simple. During the course of the class, the students are given a worksheet, opinionnaire, or test which must be handed in before the end of class. The score for the assignment is the attendance record as well.

Distributing and Collecting Equipment

Distributing and collecting equipment can be two of the most unwieldy tasks in classroom management. Activities in which each child is issued a piece of equipment can prove especially difficult if the teacher has not formulated an appropriate method for distributing a large number of items quickly. Badminton rackets can become lethal weapons if twenty students, who have already been issued the rackets, are waiting for the teacher to distribute ten more. Likewise, playground balls given to an entire class during a movement lesson can prove to be a serious distraction if the teacher decides to give instruction *after* issuing the balls.

Of equal difficulty are problems incurred when collecting equipment. Physical educators, in their zeal to use every moment possible for activity, sometimes conduct their class until the last possible minute. Once pressed for time, they dismiss their class in haste making no satisfactory arrangement for collecting equipment. They are then left with equipment heaped in a corner or worse yet, strewn across the room. The wasted time and effort which results could have been avoided easily if a proper collection plan had been adopted. Regardless of the method selected to accomplish either of these tasks, the teacher can avert a number of problems by observing the following simple rules:

1. Always check equipment before class.
2. Be sure all pieces are in good working order.
3. Check to see if there are sufficient pieces available for the activity.
4. Be sure that the equipment chosen is appropriate for both the location and the skill level of the students.
5. Place equipment in portable storage containers before class.
6. Place storage containers in a location which can be reached easily during the lesson.

Preparing before class in this manner can help minimize a number of problems which might otherwise occur.

The following methods illustrate procedures for distribution and collection using the same format. For specific classroom settings, the teacher may find it more convenient to vary both methods; that is, distribute equipment using one method and collect it using an entirely different method. Whatever the case the shortcomings for each procedure should be analyzed and corrected on paper long before the procedure is used in the gymnasium.

Singly

Each child lines up behind the storage unit, and the teacher or equipment monitor distributes an article to each individual. Collection is accomplished in the same manner. The major drawback with this method is the length of time it takes to distribute and collect with large groups.

Singly by Number

This method is similar to the first method described except that each individual in the class is assigned a number which corresponds to a numbered piece of equipment. It is each individual's responsibility to obtain his or her own equipment before activity commences and to return it to its proper place when the activity ends. This method provides the teacher with an instant and accurate record of not only who returned their equipment but the condition in which they returned it. This usually is a very satisfactory method for minimizing equipment damage and loss. When using this method, the teacher must be sure that the equipment is readily available and that the students have ample time to obtain and return their equipment.

By Group

First, a leader is chosen for each group. Then at the appropriate time during the lesson, the group leader obtains and distributes equipment to each group member. If a large variety of equipment is required by the group, the teacher should try to pack all the items in a canvas bag. This will insure that each group receives the proper amount of equipment. It will also greatly minimize the confusion which can accompany such an arrangement. Collection is accomplished in the same manner.

By Signal or Arrangement

The teacher may want to experiment with this method as an alternative to stopping the class to distribute or collect equipment. While an activity is in progress, the teacher places a large box of equipment in the middle of the floor or in some other location that is easily accessible to each student. Before the activity ends, the teacher asks each student to go to the box and choose a piece of equipment. This is done without a break in the on-going activity. When the entire class has obtained a piece of equipment, the teacher ends the initial activity and begins the activity for which the equipment was distributed. For collection, the same process is used, but in reverse.

This procedure works well with elementary school classes. For example, during a movement lesson on exploring space the teacher may ask the children to move through space at varying speeds. While the children are experimenting, the teacher places a large box of balls in the middle of the floor. While the children are moving around the room the teacher asks them to pass by the box when no one else is near it, select a ball, and continue with the movement task assigned. When each child has obtained a ball, the teacher stops the activity and begins the new activity of exploring space with balls. The same procedure is used to return the balls.

Formations

A good classroom manager must possess many skills, but in the gymnasium one of the most important skills of all is the ability to organize a group into desired formations. Because of the nature of physical education activity, it would be literally impossible to conduct a successful lesson without being able to move a group from one formation to another. The following rules should be observed during formation management:

1. Always use painted lines and circles as guidelines, when available.
2. When painted lines and circles are not available, use markers, chalk, white shoe polish, or masking tape for guidelines.

3. Try not to go from one formation to another and back again (i.e., from a circle to a line and back to a circle). Plan the lesson so that all circle activities are accomplished before you go on to the next formation.
4. If guidelines are unavailable, have the students first construct the formation in miniature and then have them enlarge it by moving back several steps.
5. When a formation is being organized, avoid having students hold hands. This tactic usually results in a pulling-and-pushing match.
6. Be sure instructions for the formation are given explicitly before students attempt to construct the formation. Give them the exact location (e.g., facing the outside wall) and size (e.g., so that everyone is shoulder to shoulder). This will help minimize confusion.

Making Geometric Figures

Methods for making any geometric figure are basically alike. The only difference is that some figures require more explicit instructions or elaborate guidelines. Here are several ways to construct simple geometric figures:

Using Lines as Guidelines. Geometric figures can be formed by having the students assemble, at regular intervals, on existing lines on the gym floor or playground.

Follow the Leader. If lines are not available, the teacher might try playing "Follow the Leader." The students are instructed to fall in behind the teacher in single file. The teacher then leads the entire class, each student following in order, into the proper formation. When the teacher completes the figure by catching up to the last person, he or she signals the class to stop. Spacing becomes something of a problem in this maneuver, but generally it works well with young students.

Using Points or Markers. The teacher locates several strategic points in a figure, such as the four points of a square. He or she then marks the points with flags, cones, or any other type of distinctive markers. The students are then told which type of figure they are making and are instructed to fill in the appropriate spaces between the markers. Care must be taken to designate the number of students preferred between each marker or overcrowding is sure to occur. This method is best suited for constructing figures with straight lines, such as squares or triangles.

Using a Signal. This method requires a training period but is well worth the time and effort when working with young students. The training period actually entails playing several variations of an organizational game during the first few class periods. The game is started simply by having the children form a circle in the middle of the gymnasium. They are then instructed to leave the circle and to get as far away as they can and get back to the circle before the teacher counts to ten. When this is accomplished easily, the teacher moves to the next step. Using the same procedure, he or she asks the children to construct other formations. From here the teacher asks the children to move at random around the gymnasium. At irregular intervals he or she will shout a formation, a location, and begin to count to ten. If the children have learned their lesson well, they will respond with the proper formation, in the proper location before the count of ten.

By Posting. (See "By Posting" under the next general heading, "Groups.")

Groups

Learning how to divide children into groups or teams is essential. The teacher who insists upon choosing captains and picking teams down to the last person for each class period not only wastes time, but also exposes some child to the ridicule of being chosen last each day. This is an unjustifiable practice and can easily be avoided. Many teachers choose squads or teams only once during a unit. They then use these fixed groups throughout all lessons during practice drills and team play. While this is very convenient, it can become somewhat boring for the student. Occasionally the teacher should vary the groupings during the period and experiment with a little different social interaction. The following suggested methods cover the gamut from the tried-and-true count off, to division by color. Each is much more appropriate and humanistic than the approach first mentioned.

Count Off

The teacher has the students form a long line, standing shoulder to shoulder. The students are then instructed to count off by the number of teams desired. If four teams are needed, for example, the teacher would ask the students to count off by fours. To be sure that each individual reports to the appropriate team, the teacher should ask the students with a given number to step forward and away from the group several steps. When the teacher is satisfied with the count, he or she then directs the teams to their position for the next activity.

By Markers or Leaders

Leaders are appointed by the teacher and placed in designated positions in the gym or field. The remaining students are instructed to stand behind the leader of their choice as long as they do not exceed the number chosen by the teacher as maximum group capacity. When this number has been reached in a line, that line is considered closed, and the students in the line are instructed to sit down and wait for directions. Markers may be used in lieu of student leaders.

Elected Captains

Captains are elected or appointed in each class. The teacher then meets with the captains as a group, after school or at some time other than during class, to choose teams. After team selections, the teacher alphabetizes the names on each team roster and posts them before the next class. Students find their names on the roster at the start of class, and from that point on they will assemble in those groups for drills and games.

By Signal

Assembly by signal is an organizational game which children love. It is also a decoding game and therefore it is even more valuable in the primary grades. The primary objective of the game is to listen for a handclap signal and to assemble in the specified group size as quickly as possible. The following code is a very simple one that could be used the first day of class:

One clap = group of one
Two claps = group of two
Three claps = group of three
Four claps = group of four

As time progresses and students become more adept at the game, the signals are made increasingly more difficult. For example:

One whistle = group of one
One handclap = group of two
One footstomp = group of three
One finger-snap = group of four

When the students become proficient at forming groups at random in this manner, the teacher can standardize the code and use it throughout the year. Then, if a certain size group is desired quickly, all the teacher needs to do is clap his or her hands. This is an especially effective method for getting many different personality groupings because the students never know which grouping is the one the teacher will finally decide upon, nor do they care. Their main objective is to get in a group as quickly as possible. Besides numerical grouping, this game can also be used effectively for organizing geometrical patterns.

Using Color, Shape, or Number

Students are given worksheets or paper cutouts when they begin class. These worksheets or cutouts have been coded by the teacher to give each student as many as three designations. For example, one student may have been given an orange triangle with a 3 printed on it, while another student may be given an orange square with a 2 on it. If the teacher wishes to form groups by color, these two students would be on the same team, but if the teacher wished to form groups by shape or number they would be in different groups.

This can be a very useful tool for forming different size groups. If two large groups, four medium groups, and eight small groups are needed during the course of the period, the teacher can use two colors, four separate shapes, and eight different number designations to solve the problem of different size groupings. It takes some thought and work prior to class, but the results are often worth the effort.

By Posting

(This method can also be used to form geometric figures.) The student assumes responsibility for finding and remembering the groupings and locations for the first and perhaps even the second activity. The students receive this information from a sign which has been posted on a bulletin board in the gymnasium before class. A simple sign, like the one shown in Figure 11.1, would look like a map giving the location and formation for the first activity or a set of activities.

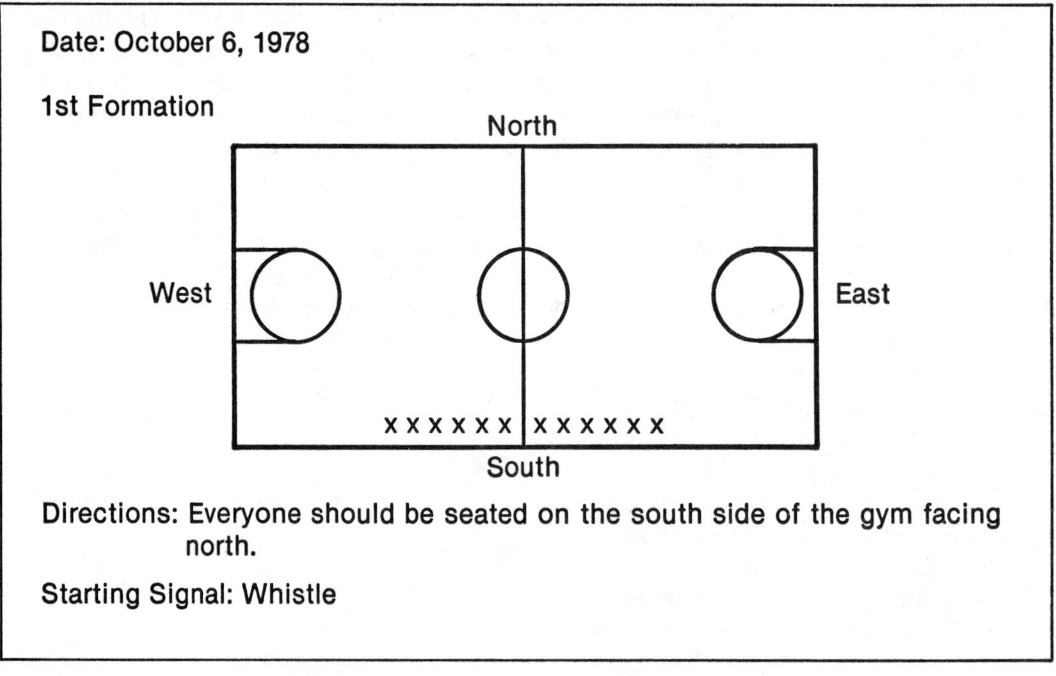

FIGURE 11.1. Simple Formation Sign.

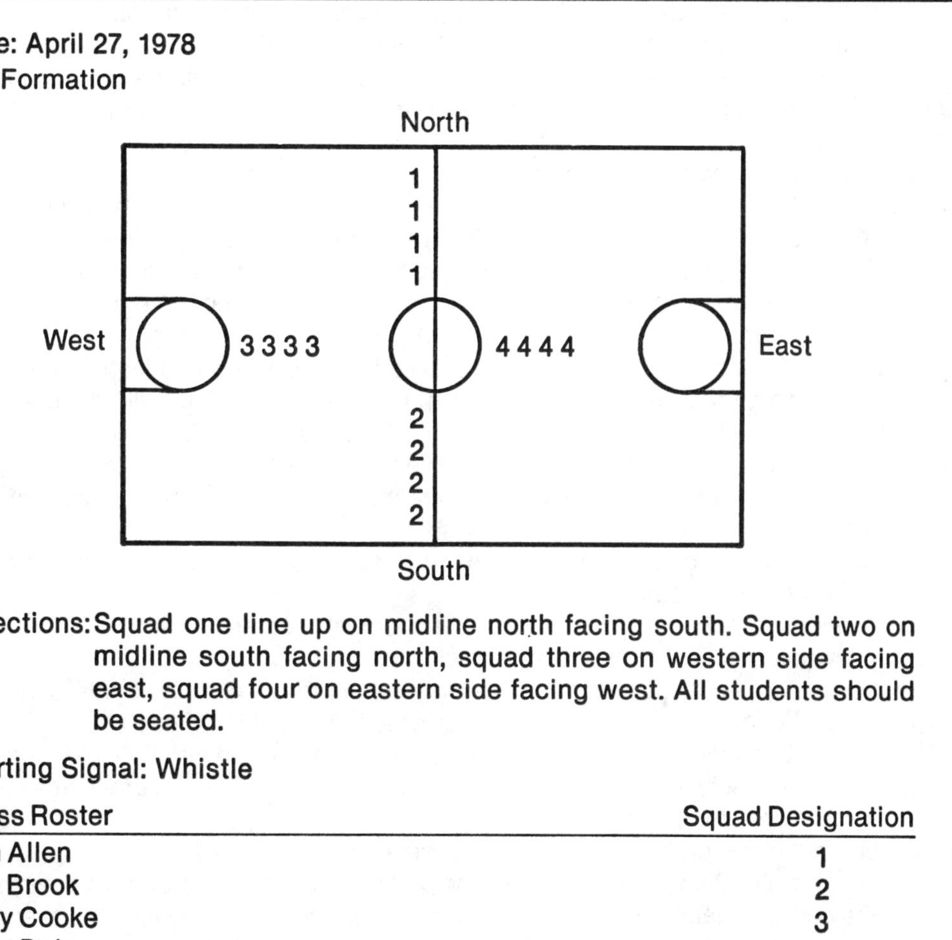

Date: April 27, 1978
1st Formation

Directions: Squad one line up on midline north facing south. Squad two on midline south facing north, squad three on western side facing east, squad four on eastern side facing west. All students should be seated.

Starting Signal: Whistle

Class Roster	Squad Designation
Dan Allen	1
Sue Brook	2
Mary Cooke	3
John Dole	4

FIGURE 11.2. More Complex Formation Sign.

If the students are very responsible and are quite capable of following explicit directions, a sign such as the one shown in Figure 11.2 may be posted.

Directions and Signals

Giving directions and using signals are two mechanical operations which can be easily learned and used to any teacher's advantage. Giving directions clearly, concisely, and succinctly is crucial. Failure to do so can result in complete confusion. When giving directions verbally, the teacher must be sure that:

1. *Everyone is listening.* Quiet is an absolute must. Those who are talking not only create a disturbance for others, their behavior necessitates repeating the instructions to avoid confusion.
2. *Instructions are given directly to the group.* Just as the teacher should have the absolute attention of the group, so should the group have the absolute attention of the

teacher. The teacher should not engage in a distracting activity, such as bouncing a ball or putting equipment away, while giving instructions.

3. *Instructions are given precisely.* Instructions should include the following information in short, concise sentences: a description of the signal for movement, location, duration, and a description of the activity as well as any other pertinent information.
4. *Time is allowed for questions.* At certain times, information is inadvertently missed by students or never mentioned by the teacher. Time should be allowed to correct either of these situations by allowing the students to ask questions.
5. *Instructions are repeated.* To insure the likelihood of the instructions being carried out completely, the teacher should repeat the instructions directly before moving the students.

Long-winded and rambling instructions should be condensed into instructions such as these: "Boys and girls, when I ask you to, I would like you to stand, walk to the equipment box, get a ball, and without bouncing it, walk back to your place and sit down quietly so that I know you are ready to begin. Any questions? Then stand, get a ball, walk to your place, and sit down." Directions of this nature force the teacher to think through the details of a given situation in an effort to be precise but concise.

Instructions may also be given in written form. Many instructors prefer working with written instruction sheets because they:

1. Allow the teacher to cover material in a logical progression.
2. Allow the students to progress at their own pace.
3. Eliminate time lag. Class can begin as soon as the first student enters the room.
4. Allow the teacher more freedom to provide individual instruction.
5. Eliminate many questions from the students in regard to what should be done.
6. Allow the teacher to engage large numbers of students in small group activities with a minimum of verbal direction.
7. Give students practice in following directions.
8. Graphically indicate to the student the points which the teacher feels are important.
9. Provide the means of diversifying activities within a given class. The teacher can elect to give instruction on several different sports during one class or to conduct one activity on many levels simultaneously.

Figure 11.3 is an example of an instruction sheet that takes attendance, conducts warm-ups, provides practice in ball-handling, and provides the location, formation, groupings, and signal for the first activity.

FIGURE 11.3. Sample Instruction Sheet.

Good morning boys and girls. Would you please find a space in the gym where you can read this paper. Please be sure you read the entire paper through at least once before beginning step 1.

STEP 1:

Look at the bottom of your paper. You should see a box with a colored x in it. This is your group color.

STEP 2:

On the folding door are four sheets of colored paper. Sign your name on the paper which is the same color as your color group.

FIGURE 11.3. Sample Instruction Sheet (cont'd).

STEP 3:

On the floor are four colored x's. Find the x which is the same color as the x at the bottom of your sheet. Move to the area around the x and do:

10 toe touches
20 sit-ups
10 long jumps

STEP 4:

Find a partner who is in the same color group that you are in. Run two laps around the gym in a counterclockwise direction with your partner. Be sure not to go inside the black line.

STEP 5:

Stay with your partner. One of you should go to the box near the blackboard and get a red ball. The two of you should go to the east side of the gym and practice the bounce pass and chest pass until the whistle blows. Be sure that you and your partner, for safety reasons, stand and throw in the same direction as the diagram shows.

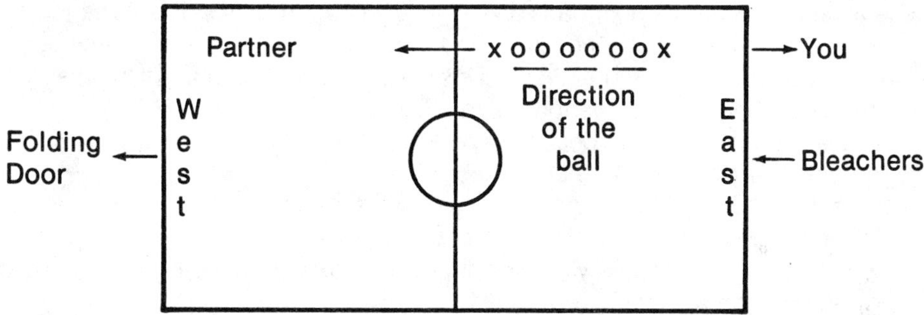

STEP 6:

When the whistle blows, return the red ball to the box and go quietly to the folding door and sit in a line in front of your colored sheet facing the bleachers.

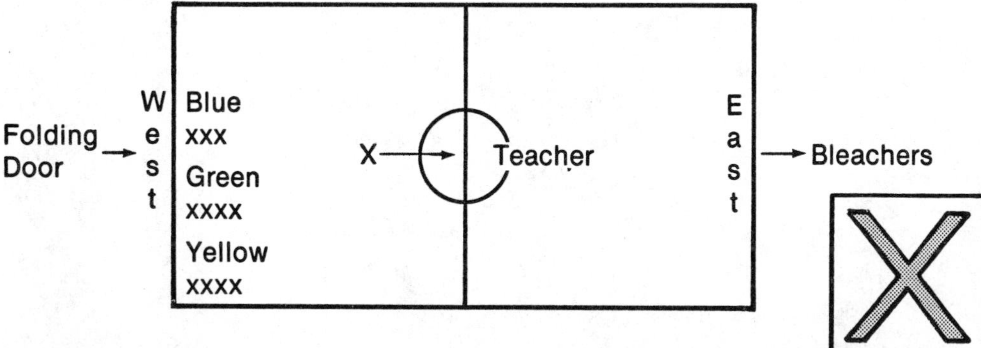

This instruction sheet was designed for elementary school students. When designing such a sheet, the teacher must be sure to use words which the students can read and understand. Instruction sheets used at a higher level can be much more elaborate, but care should still be taken to use simple language. Instruction sheets are not meant to take the place of the teacher, they are meant to act as an aid and should always be used in that manner.

Learning to give signals to which children respond immediately is imperative, especially in the case of an emergency or a situation involving safety. These signals and the appropriate student response should be established the first day of class and adhered to implicitly. Many potential accidents may be averted if the teacher can gain control immediately by simply giving a signal. Any signal is appropriate. Teachers can use a sharp blast on a whistle, a handclap, a raised hand for silence, or just their voice. The important thing is for the student to learn how to look or listen for the signal and to respond immediately by spontaneously turning in the direction of the signal, kneeling down, and becoming absolutely quiet. Teachers who use this type of crowd control need not worry about a situation getting out of hand; this method will stop any situation before it develops into a hazard.

When giving signals, teachers must be sure that they can be seen and/or heard by every student in the class. Signaling from a less desirable position means that the signal will lose some of its impact and effect. Furthermore, if an audible signal is being used, care should be taken to find a position from which the sound can be given without hurting a student's ears.

These illustrations are by no means the only possible forms of class management, they are merely a sampling; as experience is gained and as new situations arise, the teacher will devise and/or acquire many more techniques. The following important points should be remembered regarding management techniques:

1. They are an important aspect of good teaching.
2. They require detailed forethought.
3. A teacher should try to acquire a large repertoire.
4. No technique should ever be discarded.
5. Skill in managing comes with experience, but experience can and should be supported by good planning.

chapter twelve

Public Relations: A Professional Responsibility

If the state laws requiring physical education in the schools were repealed tomorrow or if economic conditions dictated drastic reductions in school spending, how would the physical education department in your local high school fare? Would the people in your community consider a structured program of physical activity vital to their children's welfare and continue their financial support, or would they consider it an extravagance that could be eliminated from the general curriculum with little consequence?

The answers to such questions depend primarily on the image your physical education department has projected to the community. If the image has been a positive one, it is most likely that the community will understand and endorse the physical education program and so continue their support in the face of a crisis. The opposite can be expected, however, if a negative image has been projected. Regardless of its intrinsic worth, an institution cannot exist in a democracy without the consent of the people, and that consent, more often than not, is based on public opinion.

This being the case, an institution, such as physical education, can assume one of the two following positions in regard to public opinion:

> It can remain passive and simply adjust to conditions it may not like but has to accept. . . . Or it can see in its true dimension the opportunity to utilize its expertise and its resources to help to shape the conditions that will determine its course.[1]

In today's marketplace, choosing the first alternative is not only risky but foolish. "In this age of cost consciousness and accountability, we can no longer expect tradition alone to protect our programs and our professions,"[2] we must do it ourselves. We must learn to effectively communicate in a positive manner with the public about who we are, what we are doing, and why, if we are to assume our continued existence.

While this is a relatively new posture in American education, it is one which cannot be taken lightly or ignored. It must be accepted as a professional responsibility equal to that of providing a thorough and efficient education for all children. Educators must realize that the

1. George Hammond, "Public Opinion: Do We Understand Its Function?" *Public Relations Journal* 32, no. 7 (July 1976): p. 9.

2. "*Speak Out,*" JOHPER 43, no. 8 (October 1972): p. 42.

only efficient and effective means of providing relevancy in education is to communicate and work with the public. A school which provides all the elements for a sound education but is not understood by the public, will be condemned as quickly as a school that blatantly ignores the needs of the learner. Learning to communicate is not a matter of choice but of necessity.

COMMUNICATING WITH THE PUBLIC: A RATIONALE

In 1969, the Charles F. Kettering Foundation financed the first of the annual Gallup Polls concerning public attitudes toward education. These surveys were directed "chiefly toward appraising the state of public knowledge and ascertaining public attitudes toward present practices, readiness to accept new programs, and ideas for meeting educational costs."[3] The data collected in the very first survey gave credence to the idea that "progress is only possible when the people are properly informed and when they are ready, through their tax dollars, to bear the cost of progress."[4] Information gleaned from these surveys has served as the basis for many of the decisions made by the educational community since the early seventies. The profession-wide resolution to communicate with the public was one such decision.

In his final remarks, Dr. Gallup made the following observations and conclusions which support the idea of strong community/school relations.

> Three of the major tasks of the public school systems in the United States can be stated as follows: first to interest a greater number of citizens in the public schools; second, to increase financial support as needs grow; third, to create a climate in the community and in the schools favorable to an improvement in the quality of education.
>
> In a sense, and as the data from this survey show, all of these problems tend to be interrelated. When the survey results dealing with the many aspects of education embraced in this survey are examined, these conclusions seem warranted.
>
> 1. While the American people seem reasonably well-informed about school activities, they are ill-informed about education itself.
>
> 2. Since they have little or no basis for judging the quality of education in their local schools, pressures are obviously absent for improving the quality.
>
> 3. Fortunately, the public would like more information about modern education — the new methods being tried and new ideas about the kind of education that is needed. In short, they need and ask for the kind of information that is presently not provided by the various media of communication. . . .
>
> 10. The public schools do a reasonably good job of interesting parents in school affairs. They do a very poor job in reaching those who do not have children attending the schools. A better way must be found to reach those persons in the community who do not happen to have children in the public schools, so that these persons

3. Stanley Elam, ed., *The Gallup Polls of Attitudes Toward Education, 1969-1973* (Bloomingfield, IN: Phi Delta Kappa, Inc., 1973), p. 1.

4. Ibid.

may become informed, involved, and active. The future of the schools to a great extent depends on success in achieving this goal.[5]

This position was reaffirmed in 1973, in the Fifth Annual Poll, when Dr. Gallup wrote:

> Included in the present survey was one of the most revealing questions asked in this series of annual surveys: In recent years has your overall attitude toward the "public" schools in your community become more favorable or less favorable?
>
> Replies to this question, and analysis of the reasons why respondents feel more favorably or less favorably toward the schools, reveal a basic fact: The more respondents know at first hand about the public schools, the more favorable are their views; the less interested and less well informed, the less favorable. Most important is the fact that persons who depend on the media for their information are most critical of the schools.[6]

From these findings two basic assumptions can be drawn: 1) it can be assumed, with reasonable certainty, that a physical education department which keeps the public continually informed about what it is doing and why is more likely to be held in high public esteem than a department which builds a wall of secrecy around itself or releases only superficial information, and 2) it can be assumed that a department which takes the time to personally interpret its actions to the public through some form of personal contact (i.e., speeches or one-on-one discussions) will fall under far less attack than the department which relies on the news media to interpret its actions. While these assumptions may prove to be true, questions still remain: Where does one begin? How does a department mobilize and initiate a school/community relations program? What can you do? Where can you go?

A NATIONAL ORGANIZATION LENDS SUPPORT

The American Alliance of Health, Physical Education, and Recreation acknowledged both the necessity for communicating with the public at the local level and the problems faced by the local physical educator, such as where to start and what to do, when they launched the Physical Education Public Information Project (PEPI), which was described as "a grand design of responsibilities for profession-wide PR."[7] The project, which aimed at promoting physical education at the grassroots level, provided the necessary guidance and succeeded in making many professionals aware of the endless possibilities available to them for communicating with the public about who they are and what they do. The public relations material displayed on the next few pages is a sample of the excellent work being distributed by the AAHPER through PEPI to enhance the image of physical education throughout the country. Ads such as these appear in countless magazines and newspapers each year in an effort to familiarize the public with what physical education is and what professional physical educators are doing to improve the health and well-being of everyone in the country. Catchy slogans such as "Move for the Health of It" have become a valuable method for making activity a watchword in American life.

5. Ibid., pp. 22-23.
6. Ibid., p. 154.
7. "Speak Out," *JOHPER* 43, no. 8 (October 1972): p. 45.

KEEP MOVING, AMERICA!

A Healthy Body and Longer Life Depend On It

Make a personal commitment to improve the quality of your life during National Physical Education and Sport Week March 1-7, 1978.

American Alliance for Health,
Physical Education and Recreation
1201-16th Street, NW
Washington, DC 20036
(202) 833-5554

AAHPER

OVER 40 DOESN'T MEAN OVER THE HILL

Neither does being 50, 60, or 70!

You're never too old to participate in sports and physical activities. In fact, a regular program of moderate physical activity can keep you feeling better, looking better, and living better no matter what your age.

You can golf, swim, jog, cycle, bowl, or play a dozen other lifetime sports. And now is the time to start.

Even if it's been a while since you last kicked up your heels, start a gradual fitness program with a check-up by your physician. So you can get back on the road to a more active, healthier life.

KEEP MOVING, AMERICA!

AAHPER

American Alliance for Health, Physical Education and Recreation
1201-16th Street, NW
Washington, DC 20036
(202) 833-5554

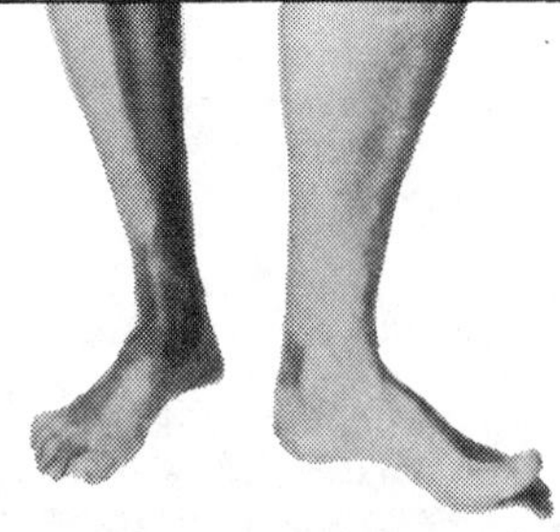

HEALTH AIDS

Use them regularly for tennis, biking, hiking, golf, jogging, swimming, or bowling. Enjoy a healthier body and a longer life.

KEEP MOVING, AMERICA!

American Alliance for Health, Physical Education and Recreation
1201-16th Street, NW
Washington, DC 20036
AAHPER (202) 833-5554

KEEP MOVING, AMERICA.

You're well on your way to a better life through physical activity. Get started on your new pair today.

American Alliance for Health, Physical Education and Recreation
1201-16th Street, NW
Washington, DC 20036
(202) 833-5554

LIFE CYCLE

Bicycling is just one of the many sports you can continue to enjoy throughout your life. And staying active can keep you feeling better . . . and living longer.

If you're not already participating in a lifetime sport, start today. Bowl, bike, hike, jog, or swim. Play tennis or golf. If you don't know how, learn how through your local department of recreation and leisure activities.

It's never too early and it's never too late.

KEEP MOVING, AMERICA!

AAHPER
American Alliance for Health, Physical Education and Recreation
1201-16th Street, NW
Washington, DC 20036
(202) 833-5554

LEARN BEFORE YOU LEAP

Knowing how to do it right makes participation in any sport safer and far more enjoyable.

Teaching individual sports skills is an important part of the *new physical education* in many schools. So children can grow into an active, healthy adulthood with less risk of injury; more self-esteem and greater confidence.

We think everyone should know how to swim. How to avoid stress and tension through sound physical activities. How to have a more rewarding existence by learning lifetime sports . . . starting right in elementary school.

Find out how good your school's physical education program is. Contact your local school board or a physical education counselor for more information.

You just may want to jump into the new physical education yourself!

KEEP MOVING, AMERICA!

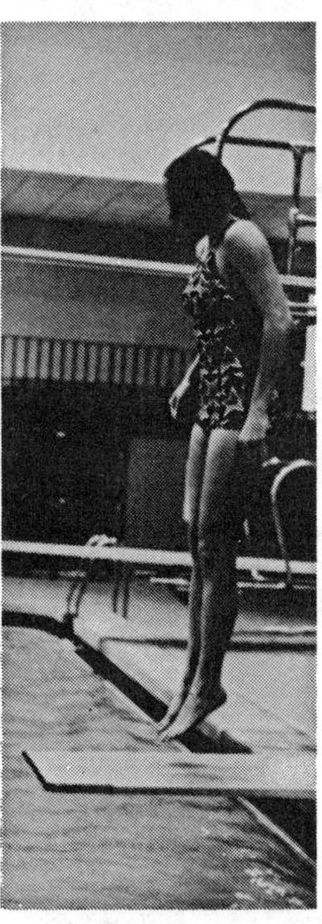

American Alliance for Health,
Physical Education and Recreation
1201-16th Street, NW/Washington, DC 20036
AAHPER (202) 833-5554

67-POUND WEAKLING

Every child needs a chance to develop good motor skills and muscle coordination through early movement education. It's the natural way to turn 67-pound weaklings into active, healthy adults.

Movement education is an important part of the *new physical education* being taught in many elementary schools around the country. But is it part of your child's curriculum?

If good physical activity skills aren't built into your child's education at an early age, he or she is being cheated out of a more fulfilling life . . . now and in the future. Learn how a good physical education program can help your child on the field and in the classroom, too. Contact your local school board or a physical education counselor for more information.

America's 67-pound weaklings deserve your support.

KEEP MOVING, AMERICA!

American Alliance for Health, Physical Education and Recreation
1201-16th Street, N.W.,
Washington, D.C. 20036
AAHPER (202) 833-5554

News Release

A Physical Education
Public Information (PEPI)
"Fill-in" for Immediate Release.

THE GAMES CHILDREN PLAY

(Washington, D. C.)---A report in Psychology Today a few years ago indicated that "Anglo-American children are not only irrationally competitive, they are almo st sadistically rivalrous."

A great many physical education specialists believe that contemporary games are partially responsible for the cooperation void which exists in the lives of many children and youth, so they are putting emphasis on games which give experience in cooperation.

It's all part of the"new physical education" according to ______ ______________________, local spokesperson for the American Alliance for Health, Physical Education, and Recreation.

"Most young children spend countless hours involved in play and games. A great deal of social learning occurs in the process. As educators, more and more we're trying to use these opportunities to teach valuable lessons about cooperation rather than only scoreboard winning.

(over)

American Alliance for Health, Physical Education and Recreation
1201-16th Street, NW/Washington, DC 20036/(202) 833-5554

Games - 2 - 2 - 2

"Games which are fiercely competitive can be destructive if they cause children to fear failure, feel rejected, lose interest in activities. Games in elementary school especially need to put more emphasis on sharing and caring.

"It's up to the physical education specialist to create such games . . . or get the children to create their own. Games should allow for total involvement of all players, all of the time. If we make spectators out of first graders, we can't very well expect the first grader to grow up being anything else."

According to a series of articles in a recent issue of the _Journal of Physical Education and Recreation_, increasingly instructors are creating and teaching new games, helping students design their own games, developing innovative games which require inexpensive equipment or no equipment, and designing games to match the developmental needs of specific children at specific ages.

To quote on author, Terry Orlick, faculty member at the University of Ottawa, "The only legitimate justification for children's games is to somehow enrich the quality of their lives . . . create fun games which help children become more cooperative, honest and considerate of others."

# # #

Without a doubt, prepackaged material (i.e., news releases, ads, and radio and TV spots) that has been prepared and distributed for widespread circulation by national organizations such as the AAHPER and the NEA has had an immeasurable effect upon the impact local educators have been able to make on their respective publics. Unfortunately, however, many professionals have come to believe that school/community relations is an elaborate publicity campaign of the Madison Avenue variety that consists primarily of clever news articles, one-minute television spots, public service announcements, and/or flashy billboards and catchy slogans.

While publicity is an important tool of public relations, it should never be considered the primary function of a planned program, nor should it ever become the dominant aspect. School/community relations must be much more than "talking at the public" about who you are and what you stand for.

SCHOOL/COMMUNITY RELATIONS — WHAT ARE THEY REALLY?

"The confusion of the publicity tool with the broader practice of public relations is understandable. The practice, in part, has evolved from publicity. Much of contemporary practice is still concerned with publicity."[8] To be effective today, however, a public relations program must be much more than a tool for disseminating information. If a public relations program is to have a positive and long-lasting effect on public sentiment, educators must be willing to provide the public with more than just superficial news releases highlighting the unusual aspects of their program. They must be willing to do more than invite the public into their classrooms for an hour of "show and tell" once a year. They must be willing to listen as well as to talk.

According to the National School Public Relations Association, public relations should be

> a planned and systematic two-way process of communication between an educational organization and its internal and external publics. Its program serves to stimulate a better understanding of the role, objectives, accomplishments, and needs of the organization. Educational public relations is a management function which interprets public attitude, identifies the policies and procedures of an individual organization with the public interest, and executes a program of action to encourage public involvement and to earn public understanding and acceptance. . . .[9]

The important aspects of this definition, those that expand the concept of public relations, are found in the phrases "systematic two-way process of communication" and "action to encourage public involvement." Both of these phrases imply a partnership between the school and the community, which is impossible to achieve when using publicity exclusively, and this partnership is important, for it makes public relations meaningful. Public relations, in this sense, becomes a day-to-day process, a part of every lesson, a daily perspective:

> Daily practice consists of a multitude of little tasks and a few big tasks. It is the application of common sense, common courtesy, and common decency. It can be

8. Scott M. Cutlip and Allen H. Center, *Effective Public Relations* (Englewood Cliffs, NJ: Prentice-Hall, Inc., 1971), p. 15.

9. Doyle M. Bortner, *Public Relations for Public Schools* (Cambridge, MA: Schenkman Publishing Co., 1972), p. 5.

> doing favors for others. It can be pleading a cause in the arena of public opinion. It can be entertaining a visitor. It can be preparing a speech or giving one. It can be a news conference or the dedication of a new building. . . . It can be writing a letter to a hurt, irate parent whose son has been expelled from college.[10]

When viewed in this light, public relations can be as simple as standing at the gym door and greeting students as they file in, or it can be as complicated as devising a curriculum with the aid of a parents' committee. The important point is that public relations is not a practice used simply to project a positive image, it is an affirmation of the public's right to involvement in education. Once this is understood and accepted, the next level of understanding must be concerned with the members of the community. Who are they, how are they organized, what are their concerns?

THE PUBLIC: WHO ARE THEY?

It is difficult, if not impossible, to deal effectively with the unknown and yet many teachers, anxious to communicate with the public, will in essence do just that. In their naivete, they will plan programs for that great unknown, the general public. They fail to realize that a public relations program for the general public is like a lesson plan for the average student; it is usually too broadly based to be meaningful to anyone.

If a public relations program is to be effective, it must be designed to meet the needs and interests of a specific segment of the population. For this reason, teachers must take care to specifically identify the various publics within their own sphere of responsibility long before they ever draw up plans for a formal program. In this way, they can be sure that every aspect of their program will reflect an understanding of their specific publics.

Generally speaking, a *public* can be defined as a group of individuals who share common beliefs, have like interests, or possess common attributes. Publics which share common beliefs or have like interests are usually easily observed because they are centered around a structured base such as religion or politics. Other publics, however, are not as prominent or as visible. This is because their members are not usually organized around a common cause, and rarely if ever are they acquainted with each other. Pubiics of this nature are organized around attributes such as age, income, or sex. Make no mistake, however, their impact can be just as devastating as their more organized, vocal counterparts.

Understanding this, it becomes apparent that 1) there can literally be thousands upon thousands of publics, and that 2) an individual can, voluntarily or involuntarily, be a member of several publics simultaneously. Take the case of Mrs. Esson who is representing Wilson Elementary School, where she is the PTA president, at a meeting on park development. During the course of the meeting, Mrs. Esson expresses her opinion on a number of topics as a member of the following publics:

1. As a mother of two school aged children who is concerned about supervision.
2. As a member of the board of directors of the Little League, who want another field.
3. As a member of the local garden club that will be responsible for the rose garden.
4. As a taxpayer who is concerned about rising taxes.
5. As a property owner whose backyard will share a common boundary with the park.

Mrs. Esson's involvement in several publics simultaneously makes the matter of working with her a little more complicated, for as mother, PTA president, and board member she is in

10. Cutlip and Center, *Public Relations*, p. 11.

favor of park development, but as a taxpayer and property owner, however, Mrs. Esson is in opposition. The wise planner will seek to provide Mrs. Esson with the kind of information that is important to her as a member of all of these publics.

Teachers can easily identify several groups within their sphere of interest that might warrant attention via a public relations program. The boys' basketball coach at the high school, who is also a physical education instructor, can randomly identify the following publics:

1. The booster club
2. The PTA
3. The players
4. The managers
5. The fans
6. The students in his class
7. The parents of the players
8. The faculty
9. The administration
10. The board of education
11. The cheerleaders
12. The general student body
13. The local news media
14. The opposing coaches and players
15. The officials
16. The junior high school students (potential players)
17. The local recreation department
18. The local taxpayers

Although the list is obviously incomplete, it has already become apparent that a public relations program aimed at all of these publics would be an impossible undertaking. At the same time, however, it should become equally apparent that none of the groups mentioned can be ignored either. In order to satisfy the needs of each group and yet remain in control of the public relations program, the basketball coach must decide which of the groups must receive direct as opposed to indirect contact and what the frequency of that contact must be. Making such a decision, the previously mentioned list might look (keep in mind this is strictly in terms of basketball) something like this:

Constant Direct Contact — by means of phone conversations, personal interviews, formal and informal conversations and meetings, and all other modes of communication as well.

1. The players
2. The managers
3. Members of the booster club
4. The local news media
5. The parents of the players

Constant Indirect Contact — by means of flyers, announcements, bulletin boards, radio shows, newspaper reports, letters, posters, and the like:

1. The fans
2. Students in the coach's class
3. Other faculty members
4. General student body

Infrequent Direct — Same as "Constant Direct," but with less frequency:

1. The board of education
2. The administration
3. The local recreation department
4. Potential players
5. Officials

Infrequent Indirect Contact — Same as "Constant Indirect," but with less frequency:
1. Taxpayers
2. Opposing coaches

A simple listing method such as this provides the teacher/coach with a means of setting priorities and giving each public the attention it needs for a specific time period. Throughout the year, this list should be revised and new groupings made as priorities shift. The local media for example, might receive frequent, direct contact during the basketball season, but infrequent, direct contact during the off-season. This type of priority listing allows the teacher or coach to concentrate effort where it is needed most.

THE TEACHER'S ROLE IN THE PUBLIC RELATIONS PROGRAM

A successful public relations program is the result of many individual efforts. Most authorities agree, however, that the single most important agent in a public relations program is the teacher. This view is based primarily on the fact that teachers are the only members of the school community who are in constant and direct contact with students.

> The children are perhaps the most influential of a school's publics. Much of the information and the attitudes held by the general public are transmitted from pupil to parent to public on the community grapevine. There is no surer route to a person's heart — or resentment — than through his child. When the program of a school system rests on a foundation of classroom accomplishment, it is like a house built on a rock. Ill-founded criticism will not overwhelm it. The pupil's role as an intermediary is a strategic one. Public relations starts in the classroom.[11]

A teacher, however, does not exist in a vacuum and, therefore, a teacher's actions do not occur in a vacuum; it is not only possible but in fact quite probable that a teacher's actions will have an effect upon others in and around the school system. Consequently, the teacher must be careful not to initiate a personal public relations program outside the structure provided by the school, for the outcome, although perhaps beneficial for the individual teacher, may be disastrous for the school as a whole. Before initiating a personal public relations program, a teacher should investigate the possibilities offered within the system-wide program to gain an understanding of the responsibilities that are assigned to each personnel level in the program's hierarchy.

In order to understand the teacher's role in relationship to the entire program, it is necessary to understand the role of each principal agent in the program as well. In most board-initiated programs, generally speaking, the principal agents are: 1) members of the board of education, 2) district superintendents and administration staff, 3) building principals, and 4) teachers. Each of these individuals has a very explicit responsibility to fulfill if the public relations program is to be potentially successful.

THE ROLE OF THE BOARD OF EDUCATION

In their collective capacity as the public policy-making body for education, the members of the school board are considered the prime movers in the school's public relations program.

11. Ibid., p. 575.

They alone have the power to create policies which initially establish the program and enable the superintendent to administer it. In some cases, these policies are quite general, allowing the superintendent great latitude, but in other cases, however, such policies explicitly define certain limits within which the superintendent's efforts must be confined.

Policies relating to public relations extend well beyond those earmarked to establish the program. They can be found in practically every chapter of the school policy manual under such titles as "School Use," "Conduct of Public Meetings," "Procedures for Handling Petitions and Criticism," "Visitation Rights of School Guests," "The Public's Right to Know," "Procedure for Handling Crises and Rumors," and others too numerous to list.

When taken collectively, these policies serve as an excellent indicator of the school board's attitudes toward its publics. Allowing inconsistencies in these policies is very poor public relations. Correcting these inconsistencies most assuredly will eliminate needless confrontation with the general community.

The board's duties concerning public relations should never enter the realm of administration. Administration of the program is strictly a management function that is assigned to the superintendent and his staff. The board's responsibilities do proceed beyond policy-making, however, into the task of evaluation. It is the function of the board to evaluate the efficiency and the effectiveness of the program which the administration has implemented. On the basis of their evaluation, the board's duties might entail making recommendations for improvements, revising present policy, or preserving the status quo.

Although the board does not actively participate in formulating or implementing the total school program, members of the board are kept very active conducting their own public relations program. Like the school, the board has a vast number of publics, the three most important being the general electorate, the school's personnel (both professional and nonprofessional) and the media. The board's efforts in this area are extremely important. A breakdown of communications at this level will drastically affect the image of the entire school district.

In summary, the board's primary responsibilities in the public relations program are: 1) to formulate operating policy, 2) to establish goals and objectives, 3) to maintain favorable relations with its internal and external publics, and 4) to evaluate the results of the program.

THE ROLE OF THE SUPERINTENDENT

As the school's chief administrator, the superintendent is charged by the board of education with the responsibility for implementing the public relations policies which have been formulated. It is in the superintendent's office, then, that policy is translated into a plan of action.

Although charged with implementing the school-wide program, the superintendent is not responsible for specific details. The details of planning are left to the individual building principals and their staff. Instead, the superintendent is responsible for the design of the framework under which the program will operate. This framework will include the general procedures for implementing the program at the community level.

The superintendent is also expected to coordinate all of the efforts made by school personnel to activate the program, and to evaluate these results in a formal manner so that he or she may report on both the proceedings and the outcomes to the board. In terms of the school-wide public relations program then, the superintendent acts as interpreter, organizer, and coordinator.

The superintendent's efforts, however, must also be directed at his or her own personal public relations program, for his or her success as a superintendent will depend heavily on relationships with the board of education, the general public, and the school staff. Here, the superintendent must work toward improving staff morale, becoming involved in community and school affairs, and gaining positive working relationships with both community and school groups. Most importantly, the superintendent must concentrate on securing the favor and the trust of the media by communicating honestly and promptly on all school matters and by always remaining available for comment. If the superintendent fails to secure the trust of the school board, the community, and the school staff at this level, this failure will undoubtedly reflect on the total school program.

THE ROLE OF THE PRINCIPAL

Whereas the superintendent is responsible for outlining a general plan, the school principal is responsible for filling in the details and giving the program an identity. Although somewhat bound by the restrictions imposed by the board and the central office, principals usually have enough latitude to enact any programs which they feel are necessitated by the circumstances of their particular school's situation. The principal's role in the public relations program is primarily that of chief supervisor and liaison between the public and the school.

As public liaison, the principal is charged with the responsibility of establishing contacts with community leaders, ascertaining the needs of the community and listening to its concerns, and involving the public in formulating solutions. This is probably one of the most crucial stages in the public relations program, since it is here, for the first time, that a school official makes immediate contact with the people on a personal and continuing basis. The problems that confront the school will be either magnified or eliminated at this point, depending on the principal's expertise in acting as the liaison.

On the supervisory level, principals act as the primary organizers and coordinators of all school activities. It is, therefore, their job to train the staff in public relations techniques and to encourage their involvement in the program. If the program is to be successful, the principals must win the total support of the staff and be able to establish themselves as leaders in this respect.

THE ROLE OF THE TEACHER

As was mentioned previously, the public's initial and possibly most lasting opinion of the school is the one that is channelled to it through the eyes of the school's clientele, the students. This simple fact puts into perspective not only the role of the teacher but also its importance, for when people question

> why a given subject should be taught in school or why it should be regarded as vital to the complete education of youth, it is largely because the true value of education through the medium of that particular subject has been misunderstood.[12]

12. Clifford Lee Brownell, *Public Relations in Education* (New York: McGraw-Hill Book Co., 1955), p. 58.

It is in this instance that teachers can be most effective in the public relations program. Operating well within the limits of the school-wide program, the teacher can add that personal touch that will bring the school community closer to the public. Teachers can create, both in their classrooms and by means of their public contacts, an openness that is conducive to winning public support.

In essence, it is the teacher's responsibility to take the public relations program that is on paper and make it an action program. Although the greatest opportunities for doing this are most often present in the classroom, there are numerous other avenues to explore. Some of these are evident in the following checklist which has been devised by the AAHPER to help professionals ascertain their public relations consciousness.[13]

> Here are fifteen ways health, physical education, and recreation professionals can personally help win community support. How do you score?
>
> 1. Do my students see the educational purpose behind their school experience?
> 2. Am I sure students do a good job of communicating these objectives to parents?
> 3. Do I keep fellow educators and administrators informed of innovations in my field?
> 4. Do I keep my eyes open for newsworthy events in my program and call them to the attention of local media through appropriate channels?
> 5. Do I encourage lay people to speak for my field as well as doing it myself?
> 6. Do I keep alert to enthusiasts in the community who could be enlisted as advisors or supporters of the school program?
> 7. Have I formulated in my own mind why I'm in the field I'm in, and have I relayed this to young people?
> 8. Do I use points of contact with the public, especially in the school environment, to get across at least one fact about the benefits of HPER programs?
> 9. Do I participate actively in state, district, and national association projects?
> 10. Am I well versed on new ideas and opinions being expressed? Am I expressing my ideas and experiences in a way that can be shared by others?
> 11. Do I use all of the resources available to me?
> 12. Am I relating to other professionals in my field toward common goals within our community?
> 13. Am I promoting the lifetime aspects and benefits of HPER learning experiences?
> 14. Have I expressed pride and appreciation to students, parents, and administrators for their participation in and support of my work?
> 15. Have I written to local and national media thanking them when they do a good job of reporting events related to my profession or when they provide public-service time?

13. "Speak Out," *JOHPER* 43, no. 8 (October 1972): p. 55.

This simple checklist illustrates perfectly that teacher involvement with public relations does not just mean staging events or preparing promotional material. It is a matter of becoming actively involved in one's profession and the community at large.

GOOD TEACHER PUBLIC RELATIONS STARTS WITH GOOD TEACHING

Good teacher public relations is truly just good teaching. Teachers who are sensitive to their students' needs, who teach students and not subject material, and who believe in what they are doing would probably find that the following suggestions are simply standard procedure for them. In truth, they can be standard procedure for any teacher who will take the time and put forth the effort to make public relations part of their lifestyle.

Get To Know Your Students

Too often, especially at the higher education levels, teachers and students have a relationship that begins and ends at an appointed hour with the clanging of a bell or the screaming of a buzzer. This type of relationship can be as sterile as the computer that scheduled the class unless teachers take the initiative to get to know their students. It's as simple as greeting the students by name at the door, or knowing that Pam is on the gymnastics team or that Craig is involved in cross-country skiing or that Carmen loves to dance. It's a matter of keeping informed and letting your students know that you appreciate their best efforts. It doesn't take a great deal of time to congratulate Peggy for being accepted to the college of her choice or to give Sam a pat on the back for the paintings he has on exhibit in the front lobby of the school. It also doesn't take a great deal of effort to go to the senior play or to write a letter to the editor of the school paper complimenting the student body for some job well done. It doesn't take much effort or time — it just takes someone who cares.

Increase Student Awareness

A common question frequently asked of elementary school children by their parents is "What did you do in school today?" Unless the student was particularly impressed by something, the answer is often one simple word — "Nothing." The physical educator can capitalize on this question by helping the children formalize their thoughts about physical education in a simple discussion after every class. Most students are excited about movement experiences. If the physical educator can help them translate this excitement into words, it is very likely that the child will answer the question with a synopsis of the physical education class.

Plan Something Special

There's no better way of showing your students that you care than by planning something special. An exercise hunt at Halloween, a turkey shoot at Thanksgiving, and a fiasco Olympics in the spring are all ways of letting students know they're special. Teachers who take the time to be interested in their class, teachers who can sense a mood change and are flexible enough to profit from the "teachable moment," and teachers who are resourceful enough to make learning a joy can do more for promoting good public relations by creating long-lasting memories than any elaborately planned promotional program ever could. A joyful experience stays with a child for an immeasurable amount of time. A series of joyful experiences can last a lifetime.

Stay in Contact with the Parents

To most people, staying in contact with parents implies open houses, conferences, or phone calls. While these are valid and important functions, there are others that can be just as effective and can reach a greater number more frequently.

The Letter

The written letter can be used frequently and creatively to communicate with parents and students alike. It is an effective means of expressing concern or recognition in a manner that is pleasant and courteous.

If the written letter is chosen as the most appropriate means of communication, the teacher should avoid formality and educational jargon. The letter should be neat, simple and to the point. If writing about a child's weaknesses, the letter should be tempered with comments of progress in other areas or suggestions of ways that the teacher as well as the parent can work to help the child.

Many of the opportunities for writing letters are inadvertently overlooked or considered too minor to be of any importance. The teacher must learn to spot these opportunities and make the best possible use of them.

The following examples show two letters, the first one was written to the parents of a varsity basketball player, the other to a child who finally succeeded in her attempts to learn a front handspring. Both were meant to convey praise and recognition in a personal way.

Dear Mr. & Mrs. Gillis:

As you probably know, basketball tryouts ended last week and Ronnie was one of two sophomores selected for the varsity squad. We are all very proud of these young ladies. Collectively, they are probably the most talented players we have ever had at Central.

When playing any sport, the participant must make many sacrifices for that single moment of victory. We hope you will support Ronnie, as we will, during those sacrifices, and be with her to share those moments of victory.

Enclosed is a game schedule. We hope you'll be able to join us frequently this season.

Please don't hesitate to call us if you have any concerns about Ronnie or the program.

Looking forward to meeting you this season, I remain

Sincerely,

Ms. Regalado

Dear Jane:

I can't tell you how proud I am of you. I've been watching you for the last two months as you worked on your front handspring, and I know that there were moments when you wanted to quit. The important thing is that you didn't. You worked hard and now you have the prize.

I'm pleased and I hope you are.

Sincerely,

Mr. Piccirillo

The letter can be either a definite asset in a teacher's personal relations program or a definite liability. The difference is usually based on one or more of the following aspects.

1. *Appearance*. Be sure your letters are neat, free of smudges, tears, or inked-in additions or deletions.
2. *Language*. Avoid abbreviations and educational jargon or multisyllabic prose. Clear, succinct language is best.
3. *Proper Grammar and Spelling*. Check all sentences for faulty syntax, misspelled words, and grammatical errors.
4. *Organization*. Be sure that your thoughts are well organized and logical so that the reader can easily grasp your message. Every mistake which goes undetected and is eventually forwarded in the letter diminishes the impact of the intended message and increases the impact of a totally unintended message. The parent who received the following letter seriously questioned the professional abilities of the teacher who wrote it, not because of his teaching methods but because of the letter he wrote.

> Dear Mrs. Johnson,
>
> I'm concirned about Billie and the poor work he's been doing lately for all of us and I'd like to enlist your help in doing something about this problem
>
> I've talked to Billie and he's insured me that there's nothing wrong but, I'd still like to see you personally.
>
> Let me know when we can meet.
>
> Respectfully,
>
> Mr. Rodgers

Newsletters

Many schools publish newsletters periodically in an attempt to keep the community informed of coming events, special programs, the school's curriculum, methods employed by teachers, and changes in rules and regulations.

The physical education department, if possible, should try to obtain a column in the newsletter for their exclusive use. It is important to advertise what is being done in the program and to solicit opinions or reactions. The easiest way to do this is with the printed word.

If the school does not publish a newsletter, the department should seriously consider publishing their own on a limited basis. Columns might include: Coming Events, How to Improve Your. . . ., Toward Better Health through Activity, Sports Events, The New Physical Education, What's Happening Here.

To be successful, a newsletter cannot be just straight reporting of school events. Although the contents should be predominately about the school community, there should also be articles about community groups or events that have a direct bearing on the subject.

The newsletter need not be exclusively written by the physical education staff. Members of the student community, booster club, or administration should be invited to submit articles as well.

Share Your Talent With The Community

Physical education runs a wide gamut of activities. One activity which can be used to introduce the parents to the instructional staff while demonstrating the potential of physical education and offering a valuable service to the community is the free university.

The free university is simply a conglomeration of activities taught by a qualified individual, and offered free of charge to those who are interested in participating. Activities can range from belly dancing to sumo wrestling and can be taught by any qualified individual in the community.

The type of activity offered is not important, but the fact that the physical education staff is endeavoring to serve the community by sharing their talents is.

Provide Demonstrations and Exhibitions

As a general rule, most parents are interested in what their children are doing in school. Probably the most popular and certainly the most enjoyable way of showing them what their children are doing is the physical education exhibition. Most departments plan their program for the spring so that they have ample time to select the activities, teach the routines, and polish the program.

The following guidelines are offered to insure success:

1. Before the exhibition date is finalized, it should be cleared through the main office to be sure that it does not conflict with the plans of another group.
2. Select a theme for the program that will serve as a guide for activity selection. Avoid stock themes which limit the imagination by suggesting stock activities.
3. Try to utilize the talents of many, if not all of the students in the school. Solicit the aid of students when planning scenery, designing costumes, selecting music, and developing the program's format.
4. Choose activities that reflect the goals of the physical education program.
5. Make the program as entertaining as possible. Select activities that have crowd appeal. There is nothing more deadly than an entire class swinging golf clubs at imaginary balls for five minutes. Avoid this type of activity unless it can be presented in an imaginative way.
6. Music is a must. It helps create a special atmosphere.
7. Be sure routines are uncomplicated and easy to learn. This will dramatically increase the number of students who will volunteer for the program. Routines that are attractive yet simple will help students maintain their self-confidence because they know that they can be successful.
8. Prepare the order of events so that the program will be fast moving. Pace is an important factor that can either enhance or curtail an audience's attention. A perceptive planner will sense this long before the program is ever presented to an audience and make the necessary adjustments.
9. Place the best activities first and last in the program. The opening activity will set the climate for the entire program so choose wisely. The finale on the other hand will leave the lasting impression so try to finish with something dramatic or exciting.
10. Plan a program that will run an hour and a half or less. A program that runs longer is bound for bad reviews. Don't forget bleachers tend to be awfully hard.
11. Enlist the aid of other faculty members to help conduct the activities backstage. Running a program single handedly can be an impossible task.
12. Provide the audience with a program, it's a great way to give credit where credit is due and to create audience anticipation.

Fixing a broken clock today

can help your child get a good job 20 years from now.

Are you and your child ready for school?

people who care about kids.

Fixing a broken clock today can help your child get a good job 20 years from now.

You can help your child get more out of school by making a connection between what he does at home and what he does at school.

For example, if you let him fix an old broken clock, you help keep him more interested in science. You connect . . . simply . . . home and school. And both work better.

There are other simple things you can do, too.

- Play dominoes to spur their interest in math.
- Ask them to make maps of the neighborhood to heighten their interest in social studies. (They're often working with maps in school.)
- Overall, show an interest in what they're doing at school. Encourage them to tell you about their day.
- Don't get in a heated discussion when you're upset. Allow time for things to cool down.
- Praise them when things go well at school — but don't get to the point where they expect lavish praise for everything they do and are disappointed when they don't get it.
- Make certain homework becomes an important part of their daily routine. Help them to develop *good* study habits.
- Give them space at home to display the things they do in school.

NEW JERSEY EDUCATION ASSOCIATION

180 W. State St. ☐ P.O. Box 1211 ☐ Trenton, New Jersey 08608 ☐ Tel: (609) 599-4561

13. Make emergency plans well in advance. What will you do if the public address system breaks down, or a child is injured, or your announcer gets laryngitis? Be sure to work out all the details before it happens.
14. Make sure all the program snags have been resolved before opening night. Confused entrances and exits, miscued records or any technical mishap can ruin the overall impression of a program. Be sure they are rehearsed with as much enthusiasm as the rest of the program.
15. Remember to formally thank those who helped make the show possible.

Get the Parents Involved

Getting parents involved in their own child's education is not always a simple task. Some parents feel that they don't possess the necessary qualifications, others insist they're too busy, and still others insist that it isn't their job, it's the school's and that's why they pay taxes. Nevertheless, the teacher should make every effort to assist those who wish to become involved and to encourage those who might be reticent.

One way to accomplish this is to invite parents into the classroom once or twice a month to act as assistants. In this way, the teacher/pupil ratio is reduced, and parents will have an opportunity to work in a meaningful way with their children. This technique is especially useful in beginner classes, such as beginning swimming.

A second method which requires less time and is usually more convenient for parents is the clinic. Parents are invited into the gymnasium for a lecture/demonstration on a topic directly related to the activity being conducted in the classroom. This is followed by an optional period of audience participation during which time the parents are invited to participate in the activity previously described. This technique is especially useful in training parents to spot gymnastics in their homes.

A third method, which is probably the most convenient but isn't as productive as the assistantship or clinic methods, is the "how to" brochure. This technique has, however, the distinct advantage of being able to cover a wide variety of topics simultaneously. To be effective, these little brochures should only cover limited topics and be written in non-technical terms. An excellent example of this type of material is displayed on the following page. It was prepared by the NJEA and circulated in supermarkets, dental offices, and the like for public consumption.

SUMMARY

Teacher public relations is a process of caring and sharing. It's caring about everything that is important in teaching, namely the students, the parents, the community, and the profession, and finding a way to share the responsibility of education with all of them. In this light, the teacher must be willing to accept public relations as a professional responsibility.

appendices

APPENDIX 1: CAFIAS

The Categories of Cheffers' Adaptation of Flanders' Interaction Analysis System

Categories	Verbal	Relevant Behaviors	Nonverbal
2-12	2		12
	Praises, commends, jokes, encourages.	Face:	Smiles, nods with smile, (energetic) winks, laughs.
		Posture:	Claps hands, pats on shoulder, places hand on head of student, wrings student's hand, embraces joyfully, laughs to encourage, spots in gymnastics, helps child over obstacles.
3-13	3		13
	Accepts, clarifies, uses, and develops suggestion and feelings by the learner.	Face:	Nods without smiling, tilts head in empathetic reflection, sighs empathetically.
		Posture:	Shakes hands, embraces sympathetically, places hand on shoulder, puts arm around shoulder or waist, catches an implement thrown by student, accepts facilities.

NOTE: Coding symbols are as follows: Teacher Environment (E) Student (S)

CAFIAS (cont'd)

Categories	Verbal	Relevant Behaviors	Nonverbal
4-14	4		14
	Asks questions requiring student answer.	Face:	Wrinkles brow, opens mouth, turns head with quizzical look.
		Posture:	Places hands in air, waves finger to and fro anticipating answer, stares awaiting answer, scratches head, cups hand to ear, stands still half-turned towards person, awaits answer.
5-15	5		15
	Gives facts, opinions, expresses ideas, or asks rhetorical questions.	Face:	Whispers words inaudibly, sings, or whistles.
		Posture:	Gesticulates, draws, writes, demonstrates activities, points.
6-16	6		16
	Gives directions or orders.	Face:	Points with head, beckons with head, yells at.
		Posture:	Points finger, blows whistle, holds body erect while barking commands, pushes child through a movement, pushes a child in a given direction.
8-18	8		18
	Student response that is entirely predictable, such as obedience to orders, and responses not requiring thinking beyond the comprehension phase or knowledge (after Bloom).	Face:	Poker face response, nod, shake, gives small grunts, quick smile.
		Posture:	Moves mechanically to questions or directions, responds to any action with minimal nervous activity, robot-like.

CAFIAS (cont'd)

Categories	Verbal	Relevant Behaviors		Nonverbal
8/-18/ ("eine"- "eineteen")	8/ ("eine") Predictable student responses requiring some measure of evaluation and synthesis from the student, but must remain within the province of predictability. The initial behavior was in response to teacher initiation.	Face:	A "What's more, Sir" look, eyes sparkling.	18/ ("eineteen")
		Posture:	Adds movements to those given or expected, tries to show some arrangement requiring additional thinking; e.g., works on gymnastic routine, dribbles basketball, *all game playing.*	
9-19	9 Pupil-initiated talk that is purely the result of the pupil's initiative and that could not be predicted.	Face:	Interrupting sounds, gasps, sighs.	19
		Posture:	Puts hands up to ask questions, gets up and walks around without provocation, begins creative movement education, makes up own games, makes up own movements, shows initiative in supportive movement, introduces new movements into games not predictable in the rules of the game.	
10-20	10 Stands for confusion, chaos, disorder, noise, much noise.	Face:	Silence, children sitting doing nothing, noiselessly awaiting teacher just prior to teacher entry, etc.	20

SOURCE: John T. F. Cheffers, Edmund J. Amidon, and Ken D. Rodgers, *Interaction Analysis: An Application to Nonverbal Activity* (Minneapolis: Association for Productive Teaching, 1974).

Additional Ground Rules

The addition of several ground rules is now necessary if we are to facilitate the use of CAFIAS.

Preliminary pilot studies indicate that it is possible to use CAFIAS with procedures similar to those of FIAS.

1. Whenever the structure of the class moves to part (coded P), a decision has to be made as to which part of the class interaction is to be coded. Observers may code any part of the lesson they so desire, using CAFIAS, but, in the absence of particular directions, the observers will follow the teacher and code his or her interaction with either the individual students or the groups with which he or she is working. Nevertheless, if another student or some part of the environment is doing the teaching, then this can be coded by CAFIAS. On most occasions, for purposes of inter-observer reliability, it is necessary to establish the specific categorization route prior to the lesson.
2. Whenever the teacher is talking and demonstrating at the same time, necessitating simultaneous coding, the observer codes the verbal symbol and encircles it. This is encoded into the matrix in both verbal and nonverbal cells.
3. In order to clarify the use of 6, CAFIAS adopts the following recommendation. When directions are being given, only the executive part of the command is coded as a 6. The information-giving section of the statement is coded as a 5. For example:

   "Group 2 will assemble the mats in the far corner in star formation." (5)

   "All right, go!" (6)

   This ground rule is consistent with Flanders' recommendation that a direction should be followed by an immediate physical movement that is observable and in response to a teacher-directed command.
4. The differentiation between a 7 used to encode encouragement and a 7 used to encode punishment.

APPENDIX 2: THE FISHMAN SYSTEM — OPERATIONAL DEFINITIONS OF SUBCATEGORIES

1. Form
   a. Auditory Augmented Feedback: Feedback provided orally.
   b. Auditory-Tactile Feedback: Feedback provided orally and by manual assistance.
   c. Auditory-Visual Feedback: Feedback provided orally and by teacher demonstration.
2. Direction
   a. A Single Student: Feedback directed to only one student, although it may be seen or heard by all students in the class.
   b. A Group of Students: Feedback directed to more than one student but less than all students, although it may be heard or seen by all students in the class.
   c. All Students in the Class: Feedback directed to the entire class.
3. Time
   a. Concurrent Feedback: Feedback provided during the performance of motor skill.
   b. Terminal Feedback: Feedback provided sometime after the performance of a motor skill.
4. Intent
   a. Evaluative Feedback: Feedback intended to provide an appraisal of the performance of a motor skill.
   b. Descriptive Feedback: Feedback intended to provide an account of the performance of a motor skill.
   c. Comparative Feedback: Feedback intended to provide an analogy related to the performance of a motor skill.
   d. Explicative Feedback: Feedback intended to provide a rationale related to the instruction for a subsequent performance of a motor skill.
   e. Prescriptive Feedback: Feedback intended to provide instructions for the subsequent performance of a motor skill.
   f. Affective Feedback: Feedback intended to provide an attitudinal or motivational set toward the performance of a motor skill.
5. General Referent
   a. The Whole Movement: Feedback provided about multiple components in the performance of a motor skill.
   b. Part of the Movement: Feedback provided about one component other than the outcome or goal of the performance of a motor skill.
   c. Outcome or Goal of the Movement: Feedback provided about the result of the performance of a motor skill.
6. Specific Referent
   a. Rate: Feedback provided about the time or duration of the movement involved.
   b. Force: Feedback provided about the strength or power expended in the performance of a motor skill.
   c. Space: Feedback provided about the direction, level, or magnitude of the movement involved in the performance of a motor skill.

SOURCE: Sylvia Fishman, "Descriptive Analysis of Teacher Behavior — The Competency Controversy," A workshop presentation given at the Eastern District Association — American Association for Health, Physical Education and Recreation Conference, Boston, Massachusetts, November 21-22, 1975.

Recording Instrument Used with the Fishman System

Tape No. ______ **Recorder** ______

Unit No.	Methodological Dimension								Substantive Dimension												
	Form			Direction			Time		Teacher Intent						General Referent			Specific Referent			
	A	AV	AT	1	2	3	C	T	E	P	C	D	EX	A	W	P	O	F	S	R	HS
1																					
2																					
3																					
4																					
5																					
6																					
7																					
8																					
9																					
10																					
11																					
12																					
13																					
14																					
15																					

APPENDIX 3
INTERACTION ANALYSIS OF THE TEACHER'S VERBAL BEHAVIOR: LOOKING AT THE "OPENNESS" v. "CLOSEDNESS" OF THE TEACHER*

Summary

This tool, "Interaction Analysis of the Teacher's Verbal Behavior: Looking at the 'Openness' vs. 'Closedness' of the Teacher," was developed to be used to analyze the verbal behavior of the teacher in the classroom. By so doing, one can determine how responsive the teacher is to the student and the amount of encouragement there is for the students to volunteer input to the teacher.

The system is formulated to rate teacher talk from the most open to the least open. A high degree of openness indicates the acceptance of many different answers or of a less structured response. A great deal of closedness indicates that only one response is accepted by the teacher. Open statements give positive feedback to the students, encouraging injection of student comments. Closed statements have an opposite effect, that is negative feedback, which tends to limit student input.

Setting and Observable Variables

Every grade level in any learning situation can be analyzed using this tool. The lesson may be coded live or from a recording.

The teacher's verbal behavior has been separated into seven general categories, A-G. Category A is the most open in nature and each category becomes progressively less open. Each category is divided into subparts. Therefore, each individual category can also be analyzed for the degree of openness or closedness within itself. The main categories studied, from most to least open, are the following: (A) Praise, (B) Questioning, (C) Lecture, (D) Directions, (E) Criticizing and Insult, (F) Discipline, (G) "OK".

Categories

A. Praising Behavior
   1. Praises answer with explanation.
   2. Praises answer and encourages other alternatives or hypotheses.
   3. Praises, but actually is seeking a different alternative or type of answer.
   4. Praises answer without explanation.
   5. Reserves praise, and makes student revise or further develop an answer.
   6. Neutral comment in response to student.

B. Questioning Behavior
   1. Creative questions — answers will be creative, imaginative, and expand in new directions.
   2. Feelings questions — freedom to express own feelings, emotion, or opinions about something.
   3. Suggestion questions — ask students if something should be changed in some way.
   4. Developmental questions — processing of facts, which must be integrated into a deeper-type answer.

*This appendix was authored by Nanciann Zimmitti Kruse.

5. Rhetorical question — question presented to the class which actually will not be answered by the students. Used to provoke thinking.
6. Lead question — ask questions in a controlled format to lead the students to the answer.
7. Factual question — memory questions.
8. Management question — questions asked to find out management procedures followed by class in case of teacher absence or forgotten actions.

C. Lecture
   1. Personal comment — story or comment of fact related or unrelated to factual material presentation.
   2. Lecturing with opened opinion bias — present facts and opinion, but indicate desire for student opinion.
   3. Joke.
   4. Lecturing without bias — straightforward facts.
   5. Lecturing with closed opinion bias — partial presentation of facts which are either opinionated or reflect some teacher bias.

D. Directions
   1. Suggestion format — suggest students follow a certain instruction.
   2. Question format — suggest students follow a certain instruction.
   3. Command format — tell students to do something.

E. Criticizing and Insult Behavior
   1. Criticize answer with explanation.
   2. Criticize student behavior with explanation.
   3. Criticize answer with no explanation.
   4. Criticize behavior with no explanation.
   5. Criticize and insult student answer.
   6. Insult without criticism.

F. Discipline
   1. Wait in silence — make no comment, but wait for students to bring themselves to order.
   2. Mild directions to bring order.
   3. Strong reprimand — threat of punishment or shouting for order.

G. "OK"
   1. Any word included within the teacher's talk which has no value other than filler or connector between phases.

Recording Process

The tally sheet is divided into columns, each of which represents a two-minute time block (see sample tally sheet that follows). It is also divided into rows, each representing a specific behavior to be observed. Within each time unit, the behaviors that occur are recorded sequentially by making an entry in the appropriate column. A comma follows each entry. When two minutes have elapsed, the process is repeated in the next column.

Analysis

After 14 minutes of coding, the row totals are tallied in the right-hand margin of the sheet. These totals show frequency of occurrence of each behavior from most to least. The position of the row totals on the tally sheet represents how open or closed a teacher is in using verbal behavior, because they are listed from open to closed on the tally sheet. The totals within each category also can be analyzed according to position for the degree of openness used.

The number of tallies per unit of time gives a rough estimate of the duration of each behavior. The greater the total number of tallies, the shorter the time spent on each individual behavior. A general pattern of transition from one category to the next can also be obtained. In each two-minute time block, the category most used is the first behavior of the pattern. Either the behavior which most often follows the first behavior or the second most-used behavior is determined to be the second behavior in the pattern.

It is hoped that this system will be used as a tool to help teachers recognize what they actually say when they teach. It should also make the teacher aware of any repetitive word or phrase used, which can become a conscious or unconscious annoyance to the students. Most importantly, it should reveal how dependent or independent teachers allow their students to be during the class by their use of open or closed verbal behavior.

TALLY SHEET

Class Size: _____ Subject: _______________

	2 min.	4 min.	6 min.	8 min.	10 min.	12 min.	14 min.	Row Totals	Category Totals
A. Praise									
1. Praise answer with explanation									
2. Praise answer and encourage									
3. Praise, but seek other answer									
4. Praise without explanation									
5. Reserve praise and develop answer									
6. Neutral comment in response to student									
B. Questioning									
1. Creative question									
2. Feeling question									
3. Suggestion question									
4. Developmental question									
5. Rhetorical question									
6. Lead question									
7. Factual question									
8. Management question									
C. Lecture									
1. Personal comment									
2. Opened lecture									
3. Joke									
4. Lecture without bias									
5. Closed lecture									
D. Directions									
1. Suggestive format									
2. Questioning format									
3. Command format									
E. Criticizing and Insult									
1. Criticize answer with explanation									
2. Criticize behavior with explanation									
3. Criticize answer without explanation									
4. Criticize behavior without explanation									
5. Criticize and insult									
6. Insult without explanation									
F. Discipline									
1. Wait in silence									
2. Mild direction									
3. Strong reprimand									
G. "OK"									

APPENDIX 4: INSTRUCTIONAL ANALYSIS*

Much criticism has been directed towards the instruction that takes place within the physical education class. For example, many claim that instruction in physical education is often repetitious, as well as presented in a nonstimulating manner. In addition, it is frequently said that physical education is not geared to the masses, but rather to a choice few gifted individuals. This tool has been designed to objectively examine the instruction which takes place within the physical education class.

Instruction was defined as the presentation of any information by the teacher or students pertaining to the subject of physical education and dwelling on the subject matter (information) of the lesson being presented. In this way, items such as moving the class from one place to another, motivating students through the use of praise, or disciplining students would *not* be considered instructional. Items such as directing students to attempt a given physical task, asking questions pertaining to physical education, or stating a fact pertaining to physical education would be instructional and thus *would* be coded as such.

Five mutually exclusive categories of instruction were developed: Direction, Form, Nature, Method of Presentation, and Length (see diagram on following page). Within these categories, fourteen mutually exclusive instructional subcategories were devised. In addition, the Method of Presentation category includes five subcategories which are *not* instructional but are often found in conjunction with the presentation of instructional information. They are frequently intertwined with periods of instruction. One therefore finds that the Method of Presentation category is divided into two parts — an educational portion and a noneducational portion. Those behaviors labeled educational pertain to the presentation of instructional information, and those labeled noneducational refer to those behaviors which are more methodological in content. Noneducational items, however, are only coded when they occur during an instructor's attempt at presenting a given piece of instruction. Such an attempt is labeled as an instructional episode.

Operational Definitions**

Instruction: The presentation of any information by the teacher or students pertaining to the subject of physical education and dwelling on the subject matter (information) of the lesson being presented. Any information presented during periods of instruction is referred to as instructional information.

Instructional Episode: A time period which begins when one first attempts to present a given piece of instructional information. An instructional episode ends when one has completed his or her attempt at presenting a given piece of instructional information.

1. Direction

   The Whole Class: Instruction directed towards the entire class.

   Part of the Class: Instruction directed towards more than one student, but not the entire class, although it may be heard or seen by the entire class. Such instruction is intended solely for the benefit of those individuals it is directed towards.

*This appendix was authored by Eugene J. Buchma.

**Credit should be given to Flanders' System of Interaction Analysis and Fishman's Procedure for Recording Augmented Feedback in Physical Education Classes for several of the categories and subcategories used in this system.

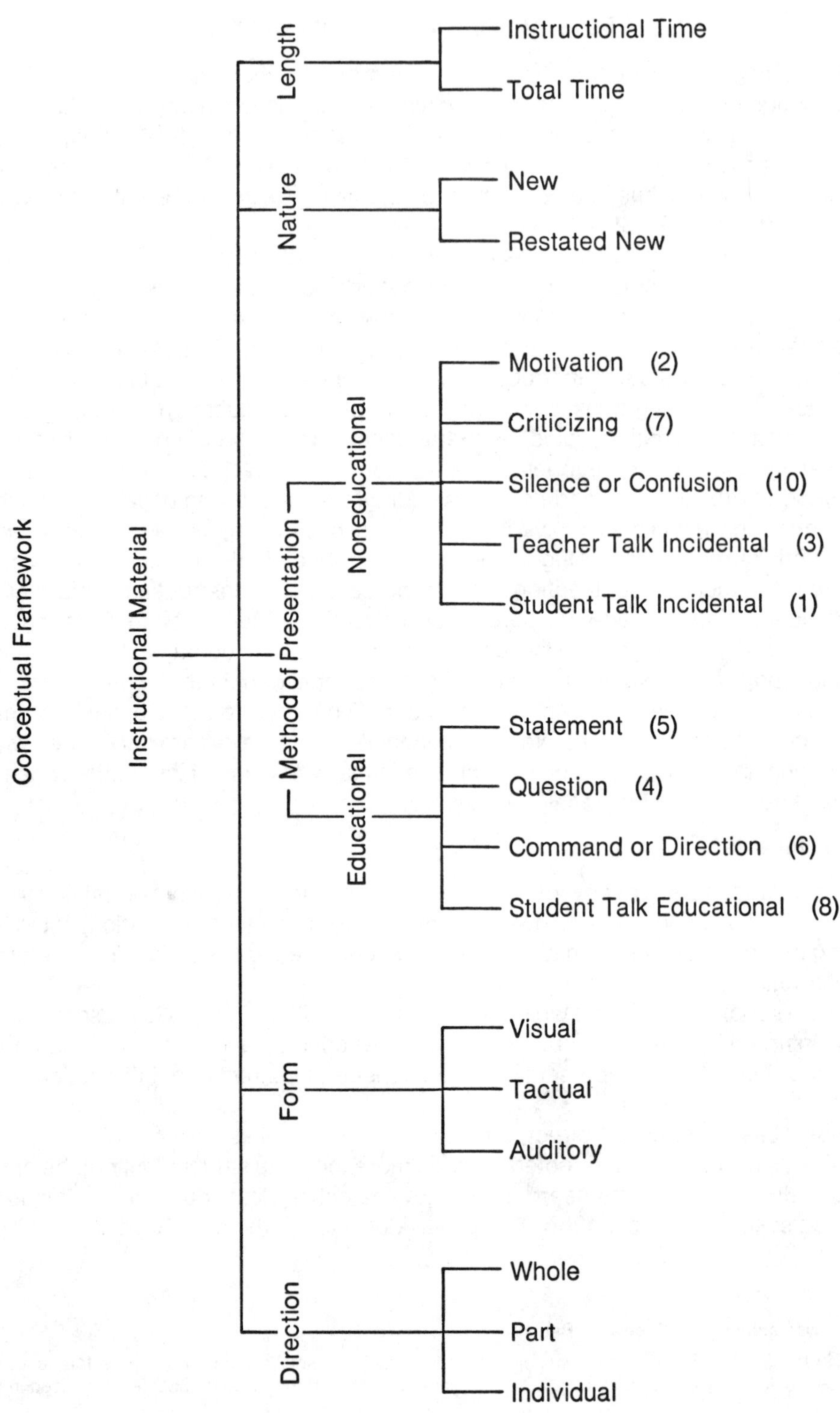
Conceptual Framework
Instructional Material
Length
Instructional Time
Total Time
Nature
New
Restated New
Method of Presentation
Noneducational
Motivation (2)
Criticizing (7)
Silence or Confusion (10)
Teacher Talk Incidental (3)
Student Talk Incidental (1)
Educational
Statement (5)
Question (4)
Command or Direction (6)
Student Talk Educational (8)
Form
Visual
Tactual
Auditory
Direction
Whole
Part
Individual

An Individual: Instruction directed towards just one individual, although it may be heard or seen by the entire class. Such instruction is solely intended for the benefit of the individual it is directed towards.

2. Form

Auditory: Instruction presented orally.

Visual: Instruction presented by an overt teacher or student demonstration. Pointing or other casual gestures are *not* considered to be visual instruction.

Tactual: Instruction presented by manual assistance in the desired motor task.

3. Nature

New Instruction: Instruction presented for the first time during a given lesson.

Restated Instruction: Instruction which was presented during the lesson and is now being re-presented or re-emphasized during the same lesson.

4. Method of Presentation

Educational

Question: Teacher asks a question pertaining to instructional information with the intent that a student or students will answer.

Statement: Teacher states a fact pertaining to instructional information.

Command or Direction: Teacher gives directions, commands, or orders pertaining to instructional information with which students are expected to comply, as well as have an opportunity to do so.

Student Talk Educational: Talk by students pertaining to instructional information.

Noneducational

Praise: Flowery words or phrases, used by the teacher for the purpose of encouraging or motivating students, which are intertwined with an instructional episode.

Student Talk Incidental: Talk by students that does not pertain to instruction, but is intertwined with the presentation of instructional information. For example, during an instructional episode a student may request permission to get a drink.

Teacher Talk Incidental: Talk by the teacher that is not instructional, but is intertwined with the presentation of instructional information. For example, while instructing, the teacher may comment, "What a nice day it is today."

Criticizing or Justifying Authority: Actions or behaviors by the teacher for the purpose of acknowledging and changing unacceptable behavior to acceptable behavior. These are intertwined with an instructional episode.

Silence or Confusion: Short periods of silence or times of confusion which the recorder is unable to interpret. These are intertwined with an instructional episode.

5. Length

Total Time: The amount of time that elapsed during a single instructional episode.

Instructional Time: The total time spent on instruction during an instructional episode. This is determined by subtracting the amount of time spent on non-educational items from the total time.

Coding Procedures

Recording is done through the use of a combination checklist and number-coding system (see chart at the end of this appendix). For each instructional episode, the first task of the recorder is to check the appropriate sections for the categories of Direction, Form, and Nature. The recorder then codes the instructional episode according to the subcategories within the Method of Presentation category. This is done by placing in the tally portion of the recording sheet, the number corresponding to the behavior being observed. A number is coded every three seconds that behavior is observed, or when the behavior changes. The codes for the Method of Presentation category are as follows: 1 — student talk, incidental; 2 — praise; 3 — teacher talk, incidental; 4 — question; 5 — statement; 6 — command direction; 7 — criticizing or justifying authority; 8 — student talk, educational; and 10 — silence or confusion.

After the completion of the lesson, the time columns for the category of Length are completed. Assuming that each coding of the Method of Presentation category represents three seconds, one can estimate the total number of seconds for each instructional episode by multiplying the total number of codings by three. Similarly, by taking into account only the educational codings, the instructional time for each episode can be determined. Simple addition of the time estimates for each individual episode will provide time estimates for the entire lesson.

Several important aspects of instruction within the physical education class can be discerned through the use of Instructional Analysis. First, the amount of time actually spent instructing is determined, as well as the amount of instructional time spent in non-educational behaviors. One can also discover how the instructional information was presented by checking the educational Method of Presentation codings. In addition, by looking at the time estimates for each instructional episode, one can see how much time was spent instructing the whole class, part of the class, or individuals; how much time was spent on new instruction versus that which was spent on restated instruction; and finally, which sensory pathways were utilized in order to present instructional information.

Instructional Analysis Checklist and Number-Coding System

	Direction			Form			Nature		Method of Presentation	Length	
Instruc. Episode	Whole	Individual	Part	Auditory	Visual	Tactual	New	Restated	1 — Student talk, incidental; 2 — Motivation; 3 — Teacher talk, incidental; 4 — Question; 5 — Statement; 6 — Command or Direction; 7 — Criticizing or Justifying Authority; 8 — Student talk, educational; 10 — Silence	Total Time	Instruc. Time
1											
2											
3											
4											
5											
6											
7											
8											
9											

APPENDIX 5: VERBS APPROPRIATE TO USE IN PREPARING OBJECTIVES

apply
assess

bring
build

change
chart
climb
codify
collect
compare
construct
contrast

define
delineate
demonstrate
describe
design
diagram
differentiate
draw

employ
explain
express

find
finish

give

hit
hold
hop

identify
imitate

keep
kick

leap
list

make
mark

name

pick
place
plan
point out
push

recite
repeat
respond
run

say
show
skip
solve
strike
swim
swing

tell
throw
toss
try

volley

walk
write

APPENDIX 6: THE LEXINGTON SECONDARY ELECTIVE PROGRAM

Submitted by: Ralph V. Lord, Jr.
School: Lexington High School, 251 Waltham Street
Lexington, Massachusetts 02173

Summary

The Lexington High School Elective Physical Education Program provides each student with a basic workable knowledge and understanding of a variety of sports activities; creates a level of skill in each activity that will enable each student to participate fully and effectively in carry-on activities; and gives a thorough appreciation of these and other activities from a spectator point of view.

A stimulating educational experience is fostered by providing facilities, equipment, and a choice of 43 activities at a variety of levels. The physical education program culminates in a well-balanced and organized intramural and interscholastic program. The interscholastic program consists of 23 sports for girls and boys totalling 49 teams at various competitive levels.

Lexington High School's enrollment is approximately 2,100 students, grades 10-12. The school is an open-campus style consisting of seven houses. Students are required to participate actively in two 55-minute periods each week. Students wishing additional classes may be accepted on a space-available condition. There are presently eight full-time physical education teachers at Lexington High School equally divided among men and women.

The school year is divided into four quarters consisting of approximately nine weeks each. Students elect two different activities each quarter, one activity for each of the two days their class meets during the week. Students are not allowed to repeat activities over a single school year unless the nature of the activity requires repetition.

Outline

Students may choose from the following activities:

Fall (1st Quarter)	Winter (2nd-3rd Quarter)	Spring (4th Quarter)
Archery I and II	Judo	Archery I and II
Tennis I	Volleyball	Tennis I and II
Golf I and II	Table Tennis	Golf I and II
Horseshoes	Weight Training	Badminton
Tetherball	Dance	Fishing
Badminton	Fencing	Fly Casting
Flag Football	Basketball	Lacrosse
Soccer	Floor Hockey	Track and Field
Field Hockey	Apparatus	Softball
Speedball	Wrestling	
	Modern Dance	
	Modern Jazz	
	Movement for Improvement	
	Self-Defense	
	Floor Exercise	

Description

At the beginning of each quarter, students select their physical education program for that quarter. Two different activities are selected, each meeting once a week for the entire quarter.

Two printed, color-coded data-processing cards are required for each student (one card for each period of physical education taken during the week). A card is given to the instructor of each activity the student elects and is utilized by the instructor to take attendance and keep cumulative evaluative records. At the end of each quarter, cards are reassigned to the instructors of each student's new activity. The cards are filed by activity and gym class to enable easy accessibility in changing a student's gym class or activity. Also, in case of a substitute teacher, all necessary records are readily available. Colored bands across the top of the cards are used to easily identify the student's class period and year of graduation. Cards are preprinted by data processing with the student's name, house, homeroom, and other pertinent information.

Conditions Specific To Program

The program is essentially held outdoors during the fall and spring seasons. However, some activities such as badminton are held indoors to facilitate better utilization of space. The second and third quarters are held in the well-equipped gymnasium and fieldhouse. The fieldhouse utilizes six to seven teaching stations each period and contains a 160-yard, 4-lane running track with specialized areas for basketball, gymnastics, volleyball, etc.

The student-teacher ratio is based on one physical education teacher for each 250 students. In addition to teaching salaries, the supply and equipment budget is allocated on the basis of $1.50 a year for each student in the high school. This budget is very satisfactory and provides very adequate funding.

SOURCE: *Ideas for Secondary School Physical Education* (Washington, D.C.: AAHPER, 1976), pp. 47-48.

APPENDIX 7: CHECKLIST FOR EVALUATION OF THE HIGH SCHOOL ATHLETIC PROGRAM

Athletic Department Personnel

I. Meeting standards of state and local certification requirements
   A. All personnel meet the letter of these requirements. Yes___ No___
   B. An attempt is made for all coaches to have at least physical education or coaching minors. Yes___ No___
   C. No nonteaching personnel are allowed to coach. Yes___ No___

II. Adequate personnel employed to meet program needs
   A. Additional staff is hired if the popularity of a sport, indicated by the number of prospects, shows demand for additional schedules and coaches. Yes___ No___
   B. Where numbers indicate, assistant coaches are provided in all sports. Yes___ No___
   C. Adequate supportive personnel are provided to insure that coaches have time for coaching. Yes___ No___
   D. Properly qualified personnel are provided to take care of the health service of the athletic program. Yes___ No___
   E. Properly qualified and certified athletic officials are obtained for all contests. Yes___ No___

III. Employment of athletic personnel as contribution to overall educational program
   A. All facets of credentials (not only winning record) are perused when personnel are selected. Yes___ No___
   B. No fringe benefits, not available to all faculty, are offered to secure athletic personnel. Yes___ No___
   C. Athletic personnel to be assigned teaching in any area must be qualified and well motivated in that area. Yes___ No___

IV. Performance of equitable professional duties
   A. Athletic personnel carry the same teaching load as other faculty, unless release from same is part of computed compensation. Yes___ No___

V. Professional, ethical, and moral standards of personnel
   A. Athletic personnel are members of general educational organizations (NEA, AAHPER, etc.). Yes___ No___
   B. Athletic personnel are members of the professional organizations appropriate to their teaching and coaching areas. Yes___ No___
   C. Some athletic personnel are leaders in their areas, as indicated by research, publications, use of new techniques, and service to professional organizations. Yes___ No___
   D. Athletic personnel operate under a code of ethics that is at least as lofty as that of NEA. Yes___ No___
   E. Athletic personnel have moral standards that at their minimum would, if emulated by their athletes when they become adults, provide a social image felt to be desirable in the community. Yes___ No___

APPENDIX 7 (cont'd)

F. Athletic personnel make positive efforts to teach the spirit as well as the letter of playing rules, sportsmanship codes, and other value areas available in sports. Yes____ No____

VI. Salary standards commensurate and equitable with established professional schedules
   A. Compensation for coaching is based on:
      1. Length of season Yes____ No____
      2. Number of participants Yes____ No____
      3. Scope of responsibility Yes____ No____
   B. Percentage scales or comparable scales are used to provide fair increments for experience. Yes____ No____
   C. Extreme differences in salary among coaches of different sports are avoided. Yes____ No____
   D. Coaching increments are not used to lure outstanding teachers in academic areas who are not qualified to coach. Yes____ No____

Students in the Athletic Program

Profile Rating Scale

na	1	2	3	4
Not applicable	Inadequate provision with little or no progress evident	Inadequate provision with some progress evident	Inadequate provision but much progress evident	Adequate provision

I. Participant
   A. Every student is given equitable opportunity to try out and participate in an athletic activity. na 1 2 3 4
   B. The program of athletic activities is designed to offer a wide variety of opportunities to meet the individual differences of the student body. na 1 2 3 4
   C. The student participates in a decision-making role in regard to athletic policies, rules, and regulations. na 1 2 3 4
   D. Regular channels of communication are established to impact program values and standards to all students. na 1 2 3 4
   E. Each student is given a complete physical examination before trying out for an athletic activity. na 1 2 3 4
   F. An adequate insurance program is provided the student to defray the cost of medical attention in case of injury. na 1 2 3 4
   G. Services are available to aid the participating student in finding the college of his choice or selecting a career upon graduation. na 1 2 3 4

APPENDIX 7 (cont'd)

H. The student is provided with the best equipment, facilities, and environment possible in view of existing minimum standards and the financial ability of the school. na 1 2 3 4

I. The participant is able to appeal to a higher authority for a redress of an arbitrary decision on the part of a coach or administrator. na 1 2 3 4

J. The participant is protected from a loss of class time by proper scheduling of athletic events. na 1 2 3 4

K. The participant is given consideration in regard to the scheduling of competition commensurate with school size and program interest. na 1 2 3 4

L. The student is encouraged to participate in a variety of sports, and if unable to participate on the varsity level, is encouraged to continue competition on the extramural or intramural level. na 1 2 3 4

M. Students are permitted to participate only in one given sport at a time. Yes____ No____

II. Nonparticipant

A. The nonparticipating student is made to feel a part of the athletic program by serving in a decision-making role in regard to athletic policies affecting the entire student body. na 1 2 3 4

B. Nonparticipating students are given preferential opportunities to attend athletic contests before the adults in the community. na 1 2 3 4

C. Nonparticipating students are encouraged to join supportive groups of the athletic program. na 1 2 3 4

D. Student leaders are given the opportunity to serve on committees for awards recognition and pep assemblies. na 1 2 3 4

E. Every effort is exerted toward directing the nonparticipant into a school-sponsored event of a physical nature to promote interest and appreciation of the values of physical activity. na 1 2 3 4

III. Evaluations

A. How well does the athletic program enrich the total school experience for both participating and nonparticipating students? na 1 2 3 4

B. To what extent does the student body view the athletic program as a valuable extracurricular experience? na 1 2 3 4

C. To what extent have policies been established to insure maximum student interest and participation in the athletic program? na 1 2 3 4

SOURCE: *Evaluating the High School Athletic Program*, National Council of Secondary School Athletic Directors, American Association for Health, Physical Education and Recreation, 1973, p. 27ff.

APPENDIX 8: HEALTH AND PHYSICAL EDUCATION SCORE CARD NO. 1 FOR ELEMENTARY SCHOOLS GRADES 1-6*

Name of School ____________________ Address ____________________

Principal ____________________ Rated by ____________________

Rating for school year ____________________ Date ____________________

Number of students enrolled: boys __________ girls __________

Score Card Summary	Maximum Score	Actual Score**
I. Program of Activities	30	______
II. Outdoor Areas	24	______
III. Indoor Areas	30	______
IV. Organization and Administration of Class Programs	36	______
V. Medical Examinations and Health Service	36	______
Total possible score	150	Total Actual ______

Percentage Score (Actual ÷ 1.5) = ______

I. Program of Activities

Maximum Score = 30 Actual Score = ______

1. Content of Primary Program (grades 1-3) includes: (1) Fundamental movements (a) locomotor, (b) axial, (2) rhythmical activities, (3) games, (4) self-testing activities, (5) relays.
   (Three activities = 2; four activities = 4; five activities = 6)

   Score ______

2. Content of Elementary Program (grades 4-6) includes: (1) athletic games, (2) rhythmical activities, (3) hunting games, (4) individual athletic events, (5) posture training, (6) relays, (7) stunts.
   (Three activities = 2; five activities = 4; seven activities = 6)

   Score ______

---

*In scoring the eight-year elementary schools, the seventh and eighth grades should be rated on the Secondary Score Card.

**Each item is to be scored 1,2,3, or more, according to scales indicated in parentheses. In the subjective scores (fair, good, and excellent), raters should make unprejudiced evaluations. If conditions are approximate but not exact, give estimated equivalent score.

APPENDIX 8 (cont'd)

3. A well-planned and detailed yearly program (course of study, including specific objectives), for each grade, is on file in the principal's office.
(Fair program = 2; good = 4; excellent = 6)

Score ________

4. A course of study committee gives consideration, at least annually, to needed revisions in the program.
(Fair committee = 1; good = 2; excellent = 3)

Score ________

5. Daily participation in class instruction period is required of all children.
(Twenty minutes daily — exclusive of recess = 2; twenty-five minutes = 4; thirty minutes or more = 6)

Score ________

6. Provision is made for adequate maintenance and sanitation of school grounds, plant, and classrooms.
(Fair = 1; good = 2; excellent = 3)

Score ________

II. Outdoor Areas

III. Indoor Areas

IV. Organization and Administration of Class Programs

Maximum Score = 36 Actual Score ________

1. Adequate supply of play equipment (2-5 balls for each class at peak load) for class instruction in all activities offered is kept in a locked box or an office cabinet.
(Fair equipment = 2; good = 4; excellent = 6)

Score ________

2. Adequate facilities for handling individual activity (adaptive) classes are available either within the school or in a central, adaptive center accessible to several schools (or the equivalent).
(Fair facilities = 1; good = 2; excellent = 3)

Score ________

3. All classroom instructors have had special training courses in health and physical education activities or are taking such courses in extension or summer schools; in larger school systems specially trained physical education supervisors are assigned, on a consultant basis, to one or more schools.
(Standards approximately met = 2-4; fully met = 6)

Score ________

APPENDIX 8 (cont'd)

4. Trained leadership is available for individual activity (adaptive) classes from the regular staff, from a consultant supervisor, or from a physiotherapy clinic.
(Standards approximately met = 1-2; fully met = 3)

Score _______

5. Appropriate activities are provided for students incapacitated for normal participation or needing special postural or orthopedic correction (classes B and C); with radically restricted cases assigned to rest at appropriate periods during the day.
(Fair program = 1; good = 2; excellent = 3)

Score _______

6. In general class instruction, emphasis is placed upon enthusiastic, joyous participation in all activities included in the program, with instruction and practice in performance fundamentals, game rules, game strategy, and social conduct standards.
(Standards approximately met = 1-2; fully met = 3)

Score _______

7. In individual activity instruction, emphasis is placed upon practicing the directed exercises at home frequently, with the cooperation of parents; upon maintaining good postural alignment at all times; and upon participating in modified sport activities for which they are fitted.
(Standards approximately met = 1-2; fully met = 3)

Score _______

8. The noon-hour and recess periods are well organized with carefully limited activities that are physiologically defensible; and with several instructors assigned each day to careful supervision of the playground and recreation hall.
(Fair organization and supervision = 1; good = 2; excellent = 3)

Score _______

9. No student is permitted to substitute clerical work, janitor work, or towel dispensing in place of physical education class activity (except during very temporary disability).
(Fair = 1; good = 2; excellent = 3)

Score _______

APPENDIX 8 (cont'd)

10. Interschool competition is not approved, but well-organized play days are staged periodically under adequate leadership.
(Play days for girls or boys separately = 2; play days for boys and girls jointly = 3)

Score ______

V. Medical Examinations and Health Service

SOURCE: William Ralph LaPorte and John M. Cooper, *The Physical Education Curriculum* (Los Angeles: College Book Store, 1968), pp. 69ff.

APPENDIX 9: CRITERIA FOR APPRAISAL OF COLLEGE INSTRUCTIONAL PROGRAMS

Philosophy and Objectives

1. The educational philosophy of the department has been formulated in writing and is subscribed to wholeheartedly by the instructional staff.
2. The departmental philosophy is in harmony with the overall educational philosophy of the college or university as stated in the appropriate publications of the institution.
3. The department philosophy is compatible with the principles set forth in the report of the President's Commission on Higher Education as they relate to the education of college men and women.
4. The major objectives of the instructional program have been formulated in writing, and these specific objectives are compatible with the overall educational philosophy of the department and the institution.
5. The major objectives of the instructional program cover the potential contributions of physical education in the area of:
   a. effective movement
   b. skill in specific activities
   c. physiological function
   d. human relations
   e. knowledge, insights, and understandings

Administration

6. In the development and conduct of the programs of physical education, the administrator is committed to action through a democratic process which includes both faculty and students.
7. The department is guided by a sound philosophy of physical education. A concerted attempt is made to interpret a broad concept of physical education to faculty, students, administration, and community.
8. The administrator gives equal consideration to the problems of men and women in regard to policy, budget, use of facilities, equipment, scheduling of classes, intramural programs, and he or she makes provision for instruction in coeducational activities.
9. The standards in the institution relating to staff qualifications, teaching load, size of classes, retirement, academic rank, and salaries apply equally to staff members in the physical education department.
10. The department promotes continuous in-service education to stimulate professional growth and improved service to students.
11. The basic instructional program is coordinated with other areas. (Intramural athletics, intercollegiate athletics, teacher education, etc.)
12. The source of financial support for the physical education program is the same as that for all other instructional areas of the institution.

13. Instruction in physical education, properly adapted, is required of all students throughout their undergraduate college careers.
14. All entering students are given a thorough physical and medical examination by home or staff physician prior to participation in the physical education program. (Followed by periodic exams.)
15. Exemption from participation in the physical education program for medical reasons is predicated upon the carefully coordinated judgment of the medical and physical education staff.
16. Students are permitted to substitute freshman and varsity sports in season for the purpose of meeting their physical education requirement, but they must return to class at the end of their sport season.
17. It is the policy of the department not to accept veteran experiences, military drill, ROTC, band, and other extracurricular participation for the required instructional program of physical education.
18. Credit and quality or grade-point value is granted on the same basis as any other area in the educational program.
19. Facilities and equipment are adequate with respect to quality and quantity.
20. Guidance and counseling of students is an integral part of physical education program.
21. Adequate supervision is provided for teaching done by graduate students and teaching fellows.
22. Comprehensive and accessible records are maintained to indicate student accomplishments within the program.
23. The department of physical education conducts a program of organized research.

Program

24. The program provides instruction in activities for every student.
25. The program provides for orientation of each student with regard to purposes, policies, and opportunities in physical education. (This may be accomplished by orientation-week programs, medical and health examinations, courses, group printed materials, and demonstrations.)
26. The program offerings are well rounded, including body mechanics, swimming, team games, rhythms, individual and dual activities, with basic requirements for each student being set up according to his or her needs.
27. The program provides specific counseling and guidance (planned and incidental, group and individual) on a very definite pattern, with appropriate referrals to other campus agencies (student health, counseling bureau, etc.).
28. The activities selected make full use of accessible community facilities.
29. The activities selected make full use of local geography and climate.

30. The program provides opportunities through coeducational classes for teaching men and women to develop skills and to enjoy together those activities which bring lifelong leisure-time satisfactions.

31. The activities selected offer opportunities for creative expression and for the development of personal resources.

32. The program provides instruction for efficient body movement in physical education and daily living.

33. The activities selected promote healthful functioning of organs and systems of the body within the limits of present physical conditions.

34. Some of the activities selected encourage all students to develop relaxation skills and to understand their importance, and provide specific opportunities for relaxation and rest where such is indicated.

35. The physical education instruction program provides a means of introducing students to the activities of the intramural program and encourages them to participate in it.

36. The physical education instruction program introduces students to, and encourages their participation in, the various recreational activities of the campus and community.

37. The physical education instruction program is integrated with other college programs and services concerned with health education.

38. Teaching methods provide progressive learning experiences through which each student derives the satisfaction in achievement which is essential for continued participation after college.

Evaluation

39. The philosophy and objectives of a department are reviewed and re-evaluated periodically.

40. All the objectives, viz., skill, knowledge, attitudes, habits, etc., are included in:
    a. the evaluation of the program
    b. the final rating (or grade) given a student. The objectives are weighted according to the emphasis given in each course.

41. Selection and use of evaluation techniques are cooperatively planned within the department.

42. Evaluative measures are selected in the light of probable psychological and physiological reactions and result in stimulation of faculty and student interest and enthusiasm.

43. Evaluation of student status and progress are determined at the beginning, during, and at the termination of the course.

44. Evaluative procedures are used to determine strengths and weaknesses of individual students and class groups and lead to guidance and help for the individual student.

45. Evaluative procedures are employed to determine strengths and weaknesses of the program for:
    a. the college student
    b. post-college life
46. Evaluative measures are employed only if the results are to be used in some way
47. Objective measurement is used whenever possible.
48. If objective measurement is not possible, subjective judgment is used for purposes of appraisal.
49. Teachers are familiar with the best available evaluation techniques and use research findings insofar as possible.
50. All students and faculty participating in a course participate in the evaluation of student accomplishments and learning, teaching effectiveness, and course content.

SOURCE: *Physical Education for College Men and Women*, Washington Conference on Physical Education for College Men and Women (Washington, D.C.: AAHPER Publication, 1954)), pp. 36-40.

index